REA's Test Prep Books Are The Best!

(a sample of the hundreds of letters REA receives each year)

" This book is a valuable tool for those taking the FTCE. It reviews every competency you'll need to know for this exam. If you're really serious about getting through this exam at the first go, then this book is a must! "

FTCE Test Taker, Jacksonville, FL

" I did well because of your wonderful prep books... I just wanted to thank you for helping me prepare for these tests. "

Student, San Diego, CA

" My students report your chapters of review as the most valuable single resource they used for review and preparation. "

Teacher, American Fork, UT

" Your book was such a better value and was so much more complete than anything your competition has produced—and I have them all! "

Teacher, Virginia Beach, VA

" Compared to the other books that my fellow students had, your book was the most helpful in helping me get a great score. "

Student, North Hollywood, CA

" Your book was responsible for my success on the exam, which helped me get into the college of my choice... I will look for REA the next time I need help. "

Student, Chesterfield, MO

" Just a short note to say thanks for the great support your book gave me in helping me pass the test... I'm on my way to a B.S. degree because of you! "

Student, Orlando, FL

(more on next page)

(continued from front page)

" The gem of the book is the tests. They were indicative of the actual exam. The explanations of the answers are practically another review session. "
Student, Fresno, CA

" I just wanted to thank you for helping me get a great score on the AP U.S. History... Thank you for making great test preps! "
Student, Los Angeles, CA

" Your Fundamentals of Engineering Exam book was the absolute best preparation I could have had for the exam, and it is one of the major reasons I did so well and passed the FE on my first try. "
Student, Sweetwater, TN

" I used your book to prepare for the test and found that the advice and the sample tests were highly relevant... Without using any other material, I earned very high scores and will be going to the graduate school of my choice. "
Student, New Orleans, LA

" What I found in your book was a wealth of information sufficient to shore up my basic skills in math and verbal.... The practice tests were challenging and the answer explanations most helpful. It certainly is the Best Test Prep for the GRE! "
Student, Pullman, WA

" I really appreciate the help from your excellent book. Please keep up with your great work. "
Student, Albuquerque, NM

" I used your *CLEP Introductory Sociology* book and rank it 99%– thank you! "
Student, Jerusalem, Israel

(more on back page)

The Best Teacher's Test Preparation for the

FTCE

Florida Teacher Certification Examination
Professional Education Test

3rd EDITION

Leasha M. Barry, Ph.D.
Assistant Professor
Division of Teacher Education
University of West Florida
Pensacola, FL

Betty J. Bennett, Ph.D.
Assistant Professor of Educational Leadership
University of North Florida
Jacksonville, FL

Lois Christensen, Ph.D.
Associate Professor
College of Education
Florida Gulf Coast University
Fort Myers, FL

Alicia Mendoza, Ed.D.
Associate Professor
Elementary Education Department
Florida International University
Miami, FL

Enrique Ortiz, Ph.D.
Elementary Mathematics Professor
University of Central Florida
Orlando, FL

Migdalia Pagan, M.S.
Instructor
College of Education
University of Central Florida
Orlando, FL

Sally Robison, Ph.D.
Professor of Mathematics Education
Florida Atlantic University
Boca Raton, FL

Otilia Salmón, Ph.D.
Associate Professor
College of Education
University of North Florida
Jacksonville, FL

Research & Education Association
61 Ethel Road West
Piscataway, New Jersey 08854

THE BEST TEACHER'S TEST PREPARATION FOR THE FTCE PROFESSIONAL EDUCATION TEST

Library of Congress Control Number 2004094576

International Standard Book Number 0-7386-0045-8

REA® is a registered trademark of Research & Education Association, Inc.,
Piscataway, New Jersey 08854.

About the Authors

Dr. Leasha M. Barry received her graduate training in Special Education, disability, and at-risk populations at the University of California at Santa Barbara. She is currently Assistant Professor in the Division of Teacher Education within the College of Professional Studies at the University of West Florida. Her work focuses on early intervention with at-risk populations, including individuals with disabilities and those who experience traumatic stress at home, and in educational and healthcare settings. Dr. Barry is interested in identifying and documenting developmentally appropriate supports and interventions that set the stage for independence and self-determination for individuals who are identified as at-risk.

Dr. Betty J. Bennett is currently an Assistant Professor of Educational Leadership at the University of North Florida. Prior to this, she taught and was an administrator in the public school system for 15 years. She earned her Ph.D. in Educational Leadership from Florida State University. She has published materials in the areas of school discipline, leadership, and curriculum and standards-based education. Research pursuits include school violence, school-wide discipline, culture, and the leader's role in assisting teachers in promoting a safe school/learning environment.

Dr. Lois Christensen is an Associate Professor within the College of Education at Florida Gulf Coast University (FGCU) in Fort Myers, Florida, where she teaches courses in curriculum and professional development, serves as on-campus coordinator for the National Council for Accreditation of Teacher Education, and is the co-director of FGCU's National Writing Project. She is a former classroom teacher, curriculum coordinator, staff development director, and grant administrator. She has taught and held administrative positions in both the Iowa and Florida Public Schools. She holds masters degrees in reading and elementary school administration from Clarke College in Dubuque, Iowa, and a doctorate in Educational Leadership and Policy Studies from Loyola University of Chicago. Her primary interest involves developing effective instructional strategies that can be built upon from current studies in brain research.

Alicia Mendoza, Ed.D., formerly chair of the Elementary Education Department at Florida International University, has held the position of Associate Professor at the same academic institution for the past twenty-nine years. Prior to coming to FIU, she was an Associate Professor at Clarion State College in Clarion, Pennsylvania and served as a consultant to Head Start classes in Western Pennsylvania. She also taught in the public schools of New York City. She earned her Ed.D. and M.Ed. at the University of Miami, and her B.A. at Queens College in New York City. Dr. Mendoza has been the recipient of a Teaching Incentive award and an Excellence in Advising award during her time at Florida International University. She is the author of numerous published articles, book chapters, and curriculum materials.

Enrique Ortiz, Ph.D., was born in Raleigh, North Carolina, but grew up in Santurce, Puerto Rico (P.R.). He earned his doctoral degree from Louisiana State University in 1987. From 1976 to 1987, he worked as a middle school mathematics teacher, curriculum specialist, instructor, and supervisor in Puerto Rico and the U.S. He worked as an Assistant Professor for the University of New Orleans from 1987 to 1989. Since 1989, he has worked as an Elementary Mathematics Professor for the University of Central Florida. He is very active in the education profession and has presented papers and in-service workshops both locally and nationally, developed curriculum materials, written professional books and articles, taught methods courses, supervised pre-service teachers, and conducted research studies in the area of mathematics education at local schools.

Migdalia Pagan, M.S., was born in Ponce, Puerto Rico, but grew up in New York City. She attended New York City's public schools through high school. She received her Bachelor of Arts in Elementary Education and Master of Science in Exceptional Education from Hunter College, New York City. She received her Specialist Degree in Multilingual and Multicultural Education from Florida State University. Ms. Pagan has taught in New York City and worked with Florida's Orange County Public Schools for twenty years. During her years with OCPS, she was a classroom teacher, an exceptional-education teacher, a curriculum specialist, a curriculum compliance teacher, a staff developer, and an educational consultant. Currently, she is a full-time instructor with the University of Central Florida, College of Education. She is also a national consultant in the areas of literacy and ESOL. Her passion continues to be teaching with and learning from both youngsters and adult students.

Dr. Sally Robison received her Bachelor of Education and Master of Education degrees from the University of Missouri-Columbia in Mathematics Education. She received her Doctorate of Philosophy from the University of Nebraska-Lincoln in Mathematics Education. For over ten years, she was a practicing teacher in the private and public schools of Missouri and Florida. For the past eight years, she has been a Professor of Mathematics Education at Florida Atlantic University. Dr. Robison has published many articles and conference proceedings, chapters in textbooks, web pages, and teaching materials that have brought her international, national, and state recognition. She has presented her research at international, national, and state conferences. Her primary research focus is on the improvement of mathematics education, integrating curriculum for improved and connected learning, teaching children of limited English proficiency with effective ESOL strategies, effective assessment practices, and using technology to enhance instruction.

Otilia Salmón, Ph.D., has been an educator for twenty-eight years in bilingual multicultural education, and specializes in foreign languages and in English as a Second Language (ESL). She obtained her doctorate at the University of Florida in Bilingual Multicultural Education. Dr. Salmón was a recipient of the Benito Juarez and Abraham Lincoln Scholarship, and studied at the University of Veracruz in Mexico. She was honored with a scholarship from UNESCO to study Communication at the UNESCO School of Communication (ILCE) in Mexico City. Dr. Salmón's first degree was from the University of the West Indies, Kingston, Jamaica. She is the author of *Spanish Grammar Can Be Easy: A Student's Companion* and *Cultural Linguistic Diversity in American Schools.* Dr. Salmón has directed ESOL and Teaching English as a Second Language (TESL) training for upcoming and practicing teachers. Dr. Salmón has taught in Mexico; Kingston, Jamaica; at the University of Florida; and at Ashland University, Ashland, Ohio, where she was Chair and professor of the Foreign Language Department. Dr. Salmón presently serves as Associate Professor at the University of North Florida in the College of Education, and also works as a consultant for the Teacher Certification exams in Spanish and English as Second Language.

About Research & Education Association

Founded in 1959, Research & Education Association (REA) is dedicated to publishing the finest and most effective educational materials—including software, study guides, and test preps—for students in middle school, high school, college, graduate school, and beyond.

REA's Test Preparation series includes study guides for all academic levels in almost all disciplines. Research & Education Association publishes test preps for students who have not yet completed high school, as well as high school students preparing to enter college. Students from countries around the world seeking to attend college in the United States will find the assistance they need in REA's publications. For college students seeking advanced degrees, REA publishes test preps for many major graduate school admission examinations in a wide variety of disciplines, including engineering, law, and medicine. Students at every level, in every field, with every ambition can find what they are looking for among REA's publications.

While most test preparation books present practice tests that bear little resemblance to the actual exams, REA's series presents tests that accurately depict the official exams in both degree of difficulty and types of questions. REA's practice tests are always based upon the most recently administered exams, and include every type of question that can be expected on the actual exams.

REA's publications and educational materials are highly regarded and continually receive an unprecedented amount of praise from professionals, instructors, librarians, parents, and students. Our authors are as diverse as the subject matter represented in the books we publish. They are well-known in their respective fields and serve on the faculties of prestigious high schools, colleges, and universities throughout the United States and Canada.

Acknowledgments

Foundational material was provided by **Julienne H. Empric, Ph.D.**, Professor of Literature, Eckerd College, St. Petersburg, FL; **Erin Spanier-Evers, M.A.**, Language Arts Coordinator, Staten Island, NY; **Christine Hudak, M.A.**, Kindergarten Teacher, School 4 Annex, Linden, NJ; **Paul Linnehan, Ph.D.**, Associate Professor of English, University of Tampa, FL; **Judy Downs-Lombardi, Ph.D.**, Educational Consultant, Temple Terrace, FL; **Donald E. Orlosky, Ed.D.**, Professor Emeritus, University of South Florida, Tampa, FL; **Gail M. Platt, Ph.D.**, Director, Learning Center, South Plains College, Levelland, TX; **Gail Rae, M.A.**, Department of English, McKee Technical High School, Staten Island, NY; **Sally Stevens, M.A.**, Pre-Kindergarten Teacher, School 4 Annex, Linden, NJ; **Christine Zardecki**, Research Associate, Rutgers University, Piscataway, NJ.

In addition to our authors, we would like to thank **Larry B. Kling**, Manager, Editorial Services, for supervising development; **Pam Weston**, Production Manager for ensuring press readiness; **Jeff LoBalbo**, Senior Graphic Designer, for providing prepress electronic prepping; **Christine Saul**, Senior Graphic Designer, for designing the cover; **Betty J. Bennett, Ph.D.**, for technically editing and proofreading the manuscript; and **Alicia Shapiro**, Project Manager for coordinating revisions. We also extend thanks to **Michael Cote** for typesetting the manuscript for the revised edition.

CONTENTS

CHAPTER 3

Competency 2: Communication   57

CHAPTER **4**

Competency 3: Continuous Improvement   83

CHAPTER **5**

Competency 4: Critical Thinking   99

CHAPTER **6**

Competency 5: Diversity   113

CHAPTER 7

Competency 6: Ethics   127

CHAPTER 8

Competency 7: Human Development and Learning   143

CHAPTER 9

Competency 8: Subject Matter   179

CHAPTER 10

Competency 9: Learning Environments 193

CHAPTER 11

Competency 10: Planning 225

CHAPTER 12

Competency 11: The Role of the Teacher   281

CHAPTER 13

Competency 12: Technology   307

CHAPTER 14

Competency 13: Foundations of Education   319

CHAPTER **15**

Competency 14: ESOL (English for Speakers of Other Languages)   **339**

PRACTICE TESTS   **387**

Practice Test 1   **389**

Practice Test 2   **443**

FTCE

Florida Teacher Certification Exam
Professional Education Test

Passing the FTCE

Passing the FTCE

About this Book

This book provides you with an accurate and complete representation of the Florida Teacher Certification Examination (FTCE) Professional Education Test. Inside you will find topical reviews designed to equip you with the information and strategies needed to pass the exam. REA also gives you two full-length practice tests, which are based on the most recently administered FTCE and contain every type of question that you can expect to encounter on test day. As with the actual test, each of ours takes two and one-half hours to complete. Following each practice test, you will find an answer key with detailed explanations designed to help you better grasp the test material.

About the Test

Who takes the test and what is it used for?

The FTCE is taken by individuals seeking initial teacher certification in Florida. Educators must pass the Professional Education Test as one of the requirements for their first five-year Florida Professional Certificate. You are eligible to take the test if you meet any one of these criteria:

- Enrolled in a college or university teacher-preparation program

- Teaching with provisional certification

- Making a teaching career change to public school teaching

If you do not do well on the FTCE, don't panic! The test can be taken again, so you can work on improving your score in preparation for your next FTCE. A score on the FTCE that does not match your expectations does *not* mean you should change your plans about teaching.

Who administers the test?

The FTCE is developed and administered by the Florida Department of Education. A test development process was designed and implemented to ensure that the content and difficulty level of the test are appropriate.

When should the FTCE be taken?

The test should be taken just before or right after graduation for those seeking certification right out of school. While the FTCE is required to teach in Florida, you may be issued a two-year temporary certificate while completing your teaching requirements and working toward passing the FTCE itself.

The FTCE is usually administered four times a year in several locations throughout Florida. The usual testing day is Saturday but the test may be taken on an alternate day if a conflict, such as a religious obligation, exists. Special accommodations can also be made for applicants who are visually impaired, hearing impaired, physically disabled, or specific learning disabled.

To receive information on upcoming administrations of the FTCE, consult the FTCE Registration Bulletin, which can be obtained by contacting:

FTCE Inquiries
Florida Department of Education
325 West Gaines Street, Suite 414
Tallahassee, FL 32399-0400
Phone: (850) 488-8198 or (813) 974-2400
Website: http://www.firn.edu/doe/sas/ftcehome.htm
        and http://www.cefe.usf.edu/requestapp.aspx

The FTCE Registration Bulletin also includes information regarding test retakes and score reports.

Is there a registration fee?

To take the FTCE, you must pay a registration fee. You may pay by personal check, money order, cashier's check, or Visa or MasterCard. Cash is not accepted.

How to Use this Book

What do I study first?

Read over the reviews and the suggestions for test-taking. Studying the reviews thoroughly will reinforce the basic skills you will need to do well on the exam. Make sure to take the practice tests to become familiar with the format and procedures involved with taking the actual FTCE.

To best utilize your study time, follow our FTCE Independent Study Schedule located at the end of this chapter. The schedule is based on a seven-week program, but can be condensed to four weeks if necessary.

When should I start studying?

It is never too early to start studying for the FTCE. The earlier you begin, the more time you will have to sharpen your skills. Do not procrastinate! Cramming is *not* an effective way to study, since it does not allow you the time needed to learn the test material.

Format of the FTCE

The Professional Education Test features 120 questions designed to assess your knowledge of the information described in the competencies included in our review sections.

The test covers the 14 teaching competencies identified by the Florida Department of Education as foundational to effective teaching. Mastery of the content included in each of the competencies is gauged by one or more items on the examination. Individual test items require a variety of different thinking levels, ranging from simple recall to evaluation and problem solving.

The competencies are broad statements written in a way that reflect the information an entry-level educator needs in order to be a truly effective teacher. Within the review section, each competency is broken down into the competency statement and a description of what the competency covers. The competencies will not be discussed in the actual FTCE test.

All the questions on the FTCE are in multiple-choice format. Each question will have four options, lettered A through D, from which to choose. You should have plenty of time in which to complete the FTCE, but be aware of the amount of time you are spending on each question so that you allow yourself time to complete the test. Although speed is not very important, a steady pace should be maintained when answering the questions. Using the practice tests will help you prepare for this task.

Computer-Based Testing

A computer-based test is also available. To register, visit http://www.cefe.usf.edu and click on "Computer-Based Testing." If you decide to take the exam on the computer, you will receive notice of Pass/Fail immediately after completing the exam. It can be scheduled at a time that is convenient for you.

About the Review Sections

The reviews in this book are designed to help you sharpen the basic skills needed to approach the FTCE, as well as provide strategies for attacking the questions.

Each teaching competency is examined in a separate chapter. All 14 competencies are extensively discussed to sharpen your understanding of what the FTCE covers.

Your schooling has taught you most of what you need to answer the questions on the test. The education classes you took should have provided you with the know-how to make important decisions about situations you will face as a teacher. Our review is designed to help you fit the information you have acquired into specific competency components. Reviewing your class notes and textbooks together with our competency reviews will give you an excellent springboard for passing the FTCE.

Scoring the FTCE

How do I score my practice test?

There are a total of 120 questions on the FTCE Professional Education Test. A score of 200 or higher, which is equivalent to 56% correct, is needed to pass. In other words, you need to answer approximately 67 questions correctly to achieve a passing score.

If you do not achieve a passing score, review the detailed explanations for the questions you answered incorrectly. Note which types of questions you answered wrong, and re-examine the corresponding review. After further review, you may want to retake the practice tests.

When will I receive my score report and what will it look like?

Approximately one month after you take the test, your score report will be mailed to you. You will receive two original score reports and are responsible for sending one to the Bureau of Teacher Certification. A copy of your score report is provided to one Florida college or university and one Florida school district. You should have requested this information on your registration application.

When you receive your score report and have passed with a 200 or higher, only the word **PASS** will be reported. If you do not pass, you will receive a numeric score and will have to retake the test.

Studying for the FTCE

It is very important for you to choose the time and place for studying that works best for you. Some individuals may set aside a certain number of hours every morning to study, while others may choose to study at night before going to sleep. Other people may study during the day, while waiting on line, or even while eating lunch. Only you can determine when and where your study time will be most effective. Be consistent and use your time wisely. Work out a study routine and stick to it.

When you take the practice tests, simulate the conditions of the actual test as closely as possible. Turn your television and radio off, and sit down at a quiet table free from distraction.

As you complete each practice test, score your test and thoroughly review the explanations to the questions you answered incorrectly; however, do not review too much at any one time. Concentrate on one problem area at a time by reviewing the question and explanation, and by studying our review until you are confident that you have mastered the material.

Keep track of your scores. By doing so, you will be able to gauge your progress and discover general weaknesses in particular sections. Give extra attention to the reviews that cover your areas of difficulty, as this will build your skills in those areas.

Test-Taking Tips

Although you may not be familiar with tests like the FTCE, this book will help acquaint you with this type of exam and help alleviate your test-taking anxieties. Listed below are ways to help you become accustomed to the FTCE, some of which may be applied to other tests as well.

Become comfortable with the format of the FTCE. When you are practicing, simulate the conditions under which you will be taking the actual test. Stay calm and pace yourself. After simulating the test only once, you will boost your chances of doing well, and you will be able to sit down for the actual FTCE with much more confidence.

Read all of the possible answers. Just because you think you have found the correct response, do not automatically assume that it is the best answer. Read through each choice to be sure that you are not making a mistake by jumping to conclusions.

Use the process of elimination. Go through each answer to a question and eliminate as many of the answer choices as possible. By eliminating two answer choices, you have given yourself a better chance of getting the item correct since there will only be two choices left from which to make your guess. Do not leave an answer blank; it is better to guess than to not answer a question on the FTCE test.

Work quickly and steadily. You will have two and one-half hours to complete the test, so work quickly and steadily to avoid focusing on any one problem too long. Taking the practice tests in this book will help you learn to budget your precious time.

Learn the directions and format of the test. Familiarizing yourself with the directions and format of the test will not only save time, but will also help you avoid anxiety (and the mistakes caused by getting anxious).

Be sure that the answer circle you are marking corresponds to the number of the question in the test booklet. Since the test is multiple-choice, it is graded by machine, and marking one wrong answer can throw off your answer key and your score. Be extremely careful.

The Day of the Test

Before the Test

On the day of the test, make sure to dress comfortably, so that you are not distracted by being too hot or too cold while taking the test. Plan to arrive at the test center early. This will allow you to collect your thoughts and relax before the test, and will also spare you the anguish that comes with being late. You should check your FTCE Registration Bulletin to find out what time to arrive at the testing center.

Before you leave for the test center, make sure that you have your admission ticket and two forms of identification, one of which must contain a recent photograph, your name, and signature (i.e., driver's license). You will not be admitted to the test center if you do not have proper identification.

You must bring several sharpened No. 2 pencils with erasers, as none will be provided at the test center.

If you would like, you may wear a watch to the test center. However, you may not wear one that makes noise, because it may disturb the other test takers. Dictionaries, textbooks, notebooks, calculators, briefcases, or packages will not be permitted. Drinking, smoking, and eating are prohibited.

During the Test

The FTCE is given in one sitting with no breaks. Procedures will be followed to maintain test security.

Once you enter the test center, follow all of the rules and instructions given by the test supervisor. If you do not, you risk being dismissed from the test and having your scores cancelled.

When all of the materials have been distributed, the test instructor will give you directions for filling out your answer sheet. Fill out this sheet carefully since this information will be printed on your score report.

Once the test begins, mark only one answer per question, completely erase unwanted answers and marks, and fill in answers darkly and neatly.

After the Test

When you finish your test, hand in your materials and you will be dismissed. Then, go home and relax—you deserve it!

FTCE Study Schedule

The following study course schedule allows for thorough preparation to pass the FTCE Professional Education Test. This is a suggested seven-week course of study. However, this schedule can be condensed if you have less time available to study, or expanded if you have more time. But be sure to keep a structured schedule by setting aside ample time each day to study. Depending on your schedule you may find it easier to study throughout the weekend. No matter which schedule works best for you, the more time you devote to studying for the FTCE, the more prepared and confident you will be on the day of the actual test.

Week	Activity
1	Take the first exam as a diagnostic exam. Your score will be an indication of your strengths and weaknesses. Make sure to take the test under simulated exam conditions. Review the explanations for the questions you answered incorrectly.
2	Study REA's FTCE Review. Highlight key terms and information. Take notes on the reviews as you work through them, as writing will aid in your retention of information.
3 and 4	Review your references and sources. The Florida Department of Education's *Domains: Knowledge Base of The Florida Performance Measurement System* may be helpful in this area. Use any other supplementary material

which your counselor or the Florida Department of Education suggests.

5   Condense your notes and findings. You should develop a structured outline detailing specific facts. You may want to use index cards to aid you in memorizing important facts and concepts.

6   Test yourself using the index cards. You may want to have a friend or colleague quiz you on key facts and items. Then, take the second full-length exam. Review the explanations for the questions you answered incorrectly.

7   Study any areas you consider to be your weaknesses by using your study materials, references, and notes. You may want to retake the tests using the extra answer sheets provided in the back of this book.

FTCE

Florida Teacher Certification Exam
Professional Education Test

Review

Competency 1:
Assessment

Definition of Competency

The teacher has knowledge of various types of assessment strategies that can be used to determine student levels and needs.

- *The teacher identifies appropriate methods, strategies, and evaluation instruments for assessing student levels, needs, performance, and learning.*

- *The teacher identifies and sequences learning activities that support study skills and test-taking strategies.*

Purposes of Assessment

(handwritten margin note, left top)
informal
observation
journals
drafts
conversation

(handwritten margin note, left middle)
formal
teacher-made tests
district exams
standardized tests

The effective teacher understands the importance of ongoing assessment as an instructional tool for the classroom and uses both informal and formal assessment measures. Informal measures may include observation, journals, written drafts, and conversations. More formal measures may include teacher-made tests, district exams, and standardized tests. Effective teachers use both formative and summative evaluations. Formative evaluation occurs during the process of learning, when the teacher or the students monitor progress in obtaining outcomes, while it is still possible to modify instruction. Summative evaluation occurs at the end of a specific time period or course, usually by a single grade used to represent a student's performance.

(handwritten note)
formative - during the process of learning, can modify instruction
summative - at the end of a specific time prd/course

Teacher-Made (Classroom) Tests

The effective teacher uses a variety of assessment techniques. Teacher-made instruments are ideally developed at the same time as the goals and outcomes are planned, rather than at the last minute after all the lessons have been taught. Carefully planned objectives and assessment instruments serve as lesson development guides for the teacher.

Paper and pencil tests are the most common method for evaluation of student progress. There are a number of different types of

(handwritten note)
paper & pencil tests - most common

questions: multiple-choice, true/false, matching, fill-in-the-blank, short answer, and longer essay. The first five tend to test the knowledge or comprehension levels. Essays often test at the lower levels, but are suitable for assessing learning at higher levels. Projects, papers, and portfolios can provide assessment of higher-level thinking skills.

If the purpose is to test student recall of factual information, a short objective test (multiple-choice, true/false, matching, fill-in-the-blank) would be most effective and efficient. The first three types of questions can be answered on machine-scorable scan sheets to provide quick and accurate scoring. Disadvantages are that they generally test lower levels of knowledge and do not provide an opportunity for an explanation of answers.

If the purpose is to test student ability to analyze an event, compare and contrast two concepts, make predictions about an experiment, or evaluate a character's actions, then an essay question would provide the best paper/pencil opportunity for the student to show what he or she can do. A teacher should make the question explicit enough so that students will know exactly what he or she expects. For example, "Explain the results of World War II" is too broad; students will not really understand what the teacher expects. It would be more explicit to say, "Explain three results of World War II that you feel had the most impact on participating nations. Explain the criteria you used in selecting these results."

Advantages of an essay include the possibility for students to be creative in their answers, the opportunity for students to explain their responses, and the potential to test for higher-level thinking skills. Disadvantages of essay questions include the time needed for students to formulate meaningful responses, language difficulties of some students, and the time needed to evaluate the essays. Consistency in evaluation is also a problem for the teacher, but this can be alleviated by using an outline of the acceptable answers.

Teachers who write specific questions and who know what they are looking for will be more consistent in grading. Also, if there are several essay questions, the effective teacher grades all student responses to the first question, then moves on to all responses to the second, and so on.

Authentic Assessments

Paper and pencil tests or essays are only one method of assessment. Others include projects, observation, checklists, anecdotal records, portfolios, self-assessment, and peer assessment. Although these types of assessments usually take more time and effort to plan and administer, they can often provide a more authentic assessment of student progress.

Projects are common in almost all subject areas. They promote student control of learning experiences and provide opportunities for research into a variety of topics, as well as the chance to use visuals, graphics, videos, or multimedia presentations in place of, or in addition to, written reports. Projects also promote student self-assessment because students must evaluate their progress along each step of the project. Many schools have science or history fairs for which students plan, develop, and display their projects. Projects can also be part of business, English, music, art, mathematics, social sciences, health, or physical education courses.

The teacher must make clear the requirements and the criteria for evaluation of the projects before students begin them. He or she must also assist students in selecting projects which are feasible, for which the school has learning resources, and which can be completed in a reasonable amount of time with little or no expense to students.

Advantages of projects are that students can demonstrate their visual, graphic, art, or music abilities; students can be creative in their topic or research; and the projects can appeal to various learning styles. Disadvantages include difficulty with grading, although this can be overcome by devising a checklist for required elements and a rating scale for quality.

project's advantages

Observations may be made for individual or group work. This method is very suitable for skills or for effective learning. Teachers usually make a list of competencies, skills, or requirements, then check off the ones that are observed in the student or group. An office skills teacher wishing to emphasize interviewing skills may devise a checklist that includes personal appearance, mannerisms, confidence, and addressing the questions that are asked. A teacher who wants to emphasize careful listening may observe a discussion with a checklist which includes paying attention, not interrupting, summarizing another person's ideas, and asking questions of other students.

Anecdotal records may be helpful in some instances, such as capturing the process a group of students uses to solve a problem. This formative data can be useful during feedback to the group. Students can also be taught to write an explanation of the procedures they use for a project or a science experiment. An advantage of an anecdotal record is that it can include all relevant information. Disadvantages include the amount of time necessary to complete the record and difficulty in assigning a grade. If used for feedback, then no grade is necessary.

Advantages of checklists include the potential for capturing behavior that cannot be accurately measured with a paper and pencil test, i.e., shooting free throws on the basketball court, following the correct sequence of steps in a science experiment, or including all important elements in a speech in class. One characteristic of a checklist that is both an advantage and a disadvantage is its structure, which provides consistency but inflexibility. An open-ended comment section at the end of a checklist can overcome this disadvantage.

Portfolios are collections of students' best work. They can be used in any subject area where the teacher wants students to take more responsibility for planning, carrying out, and organizing their own learning. They may be used in the same way that artists, models, or performers use them to provide a succinct picture of their best work. Portfolios may be essays or articles written on paper, video tapes, multimedia presentations on computer disks, or a combination. English teachers often use portfolios as a means of collecting the best samples of student writing over the whole year. Sometimes they pass on the work to the next year's teacher to help assess the needs of his or her new students. Any subject area can use portfolios, since they contain documentation that reflects growth and learning over a period of time.

Teachers should provide or assist students in developing guidelines for what materials should be placed in portfolios, since it would be unrealistic to include every piece of work in one portfolio. The use of portfolios requires the students to devise a means of evaluating their own work. A portfolio should be a collection of the student's own best work, not a scrapbook for collecting handouts or work done by other individuals, although it can certainly include work by a group in which the student was a participant.

Some advantages of portfolios over testing are that they provide a clearer picture of a student's progress, they are not affected by one inferior test grade, and they help develop self-assessment skills in students. One disadvantage is the amount of time required to teach students how to develop meaningful portfolios. However, this time can

Portfolio's advantages

be well spent if students learn valuable skills. Another concern is the amount of time teachers must spend to assess portfolios. However, as students become more proficient at self-assessment, the teacher can spend more time in coaching and advising students throughout the development of their portfolios. Another concern is that parents may not understand how portfolios will be graded. The effective teacher devises a system which the students and parents understand before work on the portfolio begins.

Standardized Testing

2 categories: norm-referenced / criterion-referenced

Standardized tests fall under two categories: criterion-referenced and norm-referenced.

In *criterion-referenced tests*, each student is measured against uniform objectives or criteria. CRTs allow the possibility that all students can score 100 percent because they understand the concepts being tested. Teacher-made tests should be criterion-referenced because the teacher should develop them to measure the achievement of predetermined outcomes for the course. If teachers have properly prepared lessons based on the outcomes, and if students have mastered the outcomes, then scores should be high. This type of test may be called noncompetitive because students are not in competition with each other for a high score, and there is no limit to the number of students who can score well. Some commercially developed tests are criterion-referenced; however, the majority are norm-referenced.

The purpose of a *norm-referenced test* is to provide a way to compare the performance of groups of students. This type of test may be called competitive because a limited number of students can

bell-shaped curve

score well. A plot of large numbers of NRT scores will resemble a bell-shaped curve, with most scores clustering around the center and a few scores at each end. The midpoint is an average of data; therefore, by definition, half of the population will score above average and half below average.

The bell-shaped curve was developed as a mathematical description of the results of tossing coins. As such, it represents the chance or normal distribution of skills, knowledge, or events across the general population. A survey of the height of sixth-grade boys will result in an average height, with half the boys above average and half below. There will be a very small number with heights way above average and a very small number with heights way below average, with most heights clustering around the average.

NRT scores are usually reported in percentile scores (not to be confused with percentages), which indicate the percent of the population whose scores fall at or below the score. For example, a group score at the 80th percentile means that the group scored as well as or better than 80 percent of the students who took the test. A student with a score at the 50th percentile has an average score.

Percentile scores rank students from highest to lowest. By themselves, percentile scores do not indicate how well the student has mastered the content objectives. Raw scores indicate how many questions the student answered correctly and are, therefore, useful in computing the percentage of questions a student answered correctly.

A national test for biology is designed to include objectives for the widest possible biology curriculum, for the broadest use of the test. Normed scores are reported so that schools can compare the performance of the students with the performance of students who the test developers used as its norm group. The test will likely include more objectives than are included in a particular school's curriculum; therefore, that school's students may score low in comparison to the norm group. Teachers must be very careful in selecting a norm-referenced test, and should look for a test that includes objectives which are the most congruent with the school's curriculum.

reliability

Schools must also consider the reliability of a test, or whether the instrument will give consistent results when the measurement is repeated. A reliable bathroom scale, for example, will give identical weights for the same person measured three times in a morning. An unreliable scale, however, may give weights that differ by six pounds. Teachers evaluate test reliability over time when they give the same, or almost the same, test to different groups of students. Because there are many factors which affect reliability, teachers must be careful in evaluating this factor.

validity

Schools must also be careful to assess the validity of a test, or whether the test actually measures what it is supposed to measure. If students score low on a test because they could not understand the questions, then the test is not valid because it measures reading ability instead of content knowledge. If students score low because the test covered material which was not taught, the test is not valid for that situation. A teacher assesses the validity of his or her own tests by examining the questions to see if they measure what was planned and taught in his or her classroom.

reliability first before validity

✳ A test must be reliable before it can be valid. However, measurements can be consistent without being valid. A scale can indicate identical weights for three weigh-ins of the same person during one morning, but actually be 15 pounds in error. A history test may produce similar results each time it is given, but not be a valid measure of what was taught and learned. Tests should be both reliable and valid. If the test does not measure consistently, then it cannot be accurate. If it does not measure what it is supposed to measure, then its reliability does not matter. Commercial test producers perform various statistical measures of the reliability and validity of their tests and provide the results in the test administrator's booklet.

Performance-Based Assessment

Some states and districts are moving toward performance-based testing, which means that students are assessed on how well they perform certain tasks. This allows students to use higher-level thinking skills to apply, analyze, synthesize, and evaluate ideas and data. For example, a biology performance-based assessment may require students to read a problem, design and carry out a laboratory experiment, then write a summary of his or her findings. He or she would be evaluated on both the process used and the output he or she produced. A history performance-based assessment may require students to research a specific topic over a period of several days, make presentations of their findings to the rest of the class, then write a response which uses what the students have learned from their own research and that of their classmates. The students are then evaluated on the process and the product of their research. An English performance-based test may require students to read a selection of literature, then write a critical analysis. A mathematics test may state a general problem to be solved, then require the student to invent one or more methods of solving the problem, use one of the methods to arrive at a solution, then write the solution and an explanation of the processes he or she used.

Performance-based assessment allows students to be creative in their solutions to problems or questions, and it requires them to use higher-level skills. This type of assessment can be time-consuming; however, students are working on content-related problems, using skills that are useful in a variety of contexts. This type of assessment also requires multiple resources, which can be expensive. It also requires teachers to be trained in how to use this type of assessment. Nonetheless, many schools consider performance-based testing to be a more authentic measure of student achievement than traditional tests.

Creating Classroom (Teacher-Made) Tests

There are fundamental professional and technical factors that must be taken into account to construct effective classroom tests. One of the first factors to recognize is that test construction is as creative, challenging, and important as any aspect of teaching. The planning and background that contribute to effective teaching are incomplete unless evaluation of student performance provides accurate feedback to the teacher and the student about the learning process. Good tests are the product of careful planning, creative thinking, hard work, and technical knowledge about the different methods of measuring student knowledge and performance. Classroom tests that accomplish their purpose are the result of the development of a pool of items and refinement of those items based on feedback and constant revision. It is through this process that evaluation of students becomes valid and reliable.

Tests serve as a valuable instructional aid because they help determine pupil progress and also provide feedback to teachers regarding their own effectiveness. Student misunderstandings and problems as revealed on tests help the teacher understand areas of special concern in providing instruction. This information also becomes the basis for remediation of students and revision of teaching procedures. For these reasons, the construction, administration, and proper scoring of classroom tests is one of the most important activities in teaching.

Principles of Test Construction

The discussion in this section is based on the following principles of test construction:

1. Tests should be constructed according to a blueprint that reflects the objectives of the content to be learned.

2. Tests should reflect the knowledge and skills intended for students to acquire in proportion to the emphasis given to the various objectives in the unit of learning being tested.

3. The type of test items provided for students to answer should be chosen according to the best testing procedures for the particular knowledge or skill the student is expected to acquire.

When a given unit or theme of instruction is prepared, the effective teacher identifies learning objectives for students. The content is then organized and materials and methods for instruction are planned that will help students achieve those objectives. Prior to the administration of tests, the teacher should have a general idea of how the class is progressing in achieving those objectives, and he or she can usually identify those students who seem to be learning better than others. But, the classroom also has a limited number of students performing at any one time, and the teacher is only sampling the performance of the students in that class. In a testing situation, the teacher has an opportunity to include every student in a common activity that has the potential to assess all students on a common task.

Self-Directed Learning and Assessment

It is important for teachers to set goals for students and use these goals when preparing lessons and tests. The goals can then later be used as a basis for creating exams.

Effective teachers not only set goals for their students, but also teach students to set and accomplish their own goals, both individually and in groups. Students need to learn how to plan for their individual learning as well as for learning with a group of students. If students are unaccustomed to setting goals, the effective teacher begins by modeling the process. The teacher explains how he or she develops goals and objectives for the class.

One way of encouraging students to set goals is to ask students to set a performance standard for themselves in regard to time needed to complete a project. For example, students might determine they will need 15 minutes to answer five questions, writing one paragraph of at least five sentences for each question. In order to accomplish this goal, the students must focus their attention very carefully and limit themselves to about three minutes per question. The teacher should then ask questions to help students determine whether the goal was realistic, and if not, what adjustments he or she needs to make.

One way to involve students in assessment could be to ask students to develop their own questions about material to be learned or to plan activities to accomplish the goals of the lesson. The highest level is to have students determine the goals for their own learning. For example, a science teacher might introduce the topic of earthquakes, then help students determine what they need to know about earthquakes and the activities and resources which will help them learn. Students also need to develop plans for products which will show that they have met their goals.

Another way to encourage self-directed thinking and learning is to use higher-level questioning strategies and to teach students to use them as well.

Test Blueprints

In order to optimize this opportunity, the classroom test must be carefully constructed by using a plan that reflects objectives, goals, and measures student learning. It is the responsibility of the teacher to identify, select, and construct test items that appropriately assess the attainment of objectives and goals. This can be accomplished by starting with a test blueprint and then preparing test items according to the blueprint. A test blueprint is a plan for the teacher to assess the relative importance of the objectives and goals to be tested and to identify the type of items or activities to be used to test for those objectives. The following discussion explains how to develop and utilize a test blueprint.

Objectives

If a unit of instruction contains several objectives, it is most likely that some objectives require more emphasis than others. The teacher should make a judgment about the degree of emphasis given to each objective so the test will reflect this proportional emphasis. This judgment is the first step in preparing a test blueprint. For example, a unit with four objectives might include the following distribution:

Objectives

I	II	III	IV
20%	30%	15%	35%

This allocation of percentages to the different objectives is the foundation on which the remainder of the blueprint will be developed. After determining the relative importance of each objective, the teacher should allot class time, provide instruction, and evaluate students according to the proportional importance of each objective. This entire process should be viewed as a cooperative effort between the teacher and the students in which they work in much the same

prepare test items while planning the lesson

manner as a coach does to make his or her team the best they can be. As the planning for instruction occurs, and as the instruction is provided, the teacher should concurrently prepare test questions that coincide with the planning and instruction. While preparing a lesson, the teacher should be making notes about test items that evaluate the intended learning of the students. By preparing test items while planning lessons, the teacher can make the instruction appropriate and increase the validity of the test at the same time. Another excellent time to prepare test items is immediately after completing the daily instruction. At this time, the learning that took place is fresh in the mind of the teacher and any special events or discussions that should be reinforced through a test can more easily be recalled.

Test Items

The test items used in an examination will vary according to the content that is being taught. The teacher must choose the type of items that will be most effective for evaluating students according to the content they have learned. Multiple-choice items may be useful to test a wide range of objectives, and an essay question may be a better choice to test for knowledge about a single event. The length and type of tests will also be influenced by factors such as time and frequency for testing. Tests will vary if they are weekly quizzes or semester examinations. Tests that have essay questions require more time than items that call for simple recognition. These are factors that must be taken into account when the test is actually assembled. However, at the time the test questions are being drafted, the most important criterion is to develop test questions that are most appropriate for the content. The questions most commonly prepared are: true/false, essay, multiple-choice, listing, matching, sentence completion, and recall.

As instruction progresses and as test items are constructed, student learning and the test development by the teacher should coincide. When the instruction and learning of the unit has nearly ended and the teacher prepares to test the students, it is time to complete the test blueprint.

For the next step in preparing the blueprint, the teacher should list the number of test items prepared under each objective according to the type of item. This step in making the blueprint is illustrated with the following example:

Objectives

Question Type	I 20%	II 30%	III 15%	IV 35%
true/false	6	8	4	11
multiple-choice	3	7	2	9
matching	0	1	0	2
essay	1	1	0	1
recall	4	6	2	8
Totals	14	23	8	31

This blueprint contains 76 test questions and includes five types of questions. Thus, a pool of items has been developed from which the teacher can prepare the test. The teacher must also take into account the relative difficulty and comparative weight of the different questions. Essay questions are more difficult than true/false questions and should carry different weight or value. The items available will limit the number of items that can be included on the examination. The resolution of these issues will determine the final length and selection of items for the test. For example, if the examination period is the length of a typical class period, the final allocation of items for the test could be as follows:

Objectives

Question Type	I	II	III	IV	Total
	20%	30%	15%	35%	100%
true/false	3	4	2	2	11
multiple-choice	3	2	3	4	12
matching	1	2	0	0	3
essay	0	0	0	1	1
recall	2	4	2	2	10
Totals	9	12	7	9	37
% of points	20	30	14	36	100

The final test prepared in this example contains 37 of the original 76 items. It includes 11 true/false items, 12 multiple-choice items, three matching items, one essay, and 10 recall items. The weight or value of each item must next be determined to make certain the value given to each objective is proportionally tested on the examination. In this case, the point value assigned to each type of item may be as follows: true/false = one point; multiple choice = two points; matching = five points; essay = 20 points; recall = three points. With these assigned values to each item, the number of points possible on this test is 100. The points to be earned for each objective are as follows: I = 20 points; II = 30 points; III = 14 points; IV = 36 points. Thus, the test reflects the emphasis given to the objectives and includes a variety of test items whose value vary with their difficulty.

Only 37 of the original 76 items were used for this test. The remaining 39 items are still valuable items and should be kept for future use. These additional items can be used to create another form of this test, which will also increase test security. Some of the items on the selected test may prove to be faulty and, therefore, they will need to be replaced by items from those placed in reserve. A filing system or a computerized schedule can be established in which each item can be analyzed and recorded. A history of that item will enable the teacher to refine the pool of items available for future testing of the objectives in each unit of instruction.

The next section in this chapter explains the criteria used for the construction of test items.

Constructing Test Questions

The most common items teachers construct for testing include essay, true/false, multiple-choice, recall or short answer, and matching. Each of these should be written according to standards that increase the chances of the test being valid, reliable, fair, and serving the unique purpose of that particular test. A brief discussion of the major considerations in constructing these test questions follows.

Constructing Essay Questions

Essay questions are asked so that the student can produce a narrative about an event or to answer a question with an explanation that cannot be provided in a better form. Essay items require more time for student responses than other types of items, and the number of essay questions on a test will depend partly on the amount of testing time available and the nature of the questions. Essay questions should be stated clearly, and they should not be overly complex. The teacher should know what an "ideal" answer is and should write a response after the question has been formulated to identify with the question and the student who will be responding. By writing a correct response, the teacher also establishes a standard for grading the student papers. After writing the preferred response, the teacher should evaluate if the question is the most effective stimulus to obtain the answer that will evaluate the objective under consideration. If the teacher determines that a correct answer is one that contains four facts and the narrative is relatively unimportant, then the test might be revised to ask students to list the four facts and save the time of writing the narrative. If the time required is excessive and unrealistic, the teacher may assign students to write an essay as an assignment in order to determine attainment of the objective.

Constructing True/False Items

True/false items are relatively easy to construct, but certain criteria are essential to avoid errors in their construction. A statement should clearly be either true or false. Statements that are conditionally true, or are true or false most of the time, are confusing and do not reliably measure student knowledge. Statements that contain absolutes provide clues that have little to do with the content. Words like never and always are examples of such words. True/false items provide a quick check on student learning and can be used for short quizzes, but their validity is suspect. The chance of guessing correctly is 50 percent and with a little knowledge and a few subtle clues in some of the questions, a student who knows very little may score at the 70 or 80 percent level on a true/false test.

Constructing Multiple-Choice Questions

Multiple-choice items contain an opening statement, which is called the stem, followed by choices, which are called alternatives. The multiple-choice test is popular in standardized testing for a very good reason. A well-constructed, multiple-choice test is the most efficient and most effective way to reliably assess student knowledge.

[handwritten margin note: > very impt.]

[handwritten annotation: multiple-choice test → most efficient & most effective way to assess student knowledge]

There are two broad categories of multiple-choice questions. Some multiple-choice questions are based on a short essay or narrative in which an event or situation is described. In these cases, several questions usually are asked about the narrative and alternatives are provided for students to select the correct answer. A single episode may provide information from which four or five test items can be written. Another more common multiple-choice item is free standing and contains all the information necessary within the single item. These are usually items with a brief stem of one or two statements followed by alternatives. In either case, the stem must be written clearly, contain no ambiguities, and direct the student with sufficient information to select the correct response. The stem must avoid clues that are unrelated to the content. For example, an item in which the stem ends with the word "an" should have alternatives that all begin with a vowel so grammatical clues do not point to the correct answer. It is also necessary to be aware of avoiding information in one question that will help a student respond correctly to another question in the test. Another error to avoid is creating a sequence of multiple-choice questions in which the answer to one question is dependent on a correct answer to another question.

4 is the preferred #0

Alternatives for Multiple-Choice Questions

The test developer must make a decision about how many alternatives to provide for each multiple-choice item. On a given test, the number of alternatives should be the same for each item. Otherwise, the different items would vary in difficulty for the wrong reasons. The preferred number of alternatives is four and the rationale for this recommendation is based on a balance of limiting the chance of guessing the correct answer and the difficulty of writing plausible alternatives.

If only two alternatives are provided in a multiple-choice item, the guessing factor is the same as in a true/false item (50 percent) and the weaknesses in true/false items exist in this case. However, two plausible alternatives are usually not too difficult to write. If three alternatives are provided, the guessing factor is reduced from 50 percent to 33 percent, which is a gain of 17 percent, but still allows considerable chance or luck to enter into the score. Again, three alternatives can usually be constructed without excessive difficulty. When four alternatives are used, the guessing factor is reduced by another 8 percent and it is usually possible to construct four plausible alternatives, but this number becomes difficult at times. If five alternatives are written instead of four, the guessing factor is only reduced by 5 percent and it is extremely difficult to construct five plausible alternatives for every item. Thus, the guessing factor and the difficulty of constructing plausible alternatives work in tandem to recommend four alternatives as the preferred number. It is also recommended that each alternative should stand alone and avoid those alternatives that say "all of the above," "none of the above," "two of the above," and so forth. The format for the items and the instructions should make it easy for the students to respond. Answer sheets for blackening in correct answers may be used if the age of the students and the nature of the test make this feasible. Usually, the teacher will ask students to mark their answers on the test and circle correct answers or write in a space provided.

Constructing Recall Items

multiple-choice items are "recognition" items

Multiple-choice items call for students to recognize the correct answer and are "recognition" items. When the student must remember the correct answer to a question, then the item is a "recall" item. Short answer questions are recall questions and they are usually written in language similar to classroom discussions. Recall items are typically constructed as direct questions or as a "fill in the blank" format. In either case, the student must supply the information rather than recognize it from a list of alternatives. Questions of this type can be difficult to score when students provide answers that are similar to the correct answer but not exactly what the teacher had in mind. Furthermore, some questions can be answered correctly although they do not answer the question. Faulty questions will encourage faulty answers. For example, the following item might be on a test, "Abe Lincoln had a reputation for being very _____." The answer the teacher had in mind is "honest." But the student who writes "tall" can make a strong case for giving a correct response. A list of responses from which the student must choose will eliminate this problem, but it also makes the item a recognition item, even if the list of choices exceeds the number of questions by a large margin. Questions that call for longer answers, such as a sentence or two, also create similar grading problems for the teacher. Careful wording of recall questions and making certain a single question is raised will strengthen the quality of recall questions.

recall items → usually constructed as direct questions or as "fill in the blank" questions.

Constructing Matching Items

The final type of question discussed here is the matching item. Matching items contain two lists, and the student is expected to match items on one list with items on another list. For example, a matching item might contain the names of states in one list and the names of state capitals in the second list. The student would be asked to match the number of one state, perhaps Indiana, with the capital, Indianapolis, which would be in the second list. These questions should avoid lengthy lists of more than six or eight items. Also, the second list should be longer than the first so that the last answer does not automatically align with the final response. If the matches the teacher wants on the test are lengthy, several items can be constructed. If the capitals of all 50 states were to be matched with their respective state, this might be tested by creating six or seven matching questions to minimize reading time and optimize testing time.

Grading matching items poses special factors. One student may match all of the items correctly while another may miss only one. Does the second student miss the entire question or receive partial credit? What constitutes a wrong answer, and is it possible to be partially correct? Most objective items are either right or wrong, but matching items pose a different situation because there are several questions to answer within the item. The teacher must decide in advance and inform the students how the matching items will be graded.

how matching items are to be graded must be told to the kids

Scoring the Test

After the test has been constructed, administered, and scored, criteria or standards of performance will be applied. With the exception of tests for total mastery, standards will include some degree of subjectivity. Custom has established a general grading scale that varies slightly in different school districts, but, typically, letter grades are attached to results on a percentage scale. That scale often looks something like this:

A = 90–100

B = 80–89

C = 70–79

D = 60–69

F = below 60.

The teacher needs to exercise professional judgment about the difficulty of the test and must make the necessary adjustments when assigning student grades. If the highest score on the test is a 95, then some recommend that all scores be raised by five points. This adjustment is based on the belief that the best student in the class deserves a score at the top of the scale and other scores should be adjusted accordingly. Under this plan, a student with a score of 58 would not fail, but would receive a 63 which would be a D.

Another grading plan is pass or fail. In this case, the student either does or does not perform the task successfully. In a swimming class, if the requirement is to swim 25 yards, then students could be graded as pass or fail. The purpose of this test may not be to see who can swim the fastest, but to make sure everyone learns to swim at least 25 yards. This latter standard is called criterion testing and can be applied in academic and skill areas of learning. It is most important that the teacher establish acceptable standards, that tests assess student acquisition of the knowledge or skills that meet these standards, and that the evaluation of the test can be done as objectively as possible.

This next section addresses procedures for evaluating and revising tests on the basis of content validity, reliability, and student response.

Evaluating and Revising Tests

After the test has been administered and scored, the teacher has a wealth of information available for analysis. This discussion will focus on a few of the most useful techniques and procedures for evaluating the test and determining how to improve it. The most obvious analysis is to determine the range and the arithmetic average of the scores of the students. Judgments about this information depend on the purpose of the test and the level of difficulty expected. If the test is designed to assess mastery, then student attainment of high scores is desirable. If the test is designed to discriminate among students according to who knows the most, then a wider distribution of scores should be expected.

Mastery

Mastery is a desirable expectation when certain fundamental knowledge must be learned perfectly to assure correct future learning. Tests of spelling or multiplication facts are examples where perfect scores should be expected. Students who make errors in these fundamental areas will be unable to learn more advanced topics, and testing for 100 percent mastery is desirable. Mastery may be operationally defined as less than 100 percent if the knowledge contains some optional areas whose failure to understand perfectly or perform exactly is still acceptable. Advanced knowledge in the sciences, subtle interpretations in literature, or performance of a skill at less than a perfect level (making seven out of ten basketball free throws) are instances where mastery may be defined as less than 100 percent. In order to define "mastery" in this context, a standard or criterion is set as a minimum below which student performance is unacceptable.

less than 100%

set a standard or criterion

Analysis of Tests

When a test is designed to categorize students according to their relative knowledge or skill, a different analysis of the test is followed. A test that discriminates students from one another along a knowledge continuum should separate those students who are most knowledgeable from those who are least knowledgeable about the content of the test. There are two kinds of analysis that help determine if the test has succeeded in doing this. One analysis requires a tally of the percent of students who answer each item on the test correctly. Any item that is missed by everyone or is answered correctly by everyone does not distinguish one student from another. If any item is answered correctly or incorrectly by everyone, then the test has determined what students know, or do not know, but it has not helped sort students according to their knowledge. Such items should be reviewed by the teacher and remain if their purpose is either to test for mastery or provide a psychological climate of success while taking the test. Items that are answered correctly or incorrectly by at least some of the students are items that have some discriminatory power. It is almost certain that on a comprehensive test most students will miss some of the questions. The further analysis described next helps determine if the test has ranked or sorted students correctly.

This second analysis is undertaken by dividing the students according to the half of the class that obtained the highest scores and the half who obtained the lowest scores. The percent who answered each question correctly in each half of the class should be compared. This comparison is done to see if any items were answered correctly by more students in the lower half of the distribution than in the upper half. Any item that has a lower percent correct by the best performing students should be reviewed and examined for grammatical or other obvious errors. A slight discrepancy should not be considered an error in the test. If 30 students take a test and the students with the 15 worst scores exceed the percent right on an item by the 15 best students by a small margin, the item is not necessarily faulty. However, a large discrepancy of 15 to 20 percentage points is a good basis for further analysis. The item may be acceptable, but it also may be ambiguous or it may punish some students for "knowing too much." By making this comparison, specific items on the test are identified that may not properly examine students and can be revised according to the weakness in the item. Some items found may be so faulty that they should not even count on the test and may be discarded in order to assign a fair final score. Weaknesses may be in the format, content, or structure. Most test items can be analyzed on this basis, and the problem with the few items that discriminate in the reverse direction are usually not difficult to detect. However, the multiple-choice question is a special case that can be analyzed more thoroughly and refined on the basis of objective data. A discussion of this further analysis of multiple-choice items is provided next.

Analyzing Multiple-Choice Questions

For the purpose of this discussion, we will assume there are four alternatives in each multiple-choice question from which students will make their selection. We will also assume that each item has been compared according to students who have the highest scores with those who have the lowest scores. The item analysis that is described next calls for a more detailed but rather easy way to evaluate multiple-choice items.

Every alternative should function and be chosen by at least someone who takes the test. In a typical class of 30 students, if each alternative is chosen by at least one student, then the item will be answered correctly by no more than 90 percent of the students. This will be true because at least three students would need to provide an incorrect answer for each alternative to be chosen. Such an item meets the standard of less than 100 percent correct and all the alternatives in the item contribute to the purpose of the item. If any alternative is not selected by the students, that item should be rewritten to either include plausible alternatives in each case or to ask for that information with a different kind of question.

In addition to the systematic analysis of test items, all student responses should be read to identify mistaken thought processes, lack of knowledge, inadequate skill, or misunderstandings the students have revealed in their responses. These errors in student thinking can be deduced from an inspection of their responses.

After completing the item analysis and comparing scores of the highest scoring and lowest scoring students, it is helpful to return to the lessons that were taught and revise lesson plans on the basis of student performance. It is also crucial to return the scored tests to the students and use their responses as a basis for further teaching. Correct answers should be praised and errors should be corrected. Re-teaching should occur to help students avoid future mistakes or misconceptions about the content of the test.

Preparation for Testing

Considerable effort is necessary to develop tests and other procedures to evaluate students. However, if the testing environment in which the student is expected to perform is neglected, the evaluative information obtained on students will be suspect. The purpose of this narrative is to describe and explain procedures for establishing a proper testing environment. The discussion in this section provides information about administering teacher-made, pencil-paper tests. In the case of standardized testing, the information provided to the proctor should be strictly followed to make certain the conditions under which the test was normed are also the conditions under which the students take the test. Performance tests that measure skill acquisition call for demonstration of proficiency in a given task. Some of the discussion that follows can be generalized to skill testing and standardized tests, but that is not the primary focus of this section. Thus, this section describes the procedures to follow in the administration of teacher-made, paper-pencil tests.

Preparation for testing includes responsibilities for the teacher and consideration for the student. The teacher's responsibility for testing begins prior to the actual testing situation. During the time when instruction and learning take place, the teacher should make certain the class understands what knowledge is especially important for them to learn. It is the responsibility of the teacher to focus learning on the critical elements of the content to be learned and to examine students on their acquisition of this critical knowledge. Tests should not be used to "trick" students by testing for obscure information. The relationship between teaching and testing should be congruent and fair.

When tests are given to students, the teacher must pay attention to the logistics and details of administering the test. The test material should be prepared sufficiently in advance to make certain it is clearly printed and void of spelling or grammatical errors. There must be enough copies for every student and some extras in case a faulty test is given out. The best possible room environment should be provided, which includes proper lighting, ventilation, temperature, and reduction of noise. The test should be scheduled to avoid conflicts with events such as fire drills or public address announcements. Confer with the principal to avoid conflicts with school activities that may interfere with a desirable testing environment. Bring extra supplies of paper and pencils for those who forget them or break their pencils during the test. Place a notice on the door that notifies others that "testing is in progress—do not disturb." Such a notice should prevent interruptions, except for emergencies. The seating in the room should allow each student to work independently and provide for adequate proctoring. These logistical matters are not entirely in control of the teacher, but any of these procedures that can be followed should be completed to assure the fairest possible test administration.

Prior to the administration of the test, the teacher should orient the students to the testing situation. The teacher should also provide assurances to the students with positive remarks that encourage them to do their best. The purpose of the test should be explained, including information about how the test results will be used and how the results are relevant to them personally. Students should be informed about when the results of the test will be reported to them and how this feedback will be provided. In some cases it is appropriate for an entire class to discuss the test results, and in other cases it is best to keep test results personal and confidential. Students should know how the results will be reported to ease their minds about this procedure, and to give them one less factor that may contribute to their test anxiety.

If the test contains any special considerations about taking the test or scoring procedures, the students should be told what they are. For example, if a test includes essay questions, they should be given reasonable parameters to help them pace their time. A single essay question can consume their entire time; if there are several questions, the students might be told to limit their writing time on each question to assure coverage of the entire examination. If certain types of questions carry more weight than others, the students should be told the point value of the different questions. True/false items might be worth one point and multiple-choice items might be worth two points. The test itself should also contain information. The time allotted for the test should be sufficient to enable all students who are reasonably well-prepared to be able to demonstrate their knowledge.

Test Administration

Students should be kept informed about the time remaining as they progress through the examination. If a clock is in the room in a conspicuous location, this may be sufficient. It may be helpful for the proctor to write the remaining time on the board in minutes such as ten, five, three, and one. As these remaining times arrive, the proctor can draw a line through the appropriate number. Thus, students can tell at a glance how much time is remaining. The proctor might suggest a pace for a long test that is divided into several sections. If students should complete the first section by a certain time, the proctor should announce, "You should have completed section one by now. If you have not done so, move on to section two." Students should be told in advance if the proctor is going to provide this information.

The Proctor

The proctor must be sensitive to the importance of time during a testing situation. The time spent before the actual testing begins should be minimal. Most students come to a testing situation ready to answer questions and do not want a long delay in getting started. In some cases, the pre-test information may even be provided in a previous session, and test materials may already be on student desks in a folder or upside down so everyone can start promptly when told to begin. Delays by the teacher prior to the testing reduces the time available for students to respond and increases test anxiety. The time provided for the test itself should be the same for everyone. Everyone should be expected to "run the same race" in order to determine the comparative knowledge each student has on the content being tested.

Proctoring the examination calls for close attention to students without "hovering" over the class in a way that may be a distraction. The proctor should not be preoccupied with other tasks during the test. Students should be instructed to remove all materials from their desks and to have an extra supply of pencils and paper. Students whose pencils break during an examination should not be allowed to go to a pencil sharpener and disturb others. The proctor can quietly supply a pencil after receiving a signal from the student. Proctors should not engage in conversation with any student during the examination. Some students may request information, such as the definition of a word. If the proctor responds, it may appear to other students that the proctor is providing unfair assistance. If all the preliminary details have been provided, if the test contains the required information, and if every student has listened and has come prepared, no student should have any questions during the examination.

The proctor must assure that all students do their own work. Crib notes, conversation between students, and signals that students may have created to help each other should all be monitored. In most cases, if the proctor is in the back of the room, the temptation for students to cheat is minimized. When students cannot see where the proctor is looking, they tend to keep their own eyes from wandering. If the room is small and desks are close, making it easy for students to look on other desks, it may be necessary to create different forms of the same test. This can be done by reversing the order of the questions or any other reorganization of the test that will protect its integrity.

Formative Feedback

After the test has been completed and collected, the teacher should score the test and give feedback to students as promptly as possible. In a discussion of the test results, it is essential to identify correct responses and express approval to the students for doing well on those items. It is important to provide overall information, such as the range of scores, the average, and the grade distribution. It is helpful to identify common errors made by students and to take time to explain the correct responses. Students may challenge answers, and a discussion of these inquiries should be provided without getting into arguments. The teacher and the students can both benefit from a discussion of items where there is a difference of opinion.

When teachers respond to student responses, they are providing feedback. Feedback can embody various dimensions, and the following four possibilities provide a framework in which teacher responses can be classified. These four types of responses are defined by recognizing that feedback may be positive or negative and it may also be responsible or irresponsible. Thus feedback may be:

I.   Positive and responsible

II.   Negative and responsible

III.   Positive and irresponsible

IV.   Negative and irresponsible

These four categories help clarify how the teacher can show acceptance of and value for student response, and also how to redirect digressions. Responses in Category I include praise for acceptable student comments which should be provided specifically, immediately, and sincerely. Responses in Category II include teacher comments that correct student errors, describe faulty logic or misinformation, and other student errors that might occur in classroom discussions. Teacher criticism in Category II should be given tactfully and be the basis for improving student learning. Category III responses are exemplified by the teacher who tolerates student errors and even gives praise for sub-standard comments by lowering standards or allowing inaccurate responses to stand without correction. Category IV responses are negative reactions by teachers to students and are delivered in a harsh and derogatory manner. Sarcasm and insults are included in Category IV responses. The two types of responsible categories (I and II) will support student responses that are acceptable and also maintain reasonable standards by correcting student responses that are not acceptable. The teacher who accepts student comments and values their remarks uses language that is responsible and maintains a relationship in which tolerance for positive and negative remarks is based on optimal student learning and mutual respect. The two types of irresponsible categories (III and IV) will either sugarcoat wrong answers and lower standards listed above, or create tension and hostility by using tactless sarcasm or insults to criticize student work. The teacher who fails to correct student errors by accepting sub-standard student responses dilutes the quality of learning and risks the loss of respect from students and colleagues who recognize such behavior. The teacher who corrects with sarcasm, or other demeaning behavior, creates tension and fear in students. A tense classroom atmosphere will reduce student cooperation, ingenuity, creativity, and the quality of classroom discussions.

Summary

An acceptable testing environment requires teachers to: (1) prepare students by emphasizing the critical knowledge for students to learn; (2) establish a setting with clear instructions and fair tests for students to complete; and (3) give feedback that praises correct responses and corrects errors and misunderstandings.

Assessment has many purposes. Above all, it is designed to provide proper feedback to the students about their progress in their academic program. It can also be used to determine the prior knowledge student possess before they begin a topic of discussion. Assessment can help to determine behavioral issues that can disrupt the learning process. For instance, behavioral assessment may look at how students work together in groups, how they organize their work, or how they pay attention to details and instructions. In addition, asking students to self assess their own work can provide great insight into the attitudes and work patterns or ethics the students are harboring inside.

Assessment should be a daily part of an effective instructional program. Assessment can provide information about how effective the lesson was, how effective the method of delivery was, how effective the curriculum meets the district goals and expectations, and how students are learning. Assessment can be viewed as a tool in determining the overall instructional effectiveness of the program, the curriculum, and the instructional delivery. Good programs continually perceive assessment as a vital and integral part of their program.

References

Further reading of these references may enhance understanding of the competency and may also increase performance on the examination.

Ainsworth, Larry, and Christinson, Jan. *Student Generated Rubrics: An Assessment Model to Help All Students Succeed.* Upper Saddle River, NJ: Pearson Learning, 1998.

Chudowsky, Naomi, and Pellegrino, James W. *Knowing What Students Know: The Science and Design of Educational Assessment.* Washington, D.C.: National Academy Press, 2001.

Hebert, Elizabeth A. *The Power of Portfolios: What Children Can Teach Us About Learning and Assessment.* Hoboken, NJ: Jossey-Bass, 2001.

Popham, W. James. *Classroom Assessment: What Teachers Need to Know* 3rd ed. Upper Saddle River, NJ: Pearson Allyn & Bacon, 2001.

Stiggins, Richard J. *Student Involved Assessment for Learning* 4th ed. Upper Saddle River, NJ: Prentice Hall, 2005.

Competency 2: Communication

Definition of Competency

The teacher has knowledge of effective communication with students, parents, faculty, other professionals, and the public, including those whose home language is not English.

- The teacher identifies appropriate techniques for leading class discussions (e.g., listening, identifying relevant information, probing, drawing inferences, summarizing student comments, and redirecting).

- The teacher identifies ways to correct student errors (e.g., modeling, providing an explanation or additional information, or asking additional questions).

- The teacher identifies nonverbal communication strategies that promote student action and performance.

- The teacher chooses effective communication techniques for conveying high expectations for learning.

Principles of Verbal Communication

There are several principles which apply to written and oral messages in the classroom. The message must be accurate. As Mark Twain said, "The difference between the right word and the almost right word is the difference between lightning and the lightning bug." Teachers in particular must be careful to use very specific words that carry the appropriate denotation (literal meaning) as well as connotation (feelings, associations, and emotions associated with the word). Content teachers must carefully teach vocabulary related to the subject area.

It is possible to be completely accurate, however, without being clear. At times a teacher may use an excessive amount of jargon from his or her subject area. While students must learn vocabulary related to the subject area, the teacher must ensure that he or she teaches the words and then reviews them so the students have practice using them. At other times a teacher may assume that students understand difficult words. Many students are hesitant to ask what a word means; teachers must be alert to nonverbal signs that students don't understand a word (confused looks, pauses in writing a word down, failure to answer a question containing the word, etc.). Taking a couple of seconds to ask students to define a word will help them understand the larger content area concepts.

Words should also be specific or concrete. The more abstract a word, the more ambiguous it will be. For example, "physical activity" is very general; "Little League baseball" is much more specific. Although students need to learn abstract words, explaining them in a concrete manner will increase their understanding. Saying that a war causes economic difficulties is general; being more specific would be to say that it reduces the amount of tax money available to cities because of money spent on munitions.

A teacher's communications must also be organized. Students will not be able to follow directions which are given in jumbled order, interrupted with, "Oh, I forgot to tell you." Effective teachers plan their directions carefully, writing them down for the students or making notes for themselves so they will give directions or explain concepts in appropriate order.

Other communication strategies include monitoring the effects of a message, or making sure that the audience actually received and understood the message. A teacher may encourage students to be active and reflective listeners by having each student summarize what another has said before making his or her own contribution.

Voice

The way a teacher uses his or her voice conveys prejudices, feelings, and emotions. When a teacher's words convey one meaning and his or her tone of voice conveys another, the students will believe the tone rather than the meaning. Students immediately know the difference between "That's a great idea" said in a low voice with a shrug, and "That's a great idea!" said with energy and a smile. A teacher's tone of voice can tell a student, "I'm asking you, but I don't think you can answer this." Messages can be modified by varying the loudness or softness, by varying the tone, by using high or low pitch, and by changing the quality of speech.

Nonverbal Communication

Even when the verbal or written message is accurate, clear, specific, and organized, nonverbal communication can confuse the message. Sometimes the nonverbal aspect of communication can carry more weight than the verbal. Nonverbal messages can be sent by the way teachers dress, the way they use their facial expressions, and the way they use their voice. Experienced educators realize that students respond better when teachers dress professionally. Most people find it easier to take seriously someone dressed in neat, clean clothes than someone in wrinkled, ill-fitting clothing. Also, students behave better when they themselves are dressed better.

Eye Contact

Facial expressions communicate a world of emotions and ideas. Teachers use many voluntary facial expressions. All students have seen "the look" from a teacher, usually when a student does something out of order. A frown or raised eyebrow can also be very effective. Although positive involuntary expressions such as smiles and laughter are appropriate, teachers should guard against involuntary negative facial expressions that convey contempt, anger, or dislike to a student.

Eye contact can be used to control interactions. Teachers often look directly at students to encourage them to speak, or look away to discourage them from speaking. "The stare" can be part of "the look" which teachers use for discipline purposes. Making eye contact with students is important when the teacher is giving instructions, sharing information, or answering questions. Many people make a habit of scanning the room with their eyes and pausing briefly to meet the gaze of many members of an audience. However, eye contact should last about four seconds to assure the person in the audience (or classroom) that the speaker has actually made contact.

Students also use their eyes, making contact with the teacher when they want to answer a question, but often looking at the floor or ceiling when they want to avoid being called on. However, teachers must be careful in making assumptions about eye contact. Research has revealed that students who are visually oriented tend to look upward while they are thinking about a response; kinesthetic learners tend to look down while they are thinking; auditory learners may look to the side. The teacher who says to a student, "The answer's not written on the floor!" may not understand the student's mode of thinking. Effective teachers who are encouraging higher-level thinking may find a classroom filled with eyes that look in various directions.

Cultural factors may also contribute to confusion about eye contact. Many cultures teach children that it is very disrespectful to look an adult in the eye; therefore, these students may stand or sit with downcast eyes as a gesture of respect. Forcing the issue only makes the students and teacher uncomfortable and actually hinders communication.

Body Language

Body language can also convey feelings and emotions to students. A teacher can emphasize points and generalizations by gesturing or tapping something on the chalkboard. If a teacher gestures too often or too wildly, students find it difficult to determine what the teacher is trying to emphasize. Too many gestures can also cause the students to watch the gestures instead of attending to the information.

Beginning teachers especially need to convey a relaxed but formal body posture, which denotes strength, openness, and friendliness. Hiding behind the desk or crossing the arms indicates timidity or even fear. A teacher who meets students at the door with a smile and even a handshake shows students he or she is confident and in control.

Expectations of Students and Communication

A teacher's expectations for student behavior can be revealed through a combination of verbal and nonverbal communication. Jere Brophy and others have researched the relationship between teacher expectations and student behavior. This research shows that teachers often communicate differently when dealing with high-achievers and low-achievers. This *— Example* behavior is not always deliberate or conscious on the part of the teacher, but it can communicate negative expectations. When dealing with high-achievers, as opposed to low-achievers, teachers tend to listen more carefully, give them more time to answer, prompt or assist them more, call on them more often, give more feedback, and look more interested. The effective communicator will be careful not to differentiate communication based on a student's achievement level.

Media Communication

Media communication has become a vital part of the classroom process. Effective teachers use a variety of audio-visuals in every class, including posters, graphs, overhead transparencies, films, videos, CD-ROMs, and laser disks.

Effective Use of Language

Effective use of language is one of the major components of learning in classrooms. New visual aids and technology have broadened the range of possibilities for instruction, but without words and their proper use the potential for learning is severely limited.

Discourse has many dimensions including verbal, non-verbal, and paralingual features. The verbal part of discourse contains the content; the non-verbal includes body language, posture, facial expressions, etc.; and the paralingual features are found in the choices of words, inflections, and subtleties of speech that portray characteristics of speakers, such as arrogance or humility. All three components communicate to students and contribute to the total message that is received.

[handwritten margin note: paralingual & choice of words, inflections & subtleties of speech]

Relationship Between Teachers and Students

Underlying the discourse that occurs in classrooms is the relationship between the teacher and students. The best relationship is one that creates a trusting confidence in each other and an environment in which opinions, information, and dialogue can be exchanged in a non-threatening classroom setting. Productive relationships with students can be built by recognizing that interactions occur within three different schemata: open relationships, closed relationships, and transitional relationships. Open relationships emerge when both participants are honest, accepting, tactful, emphatic, and active listeners. Closed relationships develop when neither participant engages in discourse that can be trusted because it is dishonest, secretive, or tactless. Transitional relationships exist when one participant is open and the other is not. Transitional relationships may become open or closed depending on how each reacts to the other over time. The teacher who behaves toward his or her students as a person does in an open relationship has the potential to establish a classroom in which honesty, trust, acceptance, empathy, and active listening become the norm. It is in such a classroom that learning through effective two-way communication is most likely to occur. Thus, the behavior of the teacher can promote the atmosphere that is most conducive to a healthy learning environment for students. If the teacher does not verbalize openly and effectively, it is not possible for the students and teacher to establish the open relationship that will be most effective in the promotion of learning. In addition to a healthy psychological classroom climate, there are technical aspects of communication that make a significant difference in learning. These aspects will be addressed next.

Knowledge about, and application of, communication principles enable a teacher to engage in successful classroom interactions with students. Successful interactions occur when learning is optimized through a partnership in learning with students. It is this positive environment that provides the best hope for teachers to a) show acceptance and value of student responses; and b) ignore or redirect digressions without devaluing student responses.

Connected Discourse

Connected discourse is discussion based on a given topic or theme, in which the information that is exchanged leads to one or more conclusions or major points. The teacher's role includes clarification of the theme or topic to make certain students know the central focus of the discussion. It is also necessary to structure questions and activities that will enable the class to reach closure on the topic under consideration.

Single questions avoid question overload, give focus for student responses, and provide students with an unambiguous task. Single questions can either stimulate higher order thinking or ask for simple recall, but when they are properly stated they are not confusing. Complex topics can be broken into smaller parts through the use of single questioning, and can be developed gradually, which will ensure that the topic will be understood better; it is best to avoid trying to do too much at once.

Marker Expressions

Marker expressions are the verbal equivalent of italics, underlining, or color marking passages in written documents. They are points of emphasis the teacher uses to help students focus on or retain the most salient information in a discussion. They can be used to give appropriate praise to students by linking a previous remark by a particular student to the emphasis at that time. For example, "You remember that yesterday John noticed how the presence of a river was a factor in the location of cities. Today, we see another example of that factor in the establishment of St. Louis."

Emphasis is a technique to help students identify and retain significant information. Teachers can prepare students for essential topics by stating, "This next topic is crucial; I want you to work extra hard at it. Ask questions about anything you do not understand." Other forms of emphasis include repetition, summarizing, and application of the knowledge. All of these methods should be utilized by actively engaging students in classroom activities.

Task Attraction and Challenge

Task attraction and challenge are methods to motivate students, and they include teacher enthusiasm for the task at hand. Teachers engage in this behavior by showing their own excitement for the learning that is about to take place. Often, teachers can alert students to the difficulty of a task and challenge them by saying that something will be hard for them to do. When properly presented, a challenge becomes the motivation for students to prove their ability.

Scrambled Discourse, Vagueness, and Question Overload

Scrambled discourse, vagueness, and question overload are teacher behaviors that make if difficult for students to stay on task. Scrambled discourse is disconnected to the theme or topic under discussion and often includes garbled verbal behavior. Vagueness is evident by the excessive use of indeterminate language (e.g. something, a little, some, much, few, things, you see, perhaps, or actually). Question overload causes confusion because multiple questions or long and involved questions are asked and the student is uncertain about what is expected.

Effective Communication

Effective teachers establish an open and trusting atmosphere that supports interaction with students. Praise is provided immediately and specifically when warranted and constructive criticism promotes learning. Teachers help students achieve by using connected discourse, single questions, marker expressions and techniques, emphasis, and task attraction and challenge.

Providing Clear Feedback to Students

One of a teacher's important functions is to respond clearly to student responses so that the student knows whether a response was correct or incorrect. In order to advance in learning the subject matter, the student requires clear guidance from the authority, the teacher. If the teacher's response is ambiguous or fuzzy, the student may be left confused, or even worse, in error.

Of course, not every question to which students respond in class has a clearly right or wrong answer. Many times, students will be asked, and should be asked, to express their judgments, opinions, values, and conclusions on topics that have many valid perspectives.

Nevertheless, teachers must frequently test, both orally and in writing, their students' knowledge of facts, objective knowledge that leaves little room for judgments or opinions. In doing so, teachers should leave no doubt in the student's mind whether his or her response was right or wrong.

It is through classroom recitations and discussions that the teacher most often responds directly to a student's answer. Here is one example of a question/student answer/teacher response sequence in which the teacher gives clear, unequivocal feedback to the student (and to the rest of the class):

Ms. Jackson: Who was the first president of the United States? Shannon?

Shannon: Benjamin Franklin?

Ms. Jackson: No, Benjamin Franklin was an important leader but he never became president. Lindsey? Who was our first president?

Lindsey: George Washington.

Ms. Jackson: That's right. George Washington was the first president of the United States.

Notice that Ms. Jackson gives a clear "no" to Shannon's answer, while at the same time reminding the class that Benjamin Franklin *is* an important figure in United States history.

Notice also that when the correct answer is given, the teacher repeats the correct answer to the entire class. This repetition helps pupils learn the name of the first president and ensures that anyone in the class who did not hear Lindsey's response now hears the correct answer.

Although the teacher's response in the above example may seem so natural and obvious that it should need no commentary, even experienced teachers might sometimes handle their response less effectively than Ms. Jackson did.

Consider the following question/student answer/teacher response sequence that begins with the same question as in the sequence above:

Mr. Lopez: Who was the first president of the United States? Roberto?

Roberto: Abraham Lincoln.

Mr. Lopez: Well, that's an interesting answer, Roberto. Many people do think that Abraham Lincoln was the greatest president we have ever had, and so in that sense he is sometimes considered "Number 1." But was he the very first president chronologically, timewise? Stacey?

Stacey: George Washington was the first president.

Mr. Lopez: So, in a sense, both Roberto and Stacey could be right. Lincoln and Washington were both great presidents. Some people think that Lincoln was the greatest; others say Washington was the greatest. But Washington was the first, at least in order of time.

Here Mr. Lopez, perhaps wishing to avoid embarrassing Roberto by saying flatly that his answer is wrong, fails to give a clear-cut, unambiguous response to an answer that is clearly wrong. Instead, he needlessly complicates the question by allowing a different meaning to the word "first"—a meaning which, most likely, neither Roberto nor anyone else in the class had entertained. What had been a simple question requiring a simple answer has become somewhat confusing.

The idea of greatness—a matter of judgment—has been introduced into a matter of historical fact.

If Mr. Lopez wishes to lead the discussion in the direction of the relative greatness of presidents, he should settle clearly and decisively the question he first raised: George Washington was the first president. Once that is made clear to everyone, he could go on to take up the question of greatness.

Notice that even at the end of the exchange Mr. Lopez still does not say unequivocally that Stacey was correct when she answered that George Washington was the first president. Instead, he qualifies his statement with the phrase "at least in order of time," a qualification likely to leave some doubt or perplexity in the minds of some of this pupils.

In considering a fact so familiar to adult Americans—that George Washington was the first president—it is good for teachers, especially teachers of the lower elementary grades, to keep in mind that many such facts may *not* be familiar and obvious to some pupils. The teacher's responsibility is to communicate such information clearly and unambiguously, as Ms. Jackson did. The teacher should not unnecessarily confuse a child, as Mr. Lopez did, by introducing a sophisticated interpretation of his own question.

Another area in which it is crucial to give clear, unambiguous feedback to the student is in making written marks and comments on papers and tests. Before returning a set of papers or tests to the class, the teacher should explain clearly any features of his or her marking system that may not be self-evident. For example, the teacher should explain that a circle around a word indicates that the word is misspelled, or that a curlicue through a word or punctuation mark means that it should be deleted.

In marking objective items on a test, the teacher should clearly indicate (with an X, for example) that an answer is wrong. If the teacher puts a question mark beside an answer, the student will be left in doubt as to what the question mark means. Does it mean that the answer is possibly correct but the teacher him- or herself is unsure? Does it mean that the answer is illegible? If so, is it wrong, or does the student have the opportunity of explaining to the teacher what was written? Some students will ask a teacher for clarification of a question mark, but others are more likely to ignore what they do not understand, and so they will learn nothing from their response or from the teacher's question mark.

When an objective answer on a test is wrong, or a word is misspelled or inappropriate, should the teacher write on the paper the correct answer or word? One's answer to this question may vary according to the grade level, the subject matter, and the individual student. In teaching the early elementary grades, it is especially important that the child be given the correct answer so that he or she would be able to compare that with his or her own answer. In later years, the teacher can shift more responsibility to the child to find out and write down the correct answers. The teacher can review the correct answers orally with the whole class and instruct the students to correct their errors. If the subject matter is relatively easy and the student can readily find the right answer or spelling in a book, then it may be best to let him or her do so. If the matter is difficult, however, and the student is unlikely to discover the correct answer without great effort, then it might be best to provide it for him or her.

Make Specific Statements about Students' Responses

While it is crucial for the teacher to indicate clearly whether a response is correct or incorrect, it is also important to encourage students' participation by praising them for intelligent, reasonable answers. In the previous section, Mr. Lopez erred by not indicating clearly that Roberto's answer was incorrect. We may assume, however, that he erred with a noble motive—the wish to find some merit in his student's response and to reward the student for his effort. The fact that he did so in an instance where the student's answer was clearly incorrect shows that it is not always possible or appropriate to find something praiseworthy in a student's response—beyond the mere fact that the student did give a serious, pertinent response.

Very frequently, however, teachers rightly pose questions that have no clearly correct or incorrect answers. They ask questions that require students to make value judgments, see implications, interpret events, both fictional and historical, express aesthetic preferences, and estimate probabilities.

In such cases, it is not only possible but highly desirable for the teacher to point out to the responding student and to the rest of the class the merits of the response. To do so is much more difficult than simply indicating that a response is correct or incorrect. It requires the teacher to listen carefully to the student's response, to ask for clarification if necessary, and to see quickly what it is about the response that deserves notice and praise.

The following example of a classroom exchange illustrates this principle. Mr. Pizzo's eighth-grade geography class is discussing the reasons why cities and towns are often founded on the banks of rivers.

Mr. Pizzo: Why do you suppose that Cairo, Rome, London, and Paris were all founded on major rivers? Jeffrey?

Jeffrey: Because the people needed to fish to eat?

Mr. Pizzo: Yes, good, that's true—the readily available food sources was certainly a prime consideration to early societies. But are fish the only benefit of rivers? What else do rivers offer people? Ilsa?

Ilsa: Transportation? Didn't they need to get up and down the rivers and out to the oceans?

Mr. Pizzo: They certainly did. To trade with faraway places it was a great advantage to be located on a navigable river. Can anyone think of another benefit?

Here Mr. Pizzo responds well to Jeffrey's answer by telling why it is partially correct. Even though Mr. Pizzo was not "looking for" this answer, he recognizes its validity. If an answer is unexpected but at least partially correct, the teacher should give the student credit for it. If the teacher had said, "Well, that's not what I was thinking of," students might get the impression that responding to questions in class is just a matter of trying to guess what is in the teacher's mind.

While recognizing the worth of Jeffrey's answer, though, Mr. Pizzo also moves beyond it by asking for further, probably more important reasons for river settlements. By doing so, he keeps the discussion going and keeps the students trying to think of reasons why so many large cities were founded on rivers.

Methods of Correcting Students' Errors

As mentioned earlier, a student's progress in learning depends in part on the effectiveness of the teacher's response to the student's error. The teacher should have a repertoire of effective ways to respond to errors and be able to select the most appropriate response for a given situation. Four productive ways of responding are to:

- simply give the correction,

- explain the error,

- provide the student with information to enable him/her to correct the error, and

- ask the student questions to enable him/her to correct the error.

Simply Give the Correction

Under what circumstances might it be best simply to correct the student? In classroom discussions or question-and-answer sessions, it is often preferable to provide a correction in a matter of fact way when the error is simple (e.g., grammar, pronunciation, word choice). In such cases, to provide explanations or ask questions in order to elicit the correction would unnecessarily slow the momentum of discussion and distract the class from the issue at hand. If the teacher provides the correction simply and quickly, the student and the rest of the class are made aware of the right response without losing the momentum of the conversation.

Consider the following situation, for example. In a history class, you are discussing the concept of laissez-faire capitalism, and one of the students mispronounces "laissez" as "layzees." It is much more efficient and less distracting from the topic simply to say the word correctly than to explain to him that "laissez" is a French word and that in "ez" endings the "z" is not pronounced. Asking the student whether he/she is sure he/she is pronouncing that correctly and whether he/she would like to reconsider the pronunciation would embarrass the student and derail the conversation.

In responding to students' papers, too, it is sometimes preferable to write in a correction rather than merely to point out that something is amiss in what the student has written. If you judge that the student will not be able to understand the nature of the error and will not be able to correct it on his own, then it is better to write in the correction. For example, a student writes in an essay the phrase "embarrassed of her braces." If the teacher were only to underline or circle the word "of," the student would probably be unable to detect what is wrong with that word. It is a matter of idiom that we say "embarrassed by" rather than "embarrassed of," and since the student has the idiom wrong, the child is unlikely to provide the correction. It is more efficient and effective for the teacher to underline or cross out "of" and write "by" above it or in the margin.

Explain the Error

Sometimes, though, it is not enough for the teacher to correct an error; he/she should provide an explanation of the error. It is especially important to do so in situations where the error occurs in the very matter that is being taught at the time. In such cases, a mere correction might not help the students understand why the given response was incorrect.

Imagine the following situation. Mr. Bielski is teaching his class how to convert improper fractions to mixed numbers. After explaining that one divides the numerator by the denominator, which results in a whole number and a fraction whose numerator is the remainder of the division operation, he gives some examples. Then, he asks the class to change the improper fraction $7/3$ to a mixed number. After a moment, one student offers the answer $4^1/_3$. Instead of just dismissing the answer as wrong, Mr. Bielski sees that the student, instead of dividing the numerator by the denominator, has subtracted the denominator from the numerator, resulting in the number 4. Mr. Bielski explains what the student has done and repeats his explanation of the correct procedure.

In writing comments on students' written work, it is sometimes necessary to explain an error or inadequacy so that the student will understand why the teacher has marked the paper a certain way. Because explanations can be very time consuming, teachers often use a system of abbreviations. An English teacher, for example, may use marginal abbreviations such as *agr* for subject-verb agreement, *frag* for sentence fragment, and so on. In doing so, the teacher must make sure, however, that all students understand the abbreviations and the principles they represent.

Provide the Student with Information

Rather than telling the student why a response is wrong, it is sometimes better to lead the student to the correct response. This technique has the advantages of prompting the student to think through the problem and of boosting his or her confidence when the student arrives at the right answer on his or her own. The only drawback is that it can be time consuming, and to use it too frequently might unduly slow the pace of the class.

Imagine that you are teaching a unit on the American civil rights movement in the 1950s and 1960s. You have just asked the class what the leaders of the movement were protesting for or against, and one student answers, "Better jobs." While this answer may be partly correct, you want the class to understand that black Americans were motivated by many more grievances than the quality of jobs. Instead of providing the further answer of "segregation in the schools, public restaurants and restrooms, and the right to vote," you might lead the student toward the answer by reminding him/her that in the 1950s and early 1960s, blacks were denied some of the social and political freedoms they enjoy today.

Ask the Student Questions

This is called the Socratic method, for Socrates practices it frequently in Plato's *Dialogues* to lead his pupils toward a deeper understanding of the truth and a rejection of their previous, uncritical responses. Few teachers are as adept as Socrates in the art of questioning, but every teacher should be able, on occasion, to ask a question or two that will help the student see the error and make the correction.

A fairly common classroom occurrence when this technique is useful is a student's misuse of a word. A student may say, for example, "This is an illusion to Shakespeare," when he means "allusion." In response, the teacher might ask the student, "Isn't an illusion a deception, something that seems real but is not? That's not what you mean here, is it?" At this point the student may be reminded that a subtle reference is called an "allusion"; if not, the teacher may have to explain the distinction between the two words.

Questioning the student is most effective, however, when the error is not just in the use of a word or in a matter of fact but in the student's thinking or reasoning. In such cases, a good teacher can help the student see a flaw in her perception of the world and so correct it. If in a discussion of French cuisine, for example, a student remarked, "French waiters are rude," the teacher might respond by asking the student why he or she says that. When the student says that he or she has eaten at two different French restaurants in town, and both times the waiter was very rude, the teacher could ask if the student thinks that two instances of rudeness are enough to make a generalization about French waiters. Isn't it possible that these two are exceptions to the rule, and that most French waiters are quite courteous? Isn't it even possible that one, or even both, of the waiters he or she encountered are usually polite but happened to be in a bad mood for some reason? Would it be fair for a Frenchman to judge Americans as loud and obnoxious after seeing two such Americans in Paris? Such a line of questioning should help the student realize that he or she was prematurely generalizing about French waiters.

The teacher should be familiar with all four ways of responding to student errors and practice using them in appropriate situations.

A teacher should recognize that ALL students are capable of learning. Although student abilities differ, it is important to maintain and communicate high expectations for learning within the classroom setting. Students will aspire to the expectations of the teacher. The teacher should believe that ALL students can learn the material, provided the material is developmentally appropriate to their students and that the student rises to the challenge.

Parent-Teacher Communication

If a student is misbehaving, the teacher should examine if the misbehavior is caused by a conflict in the classroom. If the cause cannot be determined based on classroom experience, there may be a problem at home. When a child is not responding to the teacher's efforts to stop the behavior, the teacher should contact the parents. This will allow the teacher and parents to discuss any problems that may help explain the misbehavior. The parents may be facing similar difficulties at home, or may not even be aware of a problem. Such a discussion enables the teacher and parents to work together at getting the child back on track. It is important for the teacher to express his or her feelings of concern to the parents. The parents should also be assured that the child's educational welfare and personal well-being are continuing primary concerns of the teacher.

The teacher can contact the parents using a written note, a telephone call, a meeting outside of school hours, or even a home visit if the administration approves. During the conference, the teacher should mention the incidents of misbehavior, the record of the student's daily effort if failure to accomplish assignments is the problem or part of it, the attempts made to change the negative performance, and the suggestions for solving the problem. In turn, the teacher should ask the parents about the child's attitude toward school, comments, and behavior at home. Having the student present is sometimes a useful strategy, especially if the student is omitting part of the story when talking about it at home. The parents and teacher must develop a partnership to focus on the student's well-being.

The end of any conference should include writing down the actions each participant—teacher, parent, and student—will take to improve the situation. A tentative date for meeting again, or at least for communication between the teacher and parents, should be established before the meeting ends. Within a few days, the teacher must try to find an opportunity to provide feedback to both the parents and the student about the matters discussed, especially if improvement of a negative situation is noted.

If the initial consultation with the parents is not successful at ending the misbehavior, there are a few techniques that the teacher and parents can try. A daily report may be used to provide frequent contact between the teacher and the student that allows the parents to monitor the student's behavior in the classroom. The teacher sends home a report of the student's behavior, positive and/or negative, for the parents to review, sign, and return back to the teacher the next day. This also provides the parents with a way to add their own feedback to the situation. If the behavior improves, the reports can be sent less frequently, until the student's behavior is consistently positive.

If the combined efforts of the parents and the teacher are unable to resolve the situation, they may need to consult with a school or community professional. Family or individual counseling may be another route to end the student's conflict and guide him or her back into the classroom momentum.

References

Further reading of these references may enhance understanding of the competency and may also increase performance on the examination.

Cooper, Pamela J., and Simonds, Cheri J. *Communication for the Classroom Teacher* 7th ed. Upper Saddle River, NJ: Pearson Allyn & Bacon, 2002.

Lee, Patty. *Collaborative Practices for Educators: Strategies for Effective Communication.* Minnetonka, MN: Peytral Publications, Inc., 1999.

Neall, Lucinda. *Bringing the Best Out in Boys: Communication Strategies for Teachers.* UK: Hawthorne Press, 2003.

Power, Brenda Miller. *Parent Power: Energizing Home-School Communication.* Portsmouth, NH: Heinemann, 1999.

Competency 3: Continuous Improvement

Definition of Competency

The teacher has knowledge of strategies for continuous improvement in professional practices for self and school.

- *The teacher identifies professional development experiences that will enhance teacher performance and improve student achievement.*

- *The teacher identifies ways for using data from learning environments as a basis for exploring and reflecting upon teaching practices.*

Effective Professional Development

Professional development cannot be thought of as a one-time workshop or in-service activity that is done in isolation. Rather, effective professional development occurs when there is a commitment by educators to a continuous plan of lifetime learning that begins with pre-service activities, continues into their employment in the profession and extends throughout their careers and beyond. Effective educators are lifelong learners who continuously work to hone their skills, gain new experiences, and develop new practices to enhance their teaching and quality of life. The resulting strengths of the faculty must work to complement the learning needs of an increasingly diverse body of students. In addition, professional development activities must be planned to satisfy the needs of the school as well as the needs of the individual educators. When individual *and* organizational goals are met, the results are much greater levels of commitment and success. Finally, the effectiveness of professional development is dependent on the creation of a culture that resembles a community of learning where collegiality and cooperation, which broadens knowledge and expertise, is not only allowed, it is rewarded.

Effective school programs are dependent on the extent to which employees continue to grow and develop. Professional development activities are the primary means for helping personnel reach their potential. The National Staff Development Council stated in a recent report that improvement of American education is dependent on improvement of ongoing professional development for teachers and a national plan for helping teachers fulfill their untapped potential. Research shows that quality professional development can improve student achievement. Teachers report that professional development improves their teaching, therefore, effective professional development assists school systems in reaching their primary goals of enhancing and achieving quality teaching and learning for students.

Professional Development Delivery Methods

There are many ways to engage in professional development. Some teachers prefer individual means of development while others seem to thrive more in a group situation. Neither should be pursued as the sole method of professional development. Rather, teachers should be encouraged to pursue both individual and group types of professional development. Some traditional as well as more progressive means of professional development are described here; the list is by no means exhaustive.

Case Methods

A case study is a descriptive research document, often presented in narrative form, that is based on a real-life situation or event. These cases enable teachers to explore, analyze, and examine representations of actual classrooms and school situations. Cases are presented to stimulate discussion about situations that occur in the school setting, the characters in these situations, evidence, possible solutions and conceivable ramifications for these proposed solutions. Discussions about these cases allow for differing perspectives and brainstorming that leads, in most cases, to new knowledge on the part of the participants. In addition to large or small group discussions, cases can also evoke role-playing and written analysis. Cases can be used to develop knowledge of a particular theory or to show best practices. They also allow for analysis and review, present situations, allow for problem solving on the part of the observer, and stimulate personal reflection. Early results of empirical research about using case methods and the potential for further research and development show great opportunities for those who wish to use it to pursue a deeper understanding of the process of teaching.

Action Research

In action research, teachers are encouraged to investigate topics related to their current practice. This can help teachers carry out research investigations in their own classrooms. Teachers are encouraged to identify and initiate research into classroom problems and practices that they feel should be investigated. Some tools teachers use for action research are notes, audio and visual tapes, journals, interviews, self-reflection, and observations. Teachers can pursue action research individually or with other colleagues. Teachers can share their data with others and engage in dialogue that can benefit all of those involved. Trusted teacher colleagues can assist each other in analyzing their teaching through cycles of observation, analysis and discussion of data to establish shared ideas, and methods that will improve their teaching. Practical reflection, whether individually or with colleagues, can enrich a teacher's sense of what is feasible and possible and help them transform that into effective practice.

Data gathered within the learning environment that results from day-to-day activities can also provide a means for reflection and discussion. According to the National Staff Development Council, professional development should encourage educators to develop a variety of classroom based assessment skills. These skills include

- adapting instruction based on observation and analysis of student work,

- selecting, constructing, and using assessment strategies for monitoring student learning,

- developing assessment strategies.

Educators are prone to make instructional decisions on the basis of tradition or feelings. Research based knowledge must be used to prepare the current and coming generations of students for the future. Not only must schools tap this research in shaping their professional development programs, but teachers should also be trained and encouraged to use these methods in their classrooms as a basis for exploring and reflecting upon teaching practices.

In addition to video and audiotapes of class sessions, teachers can use students' scores on tests, projects, performances, labs or other assignments to reflect on his/her quality of teaching. Common mistakes made by students or areas where class grades indicate confusion can determine content in which the teacher may wish to reexamine his/her mode of delivery of instruction. Another helpful tool is the use of a rubric or rating scale for assignments. The teacher can use the rubric to grade the students' work and ask the students to grade their own work according to the rubric. Then, a comparison of both results can indicate the students' understanding and value of the rubric.

Results of standards based exams such at the FCAT and SAT can also help a teacher assess his/her competencies. Scores of students in individual classrooms are available on these exams. Often times, teachers and administrators tend to look at areas where students have not been successful, which is helpful in determining need areas. However, concentrating also on the areas in which students have been most successful can prove helpful in professional development. When a particular teacher's students have done exceptionally well in a certain area of the test, that teacher should be encouraged to share the teaching methods that they used to foster that success with other teachers.

Educational practice should be examined and changes should be considered on the basis of sound research to which professionals have access within their classrooms, in conversations with their colleagues, within educational books, journals, websites, and through effective professional development. Equipping teachers with the skills to gather, analyze, and use relevant data to improve their teaching is a huge step toward raising student achievement.

Technology

Technology can be used to extend and make more effective much of the professional development that is currently available in schools. One method is to use it as a mode of delivery. Instead of teachers spending time commuting to off campus locations, a workshop or in-service activity can be delivered from one location to many at the same time with the use of advanced technology. This concept can also be used within a school by broadcasting a meeting either through the use of computer systems or through a television network. This type of training could be either previously taped or live. It is cautioned, however, unless the school or school system can afford an interactive technology system, that this type of training not be used exclusively, as there are many benefits to live training with the component of interaction between presenter and attendees.

Another use of technology in professional development is the use of the Internet. School systems, private individuals, and corporations offer websites for teachers that assist in many areas of instruction. Many of these services are offered free of charge or for a minimal investment. Teachers can also access professional and scholarly journals online. Many search engines for information on specific educational offerings are also available and accessible through your school district, library, and local university library system. By visiting their state government website teachers can also be kept abreast of current legislative items that impact education. Teachers should be encouraged to seek information on the Internet and to share it with their colleagues.

Mentors

Mentorship programs rely on the belief that adults have the capacity for continued growth and development, which can be facilitated by specific types of interventions that support and challenge them. A mentor relationship supports the teacher who is new to the profession, school, grade level, or subject area. The purpose of the mentor is to promote and support peer teacher growth. The mentor can help relieve insecurities of the new teacher while helping that teacher fully develop his/her talents. At the same time, the mentor is given the opportunity to experience empowerment by facilitating local change, assuming a leadership role without relinquishing the classroom, and developing teaching behaviors that blend clinical skills with practitioner-translated research and theory.

Traditionally, the desire for increased and varied responsibility within the teaching field has been fulfilled only by leaving the classroom and moving into the administrative ranks. However, the career teacher does not always wish to move into administration. Opportunities to expand the teaching role while remaining a classroom teacher are achievable through a mentoring program where established teachers are allowed to assist in the professional development of new teachers. Mentors, who must now teach their skills and experiences to another, realize a renewed level of awareness of their practice. By reexamining and reassessing their own practice along with new ideas in subject matter pedagogy and effective teaching research offered by the new teacher, mentors experience growth as well.

Reflective Learning Communities

Reflective learning communities can be formal or informal. They can be as planned as a weekly meeting of interested teachers or a impromptu conversation over lunch. The most successful learning communities, however, have particular topics, issues, or lessons that the participants plan to discuss. The time together consists of direct, honest, and productive conversations with colleagues about teaching. These discussions might result from a book or journal article that each member has read, a recent event that has occurred in the school or community, a study of a particular lesson in a particular subject area, a lesson of one of the members that was observed by the others, or a general area in need of research. This community is different from a regular faculty meeting in that the content centers on one area decided in advance that the group wants to discuss. Through both discussion and reflection, dialogue helps each member take the content and make it meaningful for themselves.

University Coursework

Many teachers seek advanced coursework or certification at local universities. Some universities work with school districts to form a collaborative approach to furthering skills or even gaining advanced certifications. In addition, if enough teachers in a particular area are interested in a course, there is a chance that the university will send a faculty member out to the school site to teach the course. Finally, entire master's degree programs in educational areas have been taught at a location away from the university campus to a cohort of teachers who live or work in that location. Depending on the area that teachers wish to study, scholarships may be available.

Professional Development Library

Within every school, there should be a place where teachers can go to gain information about their profession. Materials in a professional development library should include modern classics in the educational field, current books on educational issues, journals from various disciplines, and local, state, and federal information that impacts teaching.

Recommended Professional Development Topics

The decision as to what kinds of professional development to offer should be made, for the most part, at the school site. Obviously, some professional development decisions will be made at the district level and based on current needs in the district as a whole, and at particular school sites. However, effective professional development is created with extensive participation of teachers, principals, and parents. Many schools survey teachers as to what types of professional development they feel that they need and would like to see at the school. Another factor in planning for professional development activities is the school improvement plan. With this in mind, there is a plethora of professional development topics that can be offered in a school. The list presented here includes those activities that were most prevalent within the research and suggested by state boards of education, the National Staff Development Council, and the American Federation of Teachers.

Content Knowledge

Professional development should include deepening the content knowledge of teachers.

Data and Assessment

Teachers should be provided with instruction in the use of data and assessments to inform and instruct classroom practice including classroom assessment and action research skills. Teachers should be prepared to use disaggregated student data to monitor progress and help sustain continuous improvement. In addition, they should be able to use multiple sources of information to guide improvement, demonstrate its impact, and use this information to make decisions.

Instructional Strategies

Teachers should be provided with research-based instructional strategies to assist students in meeting rigorous academic standards and to prepare them to select and use various types of classroom assessments appropriately.

Limited English Proficient Students

Teachers should be provided with the knowledge and skills, including the appropriate use of curricula and assessments, to provide instruction and appropriate language and academic support services to Limited English Proficient (LEP) students.

Parents

Teachers should be provided with instruction as to how they can, along with principals, pupil services personnel, and school administrators work more effectively with parents and involve them appropriately. Teachers should be able to identify and use community resources to foster student learning. Professional development should promote an environment where educators feel comfortable and confident working collaboratively with other educators, parents, business and community leaders.

Pedagogy

While knowing that the content being taught is critical, teachers must also know how to help students to understand it. Therefore, professional development should provide a strong foundation in the pedagogy of particular disciplines.

Personal Self-Understanding

Teachers need greater self-understanding to keep pace with social changes and to expand their skills.

Providing a Safe and Orderly Environment

Teachers should understand and appreciate all students and be able to create safe, orderly, and supportive learning environments. Teachers should also have an understanding of a reasonable plan for discipline and safety. They should be encouraged to pursue various methods to employ discipline and safety in their classrooms.

Special Education

Teachers should be provided with instruction in methods of teaching children with special needs.

Technology

Teachers should be provided with information on the use of technology so that technology and its applications are effectively used in the classroom to improve teaching and learning in the curricula and core academic subjects taught.

Barriers to Professional Development

Without effective, ongoing professional development, quality teaching and learning in schools will not continue. If this occurs, schools will cease to improve and will become stagnant. Despite this reality, we must also look at the complexities of the day-in and day-out processes of a school that make thoughts of professional development pale to the other, more urgent duties involved in schooling our children. Teachers, researchers, and policymakers indicate that the greatest challenge to implementing effective professional development is lack of time. School schedules do not usually include time for teachers to engage in professional development activities such as consulting, observing colleagues, engaging in research, learning and practicing new skills, curriculum development, or professional reading. In the TIMSS (Third International Mathematics and Science Study), it was observed that in many Asian schools, which generally have larger class sizes than U.S. schools, teachers teach fewer classes and spend 30-40% of their day out of the classroom, conferring with students and colleagues or engaged in other professional work.

Professional development takes time for initially understanding theory and application, content knowledge, and enough formal learning time to allow this understanding to develop. Then teachers need time to integrate their new knowledge into classroom practice. Once integration is completed, teachers need time to reflect on this practice, have a dialogue with others, and be observed utilizing the new practice. Support is vital at this time to avoid teacher frustration which can cause the teacher to abort the new practice altogether. Finally, there is a need for time for feedback and discussion with colleagues to refine the new practice and to share it with others. Without this time for sharing, the new learning is isolated and other teachers and students cannot benefit from it.

A factor that seems to prevent schools from setting aside time for professional development is the prevailing school culture which considers a teacher's proper place during school hours to be in front of a class. This isolates teachers from one another and discourages collaborative work. This culture traditionally does not recognize the importance of teacher learning. For effective professional development to occur, there must be a school culture that fosters continuous improvement and that challenges traditional roles and relationships among educators. This culture must be one that recognizes that collegial support is essential and provides for ongoing and meaningful collaboration among educators. In addition, value must be placed on individual efforts and self-improvement. Incentives should be provided for those who pursue continuous improvement. The leadership in this culture must support and model lifelong learning, creativity, innovation, and the pursuit of enhanced student learning. Time must be incorporated within the school day for educators to team plan, collaborate, analyze data and student work, develop and implement instructional practices, curricula and assessments, and implement federal, state, and local mandates.

Other barriers to effective professional development include:

- Content that is not supported by staff as necessary

- Experiences that are not deep or varied enough

- New theory presented that is at odds with school policy and organization

- Individual and/or collective concerns are ignored

- Acceptance and promotion of the latest "fad" without fully understanding it or considering its implications for teachers and students in daily and long-term contexts.

As plans are made for professional development, all of these factors must be considered. Good professional development engages teachers in thinking about tough issues and difficult content, in learning with and from colleagues, and in putting to practice the resources with their students. Professional development requires the support of colleagues and administration and must include opportunities to see how others interpret and apply such knowledge; all of this takes time. In addition, it is important that practitioners are centrally involved in formulating professional development plans inclusive of how to implement the professional development and its content and activities. This fosters commitment and "buy in". Finally, the school culture should promote and provide an atmosphere that is "safe" for teachers to engage in continuous and serious reflection about what students are learning and what needs to be done to continually improve.

References

Further reading of these references may enhance understanding of the competency and may also increase performance on the examination.

American Federation of Teachers. *Principles for Professional Development: AFT's Guidelines for Creating Professional Development Programs that Make a Difference*. Washington, DC: American Federation of Teachers, 2002.

Florida Department of Education (n.d.). *Professional Development (No Child Left Behind Definition)*. Retrieved September 7, 2003 from http://www.fdoe.gov.

France, G. "Self-understanding: Professional Growth and the Role of the Teacher Counselor." *The Australian Administrator* (1982): 3(1), 1-4.

Office of Educational Research and Improvement. "The Classroom Teacher as Teacher Educator." *ERIC Digest 89-7* (1990). Retrieved September 7, 2003, ED335297.

Office of Educational Research and Improvement. "Cases, Case Methods, and the Professional Development of Educators." *ERIC Digest* (1994).

Office of Educational Research and Improvement. "Making Time for Teacher Professional Development." *ERIC Digest* (1996).

National Staff Development Council. *NSDC Standards for Staff Development.* Oxford, OH: National Staff Development Council, 2001.

Smyth, W. J., and Henry, C. "A Case Study Experience of a Collaborative and Responsive Form of Professional Development for Teachers." Paper presented at the annual meeting of the Australian Association for Research in Education, Canberra, Australia, November, 1983.

Sparks, D., and Hirsh, S. *A National Plan for Improving Professional Development.* Oxford, OH: National Staff Development Council, 2000.

Technical Education Research Center. *Teacher-initiated Research: Professional Development for Teachers and a Method for Designing Research Based on Practice. Final Report.* Washington, DC: National Institute of Education, 1981.

Webb, L.D., and Norton, M.S. *Human Resources Administration: Personnel Issues and Needs in Education.* Upper Saddle River, NJ: Prentice Hall, 1999.

Competency 4:
Critical Thinking

Definition of Competency

The teacher has knowledge of strategies, materials, and technologies that will promote and enhance critical and creative thinking skills.

- The teacher identifies a variety of instructional strategies, resources, materials, and technologies that foster critical and creative thinking.

It is one thing for teachers to have command of their subject matter. It is a given that English teachers will be able to write well, that math teachers will be able to compute and calculate, that science teachers will know and understand science, and so forth. However, it is something else—and something at least as important—that teachers know how to teach. A critical part of teaching is knowing how to question the learner. Developing critical thinking skills in students helps to develop higher level learning.

When teachers understand learners, that is, when teachers understand developmental processes common to all learners, and how environmental features and learning styles, varied and diverse, affect learning, then teachers are better able to design and deliver effective instruction. Although there may be some intuitive aspects to teaching (and it seems that some people were born to teach), teaching skills can be acquired through processes of introspection, observation, direct instruction, self-evaluation, and experimentation.

How teachers teach should be directly related to how learners learn. Theories of cognitive development describe how learners learn new information and acquire new skills. There are many theories of cognitive development, two of which will be included in this review; they are (a) the Piagetian (or Neo-Piagetian) theory and (b) information processing theory.

Piagetian theory (including Neo-Piagetian theory) describes learning in discrete and predictable stages. Therefore, teachers who understand this theory can provide students with developmentally-appropriate instruction. This theory also describes learners moving from simpler ways of thinking to more complex ways of problem-solving and thinking. For teachers, there are many important implications of this theoretical perspective. For example, teachers must create enriched environments that present learners with multiple opportunities to encounter new and unfamiliar stimuli—be they objects or ideas. Teachers must also provide learners with opportunities to engage in extended dialogue with adults; according to Piaget's theory, conversational interactions with adults are a key component in cognitive development, especially the acquisition of formal operations (or higher-ordered thinking skills). Moreover, it is important that adults (and teachers in particular) model desired behaviors; teachers must reveal their own complex ways of thinking and solving problems to students.

On the other hand, information processing theories of human development take a different approach to describing and understanding how learners learn. Based on a computer metaphor and borrowing computer imagery to describe how people learn, information processing theories begin by determining the processing demands of a particular cognitive challenge (or problem to solve) necessitating a detailed task-analysis of how the human mind changes external objects or events into a useful form according to certain, precisely specified rules or strategies, similar to the way a computer programmer programs a computer to perform a function. Thus, information processing theories focus on the process, how the learner arrives at a response or answer.

Info. Processing like Sternberg's triarchic theory of intelligence

A brief analysis of one information processing theory will serve to illustrate this point. Sternberg's (1985) triarchic theory of intelligence is a theory that takes into account three features of learning. Those three features are (a) the mechanics or components of intelligence (including both higher-ordered thinking processes, such as planning, decision making, and problem solving, and lower-ordered processes, such as making inferences, mapping, selectively encoding information, retaining information in memory, transferring new information in memory, and so forth); (b) the learner's experiences; and (c) the learner's context (including the adaptation to and the shaping and selecting of environments).

According to Sternberg, learners' use of the mechanics of intelligence is influenced by learners' experiences. To illustrate, some cognitive processes (such as those required in reading) become automatized as a result of continued exposure to and practice of those skills. Learners who come from homes where parents read and where there are lots of different reading materials tend to be more proficient readers; certainly, learners who read a lot become more proficient readers. Those learners who are exposed to reading activities and who have ample opportunities to practice reading have greater skill and expertise in reading; and in a cyclical manner, students who have skills in reading like to read. Conversely, those who lack reading skills do not like to read. Students who do not like to read, do not read; thus, their reading skills, lacking practice, fail to improve.

An information processing approach acknowledges that not only are individuals influenced by their environments and adapt to those environments, individuals also are active in shaping their own environments. In other words, a child who wants to read but who has no books at home may ask parents to buy book, or may go to the library to read, or check out books to read at home.

Information processing theory is of interest to educators because of its insistence on the idea that intelligent performance can be facilitated through instruction and direct training. In sum, intelligent thinking can be taught. Sternberg has urged teachers to identify the mental processes that academic tasks require and to teach learners those processes; he challenges teachers to teach learners what processes to use, when and how to use them, and how to combine them into strategies for solving problems and accomplishing assignments.

Teachers who wish to follow Sternberg's advice might choose to begin teaching by identifying *instructional objectives,* that is, what should students be able to do as a result of instruction. Second, teachers should analyze the objectives in terms of identifying the *instructional outcomes,* those being the tasks or assignments that students can perform as a result of achieving the instructional objectives. Third, teachers should analyze instructional outcomes in terms of the *cognitive skills* or mental processes required to perform those tasks or assignments. After following these three steps and identifying instructional objectives, instructional outcomes, and cognitive skills involved, the teacher is ready to conduct a *preassessment* (or pretest) to determine what students already know.

Instruction is then based on the results of the preassessment, with teachers focusing on directly teaching the cognitive skills needed in order for students to perform the task(s). Following instruction, teachers would conduct a *post-assessment* (or post-test) to evaluate the results of instruction. Further instruction would be based on the results of the post-assessment, that is, whether or not students had achieved expected outcomes and whether or not teachers had achieved instructional objectives.

Regardless of which theoretical perspective is adopted by teachers, and, at times, teachers may find themselves taking a rather eclectic approach and borrowing elements from several theoretical bases, it is helpful for teachers to consider if they are structuring their classrooms to satisfy learners' needs or merely their own needs as teachers. Furthermore, if the teachers' goal is to increase teaching effectiveness by facilitating learners' knowledge and skill acquisition, then teachers will engage continuously in a process of self-examination and self-evaluation.

Metacognition

Self-examination and self-evaluation are both types of *metacognitive* thinking. *Metacognition* is a term used to describe what, how, and why people know what they know when they know it. In short, it is thinking about thinking and knowing about knowing. Cognitive psychologists describe metacognition as a characteristic of higher-ordered, mature, and sophisticated thinking. Generally speaking, as learners achieve higher levels of cognitive skills, they also increase their metacognitive skills. Therefore, not only should teachers engage in metacognitive thinking, they should model that thinking for their students and encourage their students to develop metacognitive skills.

Metacognition can be understood in terms of (a) metacognitive knowledge and (b) metacognitive control (Flavell, 1987). Basically, metacognitive knowledge is what learners need to know and metacognitive control is what learners need to do. Metacognitive control, therefore, is in the hands of the learner. Teachers cannot control learners' behavior, although they can encourage and admonish. The best that teachers can do is help learners expand their metacognitive awareness and knowledge.

Awareness can be increased by talking about metacognition. Flavell has explained that there are three kinds of metacognitive knowledge, those three kinds being (a) person knowledge, (b) task knowledge, and (c) strategy knowledge.

Person knowledge falls into one of three categories: (a) intraindividual knowledge, (b) interindividual knowledge, and (c) universal knowledge. First, intraindividual knowledge is what the learner knows or understands about him- or herself. Therefore, it is important

[handwritten margin notes: metacognitive knowledge → what learners need to know; metacognitive control → in the hands of the learner (what learners need to do)]

that learners have opportunities to learn about themselves, about their interests, abilities, propensities, and so forth. For this reason (among others), it is important that learners have opportunities to learn about their own learning style and their perceptual strengths. It is also helpful for them to have opportunities to examine their personalities, values, and goals.

Furthermore, in a model that recognizes the dynamic nature of instruction, that is, one which recognizes that the learner also knows certain things and can contribute to the classroom, the teacher realizes that she or he is a learner, too. Teachers, then, can benefit from examining their own learning style, perceptual strengths, personalities, values, and goals. Moreover, it can be extremely beneficial for teachers to consider their own instructional style.

Returning to the discussion on metacognitive knowledge, the second kind of person knowledge is interindividual knowledge, how learners are alike and how they are different. Again, this is another reason why the recognition of diversity brought about by studying learning styles can inform learners and improve their cognitive performance. As they learn about their own learning style, learners also observe that their classmates have some similarities and some differences when it comes to the various elements or factors in determining learning style. Interindividual knowledge is increased as students realize that there are many different ways to learn.

Finally, the third kind of personal knowledge is universal knowledge, the knowledge that there are degrees of understanding. Examples are the realization that short-term memory is fallible and has limited capacity, that people can make mistakes, that it is easier to remember things if they are written down, that memory work requires repetition, and so forth. To examine students' understanding of universal knowledge, teachers might ask students to identify what they know about learning, for example, by asking students to write down on notecards what they know about how people learn things or by brainstorming the question in class.

The second broad category of metacognitive knowledge, according to Flavell, is task knowledge. Task knowledge includes several different variables, such as whether information is interesting or boring, or if it is new or familiar, or if it is easy or difficult. Task knowledge enables learners. to plan appropriately for undertaking tasks (for example, if something is hard to learn, then it may take more time, more concentration, and more effort) and tells them how to go about accomplishing the task (for example, if the task requires memory, then a memory strategy is needed).

Specific tasks relevant to academic disciplines can be identified by classroom teachers; however, there are academic tasks that are generally applicable to all content areas. These academic tasks include what are broadly referred to as study skills, but which are foundational skills for all learning. They include such tasks as time management, directing attention, processing information, finding main ideas, studying, and taking tests, among others (Weinstein, Schulte, & Palmer, 1988).

Flavell's final category of metacognitive knowledge is strategy knowledge, which takes into account how learners can best accomplish particular tasks and how they can be reasonably certain that they have reached their cognitive goals. Strategy knowledge also equips learners to monitor their cognitive activities and to gain confidence in their abilities. To illustrate, if the task is to find main ideas, then learners need strategies for finding main ideas. Strategies for this task include learning (a) to preview or survey reading assignments (reading headings, words in bold print; looking at illustrations and graphic aids); (b) to ask questions (What is this about? Who is this about? When did it happen? Where did it happen? How did it happen? Why did it happen?); and (c) to read the first and last sentences in each paragraph (knowing that the first and last sentences in paragraphs are most likely to be topic sentences).

Comparison/Contrast

An important higher-order thinking skill is the ability to compare and contrast two things or concepts which are dissimilar on the surface. Thomas Gordon has described a process of synectics whereby students are forced to make an analogy between something that is familiar and something that is new; the concepts seem to be completely different, but through a series of steps, students discover underlying similarities. For example, a biology teacher might plan an analogy between a cell (new concept) and a city government (familiar concept). Although they seem impossibly different, they both have systems for transportation, disposal of unwanted materials, and parts that govern these systems. By comparing something new with something familiar, students have a "hook" for the new information, which will help them remember it as well as better understand it. For example, students trying to remember functions of a cell would be assisted by remembering parts of the city government.

Questioning

There are many ways that teachers can ask questions that elicit different levels of thinking, although studies of teachers' skills in questioning often reveal frequent use of lower-level questions and infrequent use of higher-level ones.

Questions can be divided into two types, closed and open. An example of a closed question is, "What was the main character's name?" There is usually only one right answer to a closed question. Often students can point to a phrase or sentence in a book to answer a closed question.

closed question

An open-ended question requires students to think carefully about the answer. There may be more than one appropriate answer to an open-ended question. An example is, "What do you think was the most important contribution of Pascal to the field of mathematics?" Teachers who ask open-ended questions are not looking for one specific answer, rather they are looking for well-supported responses. Asking an open-ended question but requiring one specific answer will discourage rather than encourage thinking.

An example of a closed math question is, "What is 5×5?" An example of an open-ended math question is, "What is the best way to solve this problem?" The open-ended question assumes that the teacher will accept all reasonable methods of solving the problem, provided the students can explain why their method is best.

The Six Levels of Taxonomy

There are other ways to categorize questions. Benjamin Bloom, et al., developed a taxonomy of educational objectives for the cognitive domain. Teachers have used this taxonomy for a variety of purposes in addition to writing objectives, including categorizing questions and activities.

There are six levels in the taxonomy, each one building on the previous level. **The first level is knowledge**. This is similar to the closed question, with one right answer which should be obvious to students who have read or studied. Words which often elicit recall or memory answers include who, what, when, and where. Examples of knowledge-level questions include: Who developed the first microscope? What were the names of Columbus's ships? When was South Carolina first settled? Where is Tokyo?

The second level is comprehension, which also elicits lower-level thinking and answers. The primary difference from the first level is that students must show that they understand a concept, perhaps by explaining in their own words. The question "What does obfuscate mean?" would be answered on a knowledge level if students repeat a memorized definition from the dictionary and on a comprehension level if students explain the term in their own words.

The third level (first higher-level category) is application. Students take what they have learned and use this knowledge in a different way or in a different situation. A simple example of this level is using mathematics operations—addition, subtraction, multiplication, and division—to solve problems. Another example is translating an English sentence into Spanish, or applying what the students have learned about Spanish vocabulary and grammar to develop an appropriate and correct response. Another form of application is changing the format of information, e.g., create a graph from a narrative description of a survey. The key to this level is the use or application of knowledge and skills in a similar but new situation.

The fourth level is analysis, which involves taking something apart, looking at all the pieces, and then making a response. An example of an analytical question is, "How are these two characters alike and how are they different?" This question requires students to examine facts and characteristics of each individual, then put the information together in an understandable comparison. Another example is, "What are the advantages and disadvantages of each of these two proposals?" Another example might be, "Compare the wolves in *The Three Little Pigs* and *Little Red Riding Hood.*"

The fifth level is synthesis, which involves putting information together in a new, creative way. Developing a new way of solving problems, writing a short story, and designing an experiment are all creative ways of synthesizing knowledge. For example, fourth-grade science students may develop and conduct research on food waste in the cafeteria and make recommendations for changes. An example of a synthesis question is, "What do you predict will happen if we combine these two chemicals?" This question assumes students will have factual knowledge. Their predictions must be reasonable and based on prior reading and/or discussion.

The sixth level (highest level) is evaluation. This level involves making value judgments and very often involves the question "Why?" or a request to "Justify your answer." For example, students may be asked to use their analysis of two possible solutions to a problem to determine which is the better solution. Their response must be reasonable and well supported.

Evaluation-level activities must build on previous levels. Skipping from knowledge-level to evaluation-level questions will result in ill-conceived and poorly supported responses. Although teachers might use an evaluation question to provoke interest in a topic, they should make sure that students have opportunities to work at other levels as they develop their responses.

This type of questioning promotes risk-taking and problem-solving, where the teacher has established a safe environment where students are encouraged and not ridiculed for creative or unusual responses. The teacher does not expect only one specific answer, but allows students to ponder several reasonable possibilities.

Effective teachers also appreciate cultural dimensions of communication and are aware that some cultures teach their children not to question adults. These teachers explain to students that they expect questions, encourage students to ask them, but do not force the issue if students are very uncomfortable. Sometimes students may be willing to write down and turn in questions for the teacher. Teacher attitude can promote or deter questions, even by so simple a tactic as changing, "Does anybody have any questions?" to "What questions do you have?" The first question implies that no one should have questions; the second assumes that there will be questions.

Open-ended projects such as math or science fair activities will promote higher order thinking. By opening up the discussions and adapting the traditional teacher directed lesson activities so that students can openly explore solutions and approaches to problems, the role of the teacher becomes more of a moderator or mentor on the side rather than a giver of all knowledge. Provide students with the opportunity to think for themselves as they reason through their activities that encourage students to evaluate issues, form opinions and conjectures, defend their positions with adequate evidence and solid judgments, solve problems that require thinking outside of the box, and debate the pros and cons of sensitive topics or current research.

References

Further reading of these references may enhance understanding of the competency and may also increase performance on the examination.

Bentley, Richard, and Wallace, Belle. *Teaching Thinking Skills Across the Middle Years: A Practical Approach for Children Aged 9-14.* London: David Fulton Publishers, 2002.

Johnson, Andrew P. *Up and Out: Using Critical and Creative Thinking Skills to Enhance Learning.* Upper Saddle River, NJ: Pearson Allyn & Bacon, 1999.

Nosich, Gerald M. *Learning to Think Things Through: A Guide to Critical Thinking in the Curriculum.* Upper Saddle River, NJ: Prentice-Hall, 2001.

Paul, Richard W. *Critical Thinking: How to Prepare Students for a Rapidly Changing World.* Dillion Beach, CA: Foundation for Critical Thinking, 1995.

Critical Thinking Consortium
http://www.criticalthinking.org

The National Council for Excellence in Critical Thinking
http://www.criticalthinking.org/ncect.html

Competency 5: Diversity

Definition of Competency

The teacher has knowledge of cultural, linguistic, and learning style differences and how these differences affect classroom practice and student learning.

- The teacher identifies instructional and interpersonal skills and classroom practices that encourage innovation and create a positive learning climate for all students.

- The teacher selects materials and strategies that encourage learning about diverse cultural groups.

Diversity

The effective teacher appreciates human diversity. Such a person recognizes how diversity in the classroom and the community may affect learning, and creates a classroom environment in which both the diversity and uniqueness of individuals are recognized and celebrated. Effective teachers realize that students bring to the classroom a variety of characteristics, both personal and social, that create within the classroom a microcosm reflective of American society at large. Indeed, America has long held to the notion of being a "melting pot" whereby members of various racial, ethnic, religious, and national origin groups contributed to the wealth of our culture.

Ethnocentrism is a sociological term used to describe the natural tendency of viewing one's own cultural or familial way of doing things as the right, correct, or best way. Because ethnocentrism is a natural tendency, all people are likely to engage in ethnocentric thinking and behaviors at times.

Some social critics have pointed out that ethnocentrism has played a notable role in American education. They assert that educational institutions often have been guilty of assuming a Eurocentric viewpoint, that is, solely recognizing the contributions of European writers, artists, scientists, philosophers, and so forth, at the expense of those from other cultures. These critics have also noted that the contributions of men often are disproportionately recognized over like achievements of women.

In fact, David and Myra Sadker (1994) have found that teachers, both male and female, at all grade levels, are more likely to call on male than female students, are more likely to give positive reinforcement to males' correct responses than to those of females, and to provide more coaching or instructional help to males when their responses are incorrect than to females. Their research has led them to conclude that teachers are usually unaware of gender bias in their teaching, but that such bias is pervasive in American schools. Their research also has persuaded them that bias can be eliminated once teachers become sensitive to its debilitating effects on students.

The point made here is that ethnocentrism, in any form, can be damaging because it is exclusive rather than inclusive. Eurocentric, Afrocentric, and other ethnocentric perspectives are equally limited in that they narrowly focus attention on one set of ideas at the neglect of others. Therefore, effective teachers will wisely expend a degree of effort in avoiding ethnocentric thinking and behaviors. Effective teachers will attempt to include all students in all classroom activities. The race, ethnicity, religion, national origin, and gender of learners will be viewed as strengths which enable students to learn with and from each other.

Historically speaking, educational experiments have demonstrated the importance of teachers avoiding bias and ethnocentric thinking. The *Hawthorne effect*, or the phenomenon whereby what teachers expected became reality, was demonstrated when teachers were told that some students in their classes were extremely intelligent whereas others were extremely slow or mentally retarded. In fact, all students had normal range intelligence. Nonetheless, at the end of the experiment, students who had been identified to the teachers as being extremely intelligent all had made significant academic progress and were not only at the top of their class, but also performing at the top on national achievement tests. Those students who had been identified as retarded had made no progress at all; in fact, they had lost previously-made gains. Thus, it was demonstrated that teachers' expectations for students often become self-fulfilling prophecies.

In today's society, there is a considerable reference to multiculturalism. Multiculturalism, if it serves merely to separate and distinguish the accomplishments of select cultural and ethnic groups, has the potential of separating and alienating Americans. To view multiculturalism in a positive light is to acknowledge a kind of multiculturalism that embraces the accomplishments of all cultural and ethnic groups, thereby strengthening our country and society instead of fragmenting it.

Because multiculturalism and/or cultural diversity can be a controversial issue with many sides to consider, a reasonable approach to diversity for the classroom teacher is to distinguish between cultural diversity and learning diversity and to focus on diversity in learning. This approach transcends cultural boundaries and recognizes that all people have distinct learning preferences and tendencies. Furthermore, this approach acknowledges that all preferences and tendencies are equally valid and that each style of learning has strengths. The teacher who understands learning styles can validate all students in the class.

The teacher's goal should be to create a range of experiences and activities that embraces the diversity of the students. Activities should utilize appropriate materials and resources that support a multicultural experience. Activities should promote and value the diverse cultures and linguistic backgrounds of the students while maintaining equitable treatment of *all* students. Teachers should encourage shared values and expectations that create a climate of mutual respect, appropriate social behaviors that lead to acceptance, openness, and tolerance, a supportive climate of inquiry that helps students gain knowledge about the diversity of their school, families and community.

Students who are not proficient in speaking English (LEP-limited English proficient) require special consideration. The English language consists of many slang and multi-definitional words that can confuse students. Teachers need to learn the linguistic skills of vocabulary building such as concrete pictures matched to vocabulary, rewording complex statements, simplifying instructions, and modeling correct vocabulary. It must be observed that students learn to speak a language long before they are proficient at writing in that language.

Cultural diversity abounds within the classroom. This diversity, although it can correlate to ethnic diversity, can be a product of economic divergence as well. Tolerance and understanding of the varied backgrounds within the classroom will help to eliminate prejudices. In addition, teacher-parent involvement will be perceived differently depending on the ethnic and economic backgrounds of the parents within the community. Yet parental involvement is a vital part of any educational program. Sensitivity and education are needed to break the cultural barriers so the classroom becomes a safe environment that nurtures *all* children.

Many good strategies for effective teaching should be included for the diverse population. These strategies include using pictorial and concrete models to move from the concrete to the abstract, using reality when teaching vocabulary, using real world examples to make learning meaningfully connected to their world, breaking down tasks into smaller tasks so students feel a sense of accomplishment, recognizing the role of attitudes in learning, and using varied methods of teaching and cooperative learning.

strategies for teaching diverse population

Factors Affecting Learning Style

Many factors play a role in determining a student's learning style. Among those most often cited in the research literature on learning style are environmental, emotional, sociological, physiological, and psychological factors. Although there are several different models for understanding learning differences and many good instruments for assessing learning styles, the Dunn and Dunn (1993) model is one widely used in public schools with versions suitable for students in elementary and secondary classrooms. It will serve as the basis for the following discussion.

Environmental Factors

Environmental factors include students' reactions to stimuli such as sound, light, temperature, and room design. Do students prefer to study and learn with or without sound, with bright or soft lights, in warm or cool rooms, and/or with standard classroom furniture or alternative seating? Classroom teachers observe that some students are easily distracted by any noise and require absolute quiet when studying or working on assignments. On the other hand, some students seem to learn best when they can listen to music. Some researchers have found evidence that students who prefer sound learn best when classical or instrumental music is played in the background.

Light is another environmental factor with students' preferences for light appearing to be basically inherited, with family members often exhibiting the same preference. Some students prefer bright, direct illumination, while others prefer dim, indirect lighting.

Temperature and design are two other environmental factors affecting learning style. Some students will prefer warmer temperatures whereas others will prefer cooler temperatures. Finally, some students will prefer to sit in straight-backed chairs at desks while others may prefer to sit on soft, comfortable chairs or to sit or recline on the floor.

Although traditional classrooms are structured to provide quiet, brightly illuminated study and work areas with straight-backed chairs and desks, classroom teachers will observe that this environment meets the needs of only some of the learners in the class. An effective teacher will take into consideration the learning styles of all students and experiment with different room designs and study centers creating different environments in the classroom. Although classroom temperature may seem to be beyond the control of the teacher, students can be advised to dress in layers so that they can remove outer garments when they are too warm and put on more layers when they are too cool.

RITA & KENNETH DUNN

Emotional Factors

According to Rita and Kenneth Dunn, emotional factors include motivation, persistence, responsibility, and structure. To explain, some students are motivated intrinsically: they undertake and complete tasks because they see the value in doing so. Other students are motivated extrinsically: they undertake and complete tasks because they desire to please others or to earn good marks. In regard to persistence, when they undertake assignments, some students become totally and completely engaged in their work; they seem to lose track of time and can work for long periods without interruption or without feeling fatigued. Other students seem to work in short spurts of energy, needing to take frequent breaks.

When it comes to responsibility, some students are nonconforming, always doing the unexpected (and sometimes unwanted), whereas other students are conforming, always following the rules. Structure refers to whether or not students need detailed and precise instructions. Some students have lots of questions about how assignments should be done, and they desire detailed, step-by-step instructions on each phase of the assignment. Other students, however, seem to work from general concepts and are usually eager to begin assignments, often starting their work before the directions have been given.

Sociological factors include whether or not students are social learners—preferring to work in pairs or in groups—or whether they are independent learners—preferring to work alone. Another sociological factor is whether students work best under the close guidance and supervision of an authority figure (be it teacher or parent) or with a minimum of adult guidance (that is, left primarily on their own to do their work).

Physiological factors include students' preferences for food or drink while they study, what time of day they learn best, their mobility needs, and their perceptual strengths. Briefly, some students may need to eat or drink in order to effectively and efficiently learn. Rita Dunn says that to make sure that students do not abuse this privilege, she allows them to eat only carrot or celery sticks (cooked so that the snacks will not crunch when eaten by students) and to drink water. This way, she is certain that only students who really need intake when they are learning will take advantage of this concession.

Some students may learn best early in the morning, some later in the morning, some in early afternoon, and some later in the afternoon. Researchers have found that merely manipulating the time of day that certain students take tests can significantly affect their test performance.

* WHETHER STUDENTS LEARN BEST BY HEARING, DOING, SEEING

Perceptual
Strengths
1. auditory
2. visual
3. tactile
4. kinesthetic

Mobility needs refer to the fact that some students need to move around when they study, whereas other students can sit still for longer periods of time. Although all of these factors are important, and a growing body of literature tends to support the idea that these factors play a significant role in increasing students' performance and in increasing teachers' effectiveness with students, perhaps one of the most important elements in understanding learning style is to identify students' perceptual strengths. Perceptual strengths refer to students' learning modalities, such as whether they are visual, auditory, tactile, or kinesthetic learners. Basically, these perceptual modalities refer to whether students learn best by seeing, hearing, or doing.

Some students can be given a book or handout to read and then perform a task well, based on what they have read. These students tend to have visual (iconic or semantic) perceptual strength. Other students are visual learners, too, but they tend to learn best from images. These are the students who seem to recall every event, even minor details, from films, videos, or classroom demonstrations.

Although evidence indicates that less than 15 percent of the school-age population is auditory, much of the classroom instruction takes the form of teachers telling students information. Most students do not learn auditorially. Therefore, these students must be taught how to listen and learn from oral instructions and lecture.

Teachers who rely on telling students the information that is important would do well to remember that females are more likely to learn auditorially than males. Teachers should also keep in mind that whether or not students benefit from lectures is likely to depend on several other elements as well, such as whether or not the students are auditory learners, whether or not the students like the teacher, whether or not they think the information being presented is important, or whether or not they think that listening to the teacher will help them to achieve their goals.

On the other hand, there are students who do not seem to benefit much from lectures, textbook assignments, or visual aids. These students' perceptual strengths are tactile and kinesthetic. They learn from movement and motion—being able to touch, handle, and manipulate objects. Often these students may have been identified as having learning disabilities. Sometimes they have been relegated to shop or cooking classes or have found their success in athletics, music, or art. Interestingly, many of the "hands on" skills that often identify a student for a career as an auto mechanic are also important skills for mechanical engineers and surgeons.

Nature and Nurture

After experts on both sides of the argument stated their positions, the conclusion seemed to be that both *nature* (the internal variables) and *nurture* (the environment) play equally important roles in determining the outcome of individuals' growth and maturation. Again, it is important to remember the interaction of the individual with his or her environment, recalling that this view is the *dynamic* view of human development.

Before proceeding, teachers would do well to understand that perception plays an important role for learners to the extent that perception creates our individual reality. The world as we know it is a result of our selective perception. We cannot attend to all events and variables in our environment. We select certain events and variables to notice and attend to, and these phenomena which we observe form our perceptions; thus, we create our own reality. External and internal phenomena grab our attention and shape reality for each of us.

Thus, it is one thing for teachers to be aware of and sensitive to the students' environment; it is, however, impossible for teachers to see, feel, and understand the individual's environment in exactly the same way that it is seen, felt, and understood by the student.

Carol Tavris, a social psychologist and author of the book, *Anger, the Misunderstood Emotion,* notes that emotion plays a significant role in students' perceptions. For example, guilt is an emotion aroused by thoughts such as, "I should study or my parents will kill (be disappointed in) me." This is easily contrasted with the emotion of fear generated by the thought, "I should study or I will be a failure in life." Furthermore, guilt and fear can be compared to the emotion of anger which is prompted by thoughts such as, "Why should I study when my teacher is out to get me?" Today's student often sees the teacher as an enemy, not as an authority figure or a friend. Tavris has identified anger as a primary emotion experienced by many students today, and one that plays a significant role in shaping their academic perceptions, which, in turn, form their reality of classroom experiences.

Explaining further, Tavris observes that unfulfilled expectations lead to anger. For example, if a student is led to believe (by teachers, school administrators, peers, or parents and siblings) that attending class is somehow irrelevant to academic achievement, then the student who is frequently absent still has the expectation of being successful. The student's perception is that absenteeism is compatible with academic achievement. If, because of absenteeism, the student fails to master essential elements of the curriculum and does not succeed, then the student will feel anger, the appropriate and anticipated emotion.

Anger, however, can be diffused by addressing perceptions, correcting false impressions, and establishing appropriate and realistic expectations. To illustrate, if all those individuals significant to the student emphasize the importance of class attendance, then students acquire the correct perception (in this case) that attendance is important for academic achievement and that absenteeism leads to academic failure.

For the sake of illustration only, let's consider what might happen if the teacher stresses attendance and the parents do not. In this case, the best route for the teacher to take is to show empathy for the student's dilemma. The teacher can acknowledge how difficult it is for the student to attend class when the parents are not supporting attendance, but the teacher also must try to empower the student to make choices and to take responsibility for his or her own behavior.

In the situation described here, the student undergoes stress because of conflicting messages, and stress is faced by students and faculty alike. In fact, in the above example, the teacher is stressed too, because he/she faces the conflict between supporting the parents of the student and supporting that which is in the best educational interests of the student.

Stress is the product of any change; both negative and positive changes produce stress. Environmental, physiological, and psychological factors cause stress. For example, environmental factors such as noise, air pollution, and crowding (among others) create stress; physiological factors such as sickness and physical injuries create stress; and, finally, psychological factors such as self-deprecating thoughts and negative self-image cause stress. In addition to the normal stressors that everyone experiences, some students are living in dysfunctional families; some students are dealing with substance abuse and addictions; some are experiencing sexual abuse. There are numerous sources of stress in the lives of students.

Since life is a stressful process, it is important that students and faculty learn acceptable ways to cope with stress. The first step in coping with stress is to recognize the role that stress plays in our lives. A teacher might lead a class through a brainstorming activity to help the students become aware of the various sources of stress affecting them. Next, the teacher could identify positive ways of coping with stress, such as the importance of positive self-talk, physical exercise, proper nutrition, adequate sleep, balanced activities, time-management techniques, good study habits, and relaxation exercises.

Students who are stressed often become angry rather easily; however, students are not just angry. They experience a wide range of emotions and may be sad, depressed, frustrated, afraid, and, on the positive side, happy and surprised. Effective teachers realize that students' emotions as explained in this section play a significant role in students' classroom performance and achievement. Thus, effective teachers seek to create a classroom environment supportive of students' emotional needs. They have appropriate empathy and compassion for the emotional conflicts facing students, yet their concern is tempered by a realistic awareness of the importance of students attaining crucial academic and social skills that will grant them some control over their environment as they become increasingly independent and, eventually, must be prepared to be productive citizens.

Effective teachers recognize the effects of students' perceptions on the learning process and the effects of many environmental factors; as a result, they plan instruction to enhance students' self-esteem and to promote realistic expectations. It is important that teachers be able to differentiate positive and negative environmental factors, maximizing the positive variables and minimizing the negative ones. The teacher has the primary responsibility of creating a classroom environment that recognizes the different environmental factors affecting each student and that encourages each learner to excel, to achieve his or her personal best. Effective teachers work hard at creating learning environments in which all students are ready to learn—where students feel safe, accepted, competent, and productive.

References

Further reading of these references may enhance understanding of the competency and may also increase performance on the examination.

Baxter-Magolda, M. B. *Knowing and Reasoning in College: Gender-Related Patterns in Students' Intellectual Development.* San Francisco: Jossey-Bass, 1992.

Dunn, R. "The Productivity Environmental Preferences Scale (PEPS)." Paper presented at the Learning Styles Institute, Lubbock, Texas, June 5–9, 1993. (Sponsored by Education Service Center, Region XVII).

Dunn, R. and Dunn, K. "Using Learning Styles Information to Enhance Teaching Effectiveness." Paper presented at the Learning Styles Institute, Lubbock, Texas, June 5–9, 1993. (Sponsored by Education Service Center, Region XVII).

Sadker, M., and Sadker, D. *Failing at Fairness: How America's Schools Cheat Girls.* New York: Charles Scribner's Sons, 1994.

Tavris, C. "Coping with Student Conflict Inside and Outside the Classroom." Paper presented at the Texas Junior College Teachers Conference, San Antonio, Texas, February 25, 1994.

Competency 6: Ethics

Definition of Competency

The teacher has knowledge of the Code of Ethics and Principles of Professional Conduct of the Education Profession in Florida.

- The teacher applies the Code of Ethics and Principles of Professional Conduct to realistic and professional situations.

- The teacher identifies statutory grounds and procedures for disciplinary action, the penalties that can be imposed by the Educational Practices Commission against a certificate holder, and the appeals process available to the individual.

What is Ethics?

Ethics (Greek *ethika,* from *ethos,* "character," "custom") are the principles or standards of human conduct, sometimes called morals [Latin *mores, (Encarta 2003)*]. The word ethics is said to concern "a set of moral principles or values" (Merriam-Webster, 1993). In addition, Random House dictionary states that ethics are "the rules of conduct recognized in respect to a particular class of human actions" (Random House, 1987). These definitions restrict the concept of ethics to a single, universal set of rules for the human race. Moreover, ethics are alive, constantly changing and developing according to the society in which they are present. Ethical principles generated in one cultural context cannot be applied to other substantially different cultural contexts without modification.

John Dewey, an instrumentalist, raised new views on ethics around the turn of the nineteenth century. Dewey stated that, "The good is that which is chosen after reflecting upon both the means and the probable consequences of realizing the good" (Encarta, 2003). That is, morals and what is considered appropriate behavior is not intrinsic, but rather a decision, a choice that is made upon realization of the best outcome.

True contemporary ethics in the United States are based on George Moore's philosophy which purports that correct or "good" behavior is "undefinable" (Encarta, 2003). This branch of philosophy is called intuitionist. Centuries of consideration on the subject of ethical behavior in western society have required changes in the scope and nature of ethics, following Moore's dialogue that good is not a quality that may be defined. How and when, then, does society define its appropriate and inappropriate behavior?

Controversy over the capacity of educational institutions to teach and model ethics began with the early Greek philosophers even though ethics have been a part of an individual's personal morality as long as there has been life. This concept of ethical behavior as the core of education also played a significant role in the development of American education, beginning with the Puritan era through the Revolution and throughout the first century of our republic. Relevance of ethical behavior as practiced by teachers and other professionals in our modern society becomes increasingly important as people turn toward education for critical opportunities and paths to knowledge. According to Plato (first half of the 4th century BC), virtue is knowledge. Vice, or evil, is the result of ignorance, therefore people will be virtuous if they know what virtue is (*Dialogues*, Plato). Socrates believed that education could make people moral. Whatever the unethical behavior that is being practiced, society expects the education profession to address it and rectify to a standard.

Professional Ethics

The concept of professional ethics, or the values common to all of the practitioners of a specific profession, has been present since the time of the ancient Greeks. Members of the medical profession can trace their Code of Professional Ethics back to Hippocrates. The famous Hippocratic Oath includes several values which are common to many professions including recognition of privacy rights and its provision that the doctor must lead both an honorable personal and professional life. The oath's widely known admonition to "never do harm to anyone" is as applicable to the teaching profession as it is to the practice of medicine (Adams, n.d., p. 299).

Most modern professions, including widely diverse fields such as business, law, accounting, nursing, social work, and public relations, evolved and adapted specific rules of ethical behavior to provide the guidelines that are necessary to their practitioners. "It is almost definitional that a full-fledged profession is guided by a code of professional ethics" (Macmillan, 1993, p.189).

Lawrence Kohlberg defined six stages of moral development that are often examined in Western societies when a profession forms a code by which its members are to abide. Kohlberg saw the first two stages of his model as a focus on self when making an ethical decision. The person facing the moral dilemma may say, "I do not want to do this because I will be punished." The third and fourth stages are on a higher level of moral development, because there becomes concern for others' well being. A teenager in the third or fourth stage might not break curfew because a parent would be worried. The fifth and sixth stages are based on the idea that there is a universal set of morals, or ethics, that govern every person. Before his death, Kohlberg actually retracted this notion of universal morals, because he realized that the diversity present among any society would lend itself to differing morals. He did maintain that the highest level of moral development is at stage five, or determined by the principles of the individual. That is, only the person may decide for him or herself what ethical principles should be followed. The implications of Kohlberg's theory resound as professionals seek to maintain the highest level of morality and ethics within a company, a practice, and within a society. High morals are based on principles. Thus, a profession that truly wants to model ethical behavior will establish morals that every professional knows and values.

Many professional codes share certain universal ethical standards including such concepts as honesty, diversity, respect for confidentiality, continuing education, and the avoidance of discrimination. From a pragmatic perspective, the goal of a professional code is simply to "coordinate the activities of people among whom may be found a wide diversity of interests, abilities and loyalties" (Fenner, 1999).

In addition to basic universal expectations such as honesty, the practitioner of a profession has a duty to behave in a prescribed way toward colleagues, clients, the employer, and the public. The professional practitioner is "bound by a sense of the ethical dimensions of the relations among professional and clients, the public, the employing institution, and fellow professionals" (Macmillan, 1993, p. 189). Furthermore, a code of professional ethics "would include the beliefs of a particular group about what is right rather than expedient, what is good rather than simply practical, and a description of acts which members must never engage in or condone" (Katz, 1980, p.139).

Ethics and the Education Profession

A debate has long existed concerning the professional status of teachers. Although some may still argue that teaching is a vocation rather than a full-fledged profession, the increasing emphasis on accountability and educational outcomes within our society would suggest that education is more often recognized as a genuine profession. There is no debate, however, that the role that teachers play in our society is an important one. Even our courts have recognized that "by virtue of their leadership capacity, teachers are traditionally held to a higher moral standard in a community" (*Adams v. State of Florida*, 2001).

Character education, as dictated by the Character Education Partnership, dissolves any notion that there are not universal ethics. A teacher who values character education teaches the eleven principles handed down by the nonpartisan organization devoted to developing productive and moral citizens in the United States. The eleven principles of character education are:

Principle 1: Promotes core ethical values as the basis of good character.

Principle 2: Defines "character" comprehensively to include thinking, feeling, and behavior.

Principle 3: Uses a comprehensive, intentional, proactive, and effective approach to character development.

Principle 4: Creates a caring school community.

Principle 5: Provides students with opportunities for moral action.

Principle 6: Includes a meaningful and challenging academic curriculum that respects all learners, develops their character, and helps them to succeed.

Principle 7: Strives to foster students' self motivation.

Principle 8: Engages the school staff as a learning and moral community that shares responsibility for character education and attempts to adhere to the same core values that guide the education of students.

Principle 9: Fosters shared moral leadership and long range support of the character education initiative.

Principle 10: Engages families and community members as partners in the character-building effort.

Principle 11: Evaluates the character of the school, the school staff's functioning as character educators, and the extent to which students manifest good character.

(Character Education Partnership, n.d.)

Schools — reflection of our multicultural society

As the leaders and shapers of society, it is vital for educators to understand that ethical rules may evolve over time. The rules may also vary from place to place and from culture to culture. Therefore, behavior that is acceptable in one culture may be unacceptable in another. This is critical to understand, as our schools are the reflection of our multicultural society. Furthermore, certain behaviors, which were considered to be acceptable in the past, are unethical today. For example, Florida educators are now required to exercise concern for students' health by not smoking or demonstrating smoking within fifty yards of the school building.

There are many reasons for adopting a code of professional conduct for the education profession, not the least of which: "teachers and administrators have considerable power over our children. Children, being more vulnerable and powerless than most other human beings, are easily mistreated" (Howe, 1993, p. 27). It can also be said that "teachers and schools are in the business of shaping acceptable people" (Howe, 1993, p. 27). It is certainly true that schools are one of the primary sources of values transmission for children and young adults. One of the purposes of the code of professional ethics is the example that teachers must set for their students. "For ethics to work for teacher and student, schools must become places that practice the principles taught in the classroom" (ibid). The guidelines exist to be learned but, more importantly, they hope to "encourage genuine commitment to moral standards" (ibid.).

Certain basic themes are common across codes that have been adopted by educational groups. Many share the vision expressed in the preamble to the National Education Association's (NEA) code (2003):

> The educator, believing in the worth and dignity of each human being, recognizes the supreme importance of the pursuit of truth, devotion to excellence, and the nature of democratic principles. Essential to these goals is the protection of freedom to learn and to teach and guarantee of equal educational opportunity for all. The educator accepts the responsibility to adhere to the highest ethical standards.

The Code of Ethics of the Education Profession in Florida

In the State of Florida, there is a professional code of ethics, which delineates the Principles of Professional Conduct as defined by the Florida Department of Education and the Florida Education Standards Commission which educational professionals are expected to acknowledge and embrace:

"The educator recognizes the magnitude of the responsibility inherent in the teaching process. The desire for the respect and confidence of one's colleagues, of students, of parents, and of the members of the community provides the incentive to attain and maintain the highest possible degree of ethical conduct. The Code of Ethics of the Education Profession indicates the aspiration of all educators and provides standards by which to judge conduct" (NEA, 1975).

Florida educators must embrace and practice the admirable vision as described by the NEA. They must also continue their own education by staying up-to-date in their field and recognize that they are, to a certain extent, role models within the communities in which they serve.

Professionals in education should be cognizant that in their work-related activities, and in their personal lives, they are considered models of moral intentions. They should recognize that their personal problems and conflicts may interfere with their success as educators. Also, they should refrain from undertaking an activity which may interfere with their effectiveness as professionals in which there is a possibility of inflicting harm on a colleague or student to whom they have a professional obligation. Teachers should respect the rights of others who hold values, attitudes, and opinions that may differ from their own. Finally, educators should not engage in unfair and unjust discrimination based on age, gender, race, ethnicity, national origin, religion, sexual discrimination, disability, socio-economic status or any basis prescribed by law. As Kipnes (1987) noted, "Within a profession, ethics is best thought of as a collective undertaking by which practical wisdom is developed. It is a shared critical reflection upon common obligations as professionals..." (p. 30).

The Florida Education Standards Commission as expressed in the State Board of Education Rule 6B-1.001 developed Florida's code which states:

(1)   The educator values the worth and dignity of every person, the pursuit of truth, devotion to excellence, acquisition of knowledge, and the nurture of democratic citizenship. Essential to the achievement of these standards are the freedom to learn and to teach and the guarantee of equal opportunity for all.

(2)   The educator's primary professional concern will always be for the student and for the development of the student's potential. The educator will therefore strive for professional growth and will seek to exercise the best professional judgment and integrity.

(3)   Aware of the importance of maintaining the respect and confidence of one's colleagues, of students of parents and of other members of the community, the educator strives to achieve and sustain the highest degree of ethical conduct.

VERY IMPT.

educator's primary professional concern → for the student & for the dev. of the student's potential

The Principles of Professional Conduct of the Education Profession in Florida

VERY IMPT.

*The educator in the State of Florida is required to fulfill obligations to the student, to the public, and to the profession. If the individual is in violation of any of the below, he or she is subject to suspension of the educator's certificate or subject to other penalties.

Obligation to the Student:

1. Protection from harmful conditions related to learning, and/or the student's mental and/or physical health and/or safety.

2. Allow the student freedoms so as not to unreasonably restrain him/her from the pursuit of learning.

3. Never deny access to diverse points of view.

4. Never intentionally suppress or distort subject matter relevant to a student's academic program.

5. Never intentionally embarrass or disparage a student.

6. Student's legal rights are always upheld.

7. Reasonable efforts are made to protect a student from discrimination, and the educator never discriminates

based on race, color, religion, sex, age, national or ethnic origin, political beliefs, marital status, handicapping condition, sexual orientation, or social and family background.

8.   Protection from exploitation from personal gain or advantage.

9.   All personally identifiable information is kept confidential unless serving a professional purpose or required by law.

Obligation to the Public:

1.   Seeks to reasonably distinguish personal views from any organization or educational institution that he/she is associated with.

2.   Never intentionally misrepresent educational matters when communicating directly or indirectly with the public.

3.   All privileges granted by the institution should not be used for personal gain or advantage.

4.   Never accept gratuity, gifts, or favors that could influence professional judgment.

5.   Never offer gratuity, gifts, or favors for special advantages.

Obligation to the Profession:

1.   Maintains honesty in all professional dealings.

2. Never denies advantages or benefits to colleagues based on sex, age, national or ethnic origin, political beliefs, marital status, handicapping condition if otherwise qualified, or social and family background.

3. Never interferes with colleague's political or civil rights and responsibilities.

4. Makes efforts to afford every individual respect through environment by never engaging in harassment or discrimination, nor encouraging behavior that interferes with professional or work responsibilities or creates a hostile, intimidating, abusive, offensive or oppressive environment.

5. Never makes malicious or false statements about a colleague.

6. Neither uses coercive means nor promises special treatment to influence professional judgment of colleagues.

7. Does not misrepresent one's own qualifications.

8. Does not submit incorrect information in any document relating to the profession.

9. Does not submit incorrect information or fails to disclose facts on one's own or another's personal application.

10. Never misrepresents or withholds information from potential employees regarding the application process.

11. Provides to certified officials a written statement of the reasons surrounding recommendations that lead to denial of increments, significant changes in employment, or termination of employment.

12. Does not assist in entry to or continuance of any person known to be in violation of any of these ethical conditions.

13. Self-reports within 48 hours any criminal charges or convictions besides minor traffic violations.

14. Reports to authorities alleged or violations of the Florida School Code or State Board of Education Rules.

15. Seeks no reprisal from anyone under violation of the above.

16. Complies with the condition of the Education Practices Commission concerning probation, fines, or restricting scope of practice.

References

Further reading of these references may enhance understanding of the competency and may also increase performance on the examination.

Character Education Partnership. (n.d.). Eleven Principles of Character Education. Retrieved November 11, 2003, from http://www.character.org/principles/.

Fenner, D. E. W. *Ethics in Education.* New York: Garland, 1999.

Howe, H. R. "The Liberal Democratic Tradition and Educational Ethics." In *Ethics for Professionals in Education* edited by Kenneth A. Strike, and Lance P. Ternasky, pp-27-. New York: Teachers College Press, 1993.

Katz, L. G. *"Ethics and the Quality of Programs for Young Children."* In *Advances in Early Education and Day Care* edited by S. Kilmer. vol.1, pp. 137-151. Connecticut: JAI Press, 1980.

Keith-Spiegel, P., et al. *The Ethics of Teaching: A Casebook* 2nd ed. Mahwah, N.J.: Erlbaum, 2002.

Kipnes, K. "How to Discuss Professional Ethics." *Young Children.* Washington D.C.: National Association for the Education of Young Children (NAEYC), 1987.

Macmillan, C.J.B. "Ethics and Teacher Professionalization." In *Ethics for Professionals in Education,* edited by P. Lance Ternasky, pp. 189-. New York: Teachers College Press, 1993.

Merriam-Webster. *Merriam-Webster Collegiate Dictionary.* 10th ed. Springfield, MA: Merriam-Webster, 1993.

Random House. *Random House Dictionary of the English Language. Unabridged 2nd ed.* New York: Random House, 1987.

Rudder, C. F. "Ethics and Educational Administration: Are Professional Policies Ethical?" In *Ethics in Education* edited by David E.W. Fenner, pp.43- . New York: Garland, 1999.

Slattery, P. and Rapp, Dana. *Ethics and the Foundations of Education: Teaching Convictions in a Postmodern World*. Upper Saddle River, NJ: Pearson Education, Inc., 2003.

Strike, K. A. and Ternasky, P. Lance. *Ethics for Professionals in Education*. New York: Teachers College Press, 1993.

Adams, F. Translation by Francis Adams. New York: Loeb. Vol. I, p. 299-301.

National Education Association. (2003). NEA: Code of Ethics of the Education Profession. Retrieved November 14, 2003, from http://www.nea.org/code.html.

Chapter 8

Competency 7: Human Development and Learning

Definition of Competency

The teacher has knowledge of how to apply human development and learning theories that support the intellectual, personal, and social development of all students.

- The teacher identifies patterns of physical, social, and academic development of students.

- The teacher identifies motivational strategies and factors that encourage students to be achievement and goal oriented.

intervention → always w/ students w/ disabilities

- *The teacher identifies activities to accommodate different learning needs, developmental levels, and experiential background.*

- *The teacher applies knowledge of learning theories to classroom practices.*

- *The teacher identifies characteristics of, and intervention strategies for, students with disabilities.*

This competency addresses the importance of understanding theoretical orientations to both human development and learning and how to apply the principles of these orientations to school settings for all students. Understanding and being able to apply developmental and learning theories in the classroom includes skill in motivation, accommodation of lesson plans, strategy use, and assessment of need, developmental ability, and experience for all students. Teachers who have mastered this competency can identify individual student needs through appropriate assessments and create corresponding curriculum and instruction that meets the needs of all students in the class.

Physical, Social, and Academic Development

Physical Development

Physical changes play a significant role in the development of children as they gradually gain control of their body's movement and function. As they develop physically, children refine their motor skills, which enable them to engage in increasingly complex lessons and activities. It is important for teachers to be able to identify patterns of physical development so that they can create educational activities that are developmentally appropriate for their students' physical abilities.

Children between the ages of three and four have mastered standing and walking. These children are developing gross motor skills including the ability to hop on one foot or balance, climb stairs without support, kick a ball, throw overhand, catch a ball that has bounced, move forward and backward, and ride a tricycle. Children between the ages of three and four are also developing fine motor skills such as using scissors, drawing single shapes, and copying shapes such as capital letters.

By age four or five, when most children enter school, they are developing the gross motor ability to do somersaults, swing, climb, and skip. These skills require increasing coordination. In addition, children at this age can begin to dress themselves using zippers, buttons, and possibly tying shoes. They can eat independently using utensils. Children at this age are increasingly capable of copying shapes including letters and numbers. They can cut and paste, and can draw a person with a head, body, arms, and legs.

These skills develop quickly. By age six children can bounce a ball, skate, ride a bike, skip with both feet, and dress themselves independently. As the student develops year by year, the physical skills, both fine and gross motor, become increasingly complex involving more muscles and more coordination. By age nine children can complete a model kit, learn to sew, and cook simple recipes. By age ten children can catch fly balls and participate in all elements of a softball game. Knowing these basic milestones that most will achieve by a certain age will assist teachers in making decisions about academic lessons and tasks. In addition, teachers may be able to identify children who may not be reaching their developmental milestones with the rest of the class.

The onset of puberty is an important physiological milestone to recognize in students. Increasing numbers of students are reaching the onset of puberty at younger ages in elementary school. Girls, on average, reach maturational milestones before boys by about one to two years. During this time, children grow at a rate comparable only with the first year of life. Puberty includes dramatic changes in skeletal, muscular, and reproductive systems. Students will experience changes in weight, height, strength, and sexual characteristics including hair growth, voice changes, as well as physical shape and function. Many glands and organs also change during this time. Some organs become larger and gland composition and function will alter. For instance, the sweat glands change during this time so students now need to use deodorant. In addition to bodily characteristics, there is a change in bodily feelings, and there is an increase in sex drive.

The physical development of students in puberty is so dramatic that it can become a major concern for students at this age and interfere with their academic and social development as well. Physical changes may cause embarrassment to both females and males when they draw unwelcome attention; moreover, these changes almost always create discomfort as adolescents find the body they were familiar and comfortable with to be quite different, sometimes seemingly overnight.

In sum, the physical ability of students to engage in simple to complex activities in school gradually increases as they develop. Classroom and playground activities must be adjusted and adapted to be developmentally appropriate for the specific skill levels of students. To this end, it is important for teachers to be able to identify the physical development patterns of their students.

Social Development

Schools, regardless of grade level, are social places. Students form social relationships with adults, peers who are their own age, and students who are in different age and developmental groups other than their own. In the social environment of a school, teachers can encourage social development through their interactions with students.

Eric Erickson's psychosocial theory

Eric Erickson's theory of social development, or *psychosocial theory*, is commonly used in education to provide us with a way to think about the social and emotional development of students. Erickson used stages to describe social development. These stages and the approximate age ranges in which children struggle with each stage can help teachers identify the patterns of social development of their students.

birth -1 sense of trust & benevolence to society

From birth to about one year of age, children develop a sense of trust and benevolence of society. While this stage of social development occurs long before a child enters the classroom, it is important to recognize as a stage of social development.

1-3 -sense of autonomy

When children reach about one to three years of age they develop a sense of autonomy. Autonomy can be seen in any typically developing two-year-old who insists on accomplishing a task independently. Children at this stage of social development begin to refuse help and try to accomplish tasks on their own that previously were done for them. Teachers can encourage autonomy in their students by allowing students to try new things, make mistakes, and make messes as they try to accomplish tasks so that students can learn from those experiences.

3-6 sense of initiative

As children enter school, three to six years of age, they are developing a sense of initiative. Initiative can be seen in children who independently explore, make decisions, and investigate their world. Teachers can encourage initiative by providing positive feedback for student attempts at taking initiative regardless of the outcome. The social interaction of a teacher acknowledging a student's attempt or initiative is what motivates the student at this stage.

6-12 sense of industry & competence
need for mastery in tasks

As children progress through elementary school, six to twelve years of age, they develop a sense of industry or a need for mastery and competence in tasks they face. At this stage of social development, students seek out challenges and enjoy accomplishing tasks. Teachers can encourage industry by engaging students in tasks that are challenging, but not so challenging that the student always fails. Students are motivated by their success when they have a healthy sense of industry. Similar to initiative, students who are developing a sense of industry are motivated by teachers who acknowledge their accomplishments.

12-18 identity dev't

During adolescence, twelve to eighteen years of age, children are developing their identity. Students in this stage of social development often rebel against society in an effort to define their identity. Teachers can encourage students to develop their sense of identity by offering a stable and consistent learning environment. They should encourage discussion and activities that facilitate the student to think about their role in society, societal affiliations such as political groups, education or career goals, and family or cultural values.

- continuous process

Academic Development

Identifying the academic development of individual students is imperative for teachers to create developmentally appropriate experiences for students. Academic development is a

Jean Piaget's Theory of Intellectual Dev't.

continuous process that follows a specific sequence in which skills build from one stage to the next. Although age ranges are associated with academic developmental stages, teachers should realize that milestones are reached at very different chronological ages in individual students.

One way to conceptualize academic development is to employ Jean Piaget's Theory of Intellectual Development. Piaget used four stages to describe intellectual development. Children between the ages of birth to two use their senses and developing motor skills to learn about the world around them. Accordingly, this is called the **sensorimotor stage**. In this stage, children learn cause and effect relationships between their actions and reactions in the environment. Their learning is focused on what they can personally perceive.

When children enter school, between two and seven years of age, they are likely experiencing the **preoperational stage of development**. In this stage students are learning about concrete concepts that they come into contact with in their experience. Children in this stage demonstrate a rapid increase in language skills with many errors in their language use. Children are able to comprehend symbols and pictures as representations of concrete ideas.

When children are between seven and eleven years of age, they are likely experiencing the **concrete operational stage of development**. Children in this stage of development are learning to use logical reasoning with concrete materials. Students in this stage can form categories using multiple characteristics and can create hierarchies using subcategories.

Finally, adolescents and adults are in the **formal operational stage of development**. When students reach this stage they can begin to think about abstract concepts, use logical systematic reasoning, and can apply their conclusions to new problems. In this stage students can comprehend symbols as representations of abstract concepts necessary for understanding higher order mathematics, chemistry, and physics.

Teachers' understanding of academic development assists them in creating appropriate lesson plans that their students will benefit from and be successful in completing. It is important for teachers to realize that there are other theorists who view academic development differently than Jean Piaget's four stages.

Another influential theorist, Lev Vygotsky, viewed academic development as a continual building of skills where each child in a class has an individual "zone of proximal development." From this perspective, as students learn and develop academically, their zone of proximal development shifts. Based on an individual student's zone of proximal development, teachers should create lessons that "scaffold" student learning. This means that lessons should take into account a student's current understanding, provide the knowledge that is missing to complete a lesson, and support the student as he or she completes the lesson and gains this new knowledge.

Regardless of the perspective taken, academic development is serial in nature in that skills build on each other. A student cannot understand the concept of multiplication until they understand the concept of addition. They might be able to learn rote multiplication facts without the understanding of addition, but they will not understand the concept of multiplication. It is important for teachers to understand and be able to assess the academic development of their students so they can develop lesson plans that address individual student need and component skills necessary to encourage student academic success.

Lev Vygotsky different from Piaget

Academic Devt. is serial – skills build on each other

Motivational Strategies

The construct of motivation is what we use to explain why some students will read every book in their classroom, just for the fun of it, while others will read so that they can do well on a test, and some will not read for any reason, even if they know how. In this example, the student who reads for the fun of it is *intrinsically* motivated to read, while the student who reads so that they will perform well on an exam is *extrinsically* motivated to read. Finally, the student who will not read is simply not motivated at all.

What is motivating to one student will not necessarily be motivating to another. Furthermore, what was motivating last week to a child may not be motivating in the future. Motivation, like reinforcement can only be determined after it is exhibited and depends on many factors. It is difficult to know for sure what will and what will not be motivating to a classroom of students. Knowing this, it is the teachers' job to identify what is motivating for their students and use that information to attempt to increase motivation in their students' future assignments.

Educators employ behavioral, cognitive, and humanist perspectives to think about motivation. Each perspective provides insight into how motivation works and how motivation can be used in the classroom. Teachers should be able to identify the application of each theory in practice in their classroom.

Behavioral Perspective of Motivation

If we choose to follow behavioral theory, it is easy to think of motivation as similar to reinforcement. Extrinsic motivation can be explained using behaviorism by individuals who are likely to be motivated to complete assignments if they are reinforced for doing so. Similarly the task or assignment itself may be reinforcing and therefore intrinsically motivating. If no reinforcement is given or the task itself is not reinforcing, then students will not be motivated to participate.

Cognitive Perspective of Motivation

Cognitive theorists choose to view motivation as a cognitive need rather than as behavioral reinforcement. A simple way to explain this view is with the idea of schema. Basically, children come to a task with a basic set of beliefs or schema for that situation. When the task is challenging, that is their current set of beliefs are not sufficient to complete the task, they are forced to accommodate and assimilate their beliefs and the information they receive to create a new set of beliefs, or modified schema, that is sufficient to complete the task. The creation of the new set of beliefs is learning. From this perspective motivation is the drive to have the world make sense, be predictable, orderly, and consistent.

Humanist Perspective of Motivation

Humanists choose to view motivation as an innate drive to seek out fulfilling experiences and activities to achieve individual full potential. Basically, from this perspective, if the activity will provide growth, then people will be motivated to complete the activity. Humanists believe that we naturally will be motivated to be all we can be without manipulation from reinforcement or a need to create order.

Schema
to
set of
beliefs

Factors that Influence Motivation

Regardless of the theoretical perspective chosen to explain motivation, there are common personal factors that affect motivation in individual students. An individual's personal state can mitigate motivation. For instance, arousal can have enhancing or detrimental effects on motivation depending on the amount. When individuals experience optimal arousal, they are awake and alert and reacting to their environment. When someone is aroused to the point of anxiety, as is the case with test anxiety, then motivation and performance decrease. Similarly, if someone is not aroused enough, say they are very tired, for instance, they will likely perform poorly as well.

Motivation can also be influenced by an individual's needs at that moment. If an individual's basic needs are unmet, they are likely to be unmotivated to perform other tasks. For instance, if an individual does not have breakfast, their basic needs have not been met and their motivation to accomplish tasks may decline. The relationship between motivation and need can also explain the drives in the cognitive and humanist perspectives. These perspectives interpret need broadly and include the need to create order, the need to understand, the need for affiliation, the need for approval, and the need to achieve full potential.

Another personal factor that can influence motivation is personal beliefs including self-efficacy and self-esteem. At different developmental stages, children view effort and their ability differently. Young children often believe that the more effort they exert, the greater their ability will be. These children are motivated to put forth effort because they believe they will achieve more if they do. As children age, however, they tend to view ability as a trait that is constant. They tend to begin to believe that if they have to put a lot of effort into something, they are less able than a peer who can complete the task effortlessly.

Handwritten margin notes:

1. indiv's personal state
2. indiv's needs
3. personal beliefs
   a. self-efficacy
   b. self-esteem
4. indiv's ability to set goals for himself
   3 criteria
   a. highly specific
   b. attainable
   c. challenging that won't discourage
5. indiv's ability to self-regulate learning

This developmental change is important to realize when working with children of different ages.

An individual's ability to set goals for themselves can also influence motivation. Some students know how to set a reasonable goal and then work toward that goal until it is achieved. Other students do not have this ability. Teachers have the opportunity to teach students how to set goals for themselves to increase motivation.

Teaching students how to set goals should include three criteria. An effective goal should be highly specific, attainable in the immediate future, and challenging without being so challenging that it is discouraging. Students are motivated by successful goal completion. Setting small, attainable goals will likely increase the chances that students will respond positively.

Similar to the ability to set personal goals, some students are able to self-regulate their learning, while others do not. Teaching students to self-regulate their learning involves metacognitive skills. Students who self-regulate are able to think about their own thoughts and use of strategies needed for a particular task. Then, they are able to set goals for themselves, apply strategies for achieving those goals, and self-monitor their attainment of those goals. Self-regulation is an important and effective tool that teachers can employ to help increase individual student motivation.

Teachers can use several basic classroom strategies to attempt to increase motivation in their students. For instance, teachers can provide clear, well-planned instructions for activities to decrease frustration. Teachers can provide models of what is expected, rubrics to provide guidance on assignments, and clear objectives or goals for each assignment. Accordingly, assessment of student achievement should always be clearly and obviously linked to the assignment's goals and objectives. Teachers can also increase motivation by communicating genuine interest or enthusiasm both in the topic and when providing praise or reinforcement. In addition, teachers who set clear expectations for their students are likely to increase the motivation of their students.

Teachers can also use specific instructional strategies to increase motivation in their classroom. Teachers should try to increase arousal to an optimal level when they introduce a new topic or activity. This can be accomplished by attracting students' curiosity, timing the introduction after a physical activity, or by any other means of attracting student attention. Another strategy that teachers can employ to increase motivation is to personalize lessons for students. Excellent teachers try to bring the student into the lesson and challenge the student to apply what they are learning to themselves or a familiar situation. This process of personalization increases individual student investment in an activity and increases their motivation to participate in it. Teachers can also give the students a choice in their lessons to increase motivation. Offering a variety of activities increases the chances that one of the activities will appeal to the student and their investment in making the decision increases their motivation.

Teacher feedback can be an effective strategy for increasing motivation. Rewarding success or attempts with reinforcement may increase extrinsic motivation. To increase intrinsic motivation, teachers can use feedback that focuses student attention on the intrinsic value of the assignment, task, topic, or activity. Rather than simply congratulating students for completing an assignment, teachers can comment on innate feelings of pride, accomplishment, understanding, ability, and skill.

Teachers can also influence motivation by manipulating environmental factors in their classrooms. As we reviewed earlier, student motivation is influenced by individual needs. Creating a learning environment that satisfies students basic needs will help increase the chances that they will be able focus on their work. The classroom environment should be safe and well-organized to foster feelings of security and minimize distraction.

Increasing motivation can be one of the most challenging aspects of teaching in a classroom setting. It is important to remember the individual and ever changing nature of what is motivating to students. Teachers should not be discouraged when a technique is not effective for all students. Teachers should remember that motivation in their classrooms is difficult to control but can be influenced by the strategies they choose to employ.

Accommodating Different Learning Needs, Developmental Levels, and Experiential Backgrounds

To successfully adapt and accommodate activities for students, teachers must first accurately assess their students' learning needs, developmental level, and experiential background.

Individual experience can also be assessed. Based on accurate assessment information, teachers can provide accommodations, adapt materials, and develop activities that are appropriate for individual students' ability based on need, development, and experience.

The Importance of Assessment

[handwritten: in 1. adaptive behavior 2. emotional devt. 3. communication or lang. skills]

Teachers can identify activities to accommodate different learning needs, developmental levels, and experiential backgrounds by assessing individual student ability. Assessments of ability include the student's abilities in the areas of adaptive behavior, emotional development, and communication or language skills. Other informative assessments include formal and informal student observation, ecological inventories, criterion-referenced testing, curriculum-based testing, portfolio assessments, and assessments of student preferences and choices.

Using assessment information, teachers can identify individual strengths and weaknesses. Based on these strengths and weaknesses, activities, lessons, and tasks for specific learning goals can be modified and accommodated so that all learners in a classroom can accomplish them and achieve the learning goal. A student's individual weaknesses will guide teachers in determining activities which will need to be accommodated. Similarly, a student's individual strengths will lead teachers to ways to accommodate a given activity.

To illustrate, if there is a learning goal that each student will be able to identify the capitals of all fifty states in the United States, there should be a variety of activities designed to teach this learning goal. One activity might include playing a game on the black top outside where the United States map is painted. If there is a student with a physical disability, this game may need to be accommodated for them. A teacher might ask that student to call out the state capitals so they can participate meaningfully in the activity while other students run to each state where the capital is located. Another activity might involve writing the name of each capital in the appropriate state on a map. If there is a child that is not yet able to write or who uses alternative methods of communication, that child can indicate which state and which capital match by pointing on a map. Or the child can use a matching task that does not require writing or identifying words to complete the learning goal of knowing which capital is in each state. Similarly, all children will have strengths and weaknesses. Teachers need to identify the strengths and weaknesses of each student to know what activities will need to be accommodated and how they should be changed so all students can be successful.

Operational Definitions of Learning Goals

Any learning goal can be defined in behavioral terms using an operational definition. An operational definition includes a clear and precise description of the learning goal that should be performed as well as an accurate means to measure that goal as students strive to achieve it. Operational definitions are important to use when defining all learning goals including academic, behavioral, and social skill goals. The operational definition helps clarify exactly what each individual student is striving to achieve, and what accommodations are being made, so that all teachers who interact with that student are aware of the goals and will understand the specific intent of each goal.

Operational Definitions as Academic Goals

Operational definitions should be used to identify academic goals. The definition should include both a description and a means of measuring the academic goal. To describe an academic goal, think about what behaviors students will exhibit who have achieved the goal. A description might include the level of comprehension a student will demonstrate after reading a section of text. A description might include a particular type of math problem that a student should be able to answer correctly in an oral or written format. A description might include the student's ability to discuss elements of a culture they have been studying in social studies. In some way, all learning goals can be described using behavioral terms. Next, the description needs to be accompanied by a means of measuring that behavior. Measurement can be in the form of direct measures such as rate, duration, or inter-response time or indirect measures such as whole or partial intervals or momentary time sampling.

Using operational definitions to identify academic goals makes assessing student success easier. The measurement needed for assessment is included in the definition. Any teacher who comes in contact with that student can use the same operational definition and assess that student's progress toward the goal.

Operational Definitions as Behavioral Goals

Operational definitions can also be applied to behavioral goals. Student behavior is a common issue in many classrooms. Teachers can use operational definitions for appropriate behaviors they want to increase in their classrooms as well as inappropriate behaviors that they wish to decrease in their classrooms. Again, the operational definition needs to include a description of the behavioral goal as well as a means of measuring that behavior.

An operational definition of a behavioral goal needs to specifically address what the behavior of a child who has reached the goal should look like. The description should be written using positive terms. Teachers have a tendency to focus on the behavior that they want to stop rather than the appropriate behavior they want to increase. If a teacher wants a student to sit in their seat rather than run around the classroom all of the time, the goal can be written in the positive direction and focus on what the child should be doing, sitting in the seat, rather than focusing on what the child should not be doing. All too often behavior plans focus on the negative side of things and we forget to include the most important part which is describing what the child should be doing instead and how we will teach that child to exhibit those behaviors.

Operational Definitions as Social Skill Goals

Just as an operational definition can be used to identify academic and behavioral goals, the same principles can be applied to goals in social skills. Social skills can be described in behavioral terms by thinking about the behaviors exhibited by children who have reached the goal. After describing the social skill to be learned, teachers must remember to include a means to measure that goal.

The same measurements are used to assess behavioral aspects of academic, behavior, and social skill goals using operational definitions. To recap, measurement can be direct measures such as rate, duration, or inter-response time or measures can be indirect such as partial or whole intervals or momentary time sampling.

Task Analysis

An excellent way to identify activities that need to be adapted for students is to use a task analysis. A simple task analysis is a technique that addresses component parts of learning goals that need to be adapted as well as provides a means of measuring student progress toward a learning goal. Task analysis can be used with students with any level of learning need, developmental ability, or experience.

Once a learning goal is defined using an operational definition, the behavioral description of the goal can be broken down into component parts, steps, or skills needed to complete the goal. The component parts, steps, or skills can be easily recognized by attempting to complete the goal yourself or watching someone else complete the goal and noting each behavior that must be performed to accomplish the goal. Some learning goals will not need to be broken down into component steps while others will, depending on the learning needs, developmental level, and experience of each individual student.

Once the component parts, steps, or skills are identified, the task analysis can be validated by prompting and assisting the student through the steps to see if the goal is achieved or if additional steps and accommodations need to be made. The student will likely have trouble with some steps, indicating that they need to be further broken down, additional component skills are necessary, or adaptations or accommodations need to be made. Adaptations and accommodations should be made that are not stigmatizing, that are age appropriate, and that facilitate independence for the student. The student will likely complete other steps easily without prompting or assistance, indicating they can be consolidated into larger steps in the analysis.

After making accommodations and revising the steps and component skills in the task analysis, the task analysis should be re-written on a data collection sheet in a logical order that includes student initiation and termination of the task. The data collection sheet can be used as a guide for teaching the student the steps and component skills needed with the necessary accommodations to achieve the learning goal. As teaching continues, data can be collected on student progress on each step and skill to assess if the student is making progress or if they are having trouble with a specific step. Further accommodations and adjustments to steps can always be made to facilitate success for individual students.

Applying Learning Theories in the Classroom

Effective teachers are able to apply their knowledge of learning theory in practice in their classrooms. Teachers have to determine how to match what needs to be taught with the specifications of those who need to learn it. The successful teacher spends considerable time becoming familiar with required instructional objectives, curriculum, and texts. Time is also spent evaluating the physical, social, and academic development of their students to assess individual differences and learning needs. The effective teacher must then be organized enough to choose and sequence learning activities before the school year begins, but flexible enough to adapt these activities after becoming acquainted with the special needs of specific students.

Educators use behavioral, cognitive, and social learning theories as perspectives to explain human learning. Each perspective provides insight into human learning processes. Teachers should be able to identify each learning theory in practice in their classroom.

Behavioral Perspective of Learning Theory

Theorists of the behavioral perspective, such as Skinner, Pavlov, and Watson, define learning as a change in behavior. Behavioral theorists do not consider internal cognitive processes as a part of learning. Further, behavioral theorists view the learning process as an association between stimulus and response reactions and subsequent behavior change.

Implementing behavioral learning theory in practice involves creating an educational environment in which educational stimuli can be presented and behavioral responses can be observed and measured. Educators who apply behavioral theory use methods such as drill and practice. Drill and practice employs repetition of the stimulus response relationship in an effort to habit train students to respond correctly. For instance, many teachers use drill and practice to teach math and reading skills.

Other applications of behavioral theory to the classroom involve habit training. Teachers who want to teach new stimulus response relationships can do so by methods of exhaustion in which the stimulus response is repeated to such an extent that the individual literally exhausts him or herself and no longer is motivated to perform the behavior. This strategy is useful for decreasing inappropriate behavior. Other methods of habit training involve systematic exposure to increasing intensity of a stimulus so that an individual does not pay attention to it and therefore does not produce the associated behavior. An excellent example of this method is the use of successive approximations toward a standardized exam for those who experience test anxiety.

Behavioral theory also provides excellent ways to promote appropriate behavior in the classroom. Teachers should know how to conduct functional assessments and analysis of behaviors and understand how to write behavior support plans accordingly. Often times, behavior support plans include teaching new, replacement, or competing behaviors in the formation of new stimulus response relationships.

The behavioral perspective applied in classroom settings is also represented in teachers' use of reinforcement. Classrooms that use token economies or point systems are applying behavioral theory in practice. Reinforcement in behavioral theory is inseparable from motivation. Thus, it is important for teachers to understand the relationship between motivation and learning.

Cognitive Perspective of Learning Theory

Cognitive theorists, such as Piaget and Vygotsky, define learning as the changes in mental associations that take place from experience. Cognitive theorists view learning as a process that occurs internally in which people are constantly interpreting and organizing information. Further, cognitive theorists believe that students are ultimately responsible for their own learning in that they have control of their own mental processes and metacognition.

Cognitive theory applied to classrooms can be seen when teachers use multiple forms of instruction to teach one idea. The multiple forms of instruction are designed to activate cognitive processing in several ways, which according to cognitive theory strengthens the associations of information in the brain. Teachers who follow a cognitive perspective are concerned with what students are learning as well as the process they use for learning that information. Teachers who use visual aides in addition to expository instruction are applying cognitive theory in practice.

Cognitive theorists focus on academic and cognitive developmental stages to guide instruction and lesson planning. Teachers who are influenced by cognitive theory will consider Piaget's developmental stages or Vygotsky's zone of proximal development of each child in their classroom and plan lessons accordingly. For example, teachers who use a cognitive perspective will tend to use strategies such as manipulatives in math lessons for those who need concrete examples of abstract ideas.

Teachers can also apply cognitive theory in their classes by assisting students in the organization of information. According to cognitive learning theories, students are more likely to recall information if they can associate new knowledge with information they already know. Purposefully relating new content to old content helps students create these links in their knowledge. In addition, this also helps students to accommodate the new information into their existing schema or information processing organization. Teachers who use advanced organizers are actively applying cognitive theory in practice by assisting their students in organizing information.

Teachers who continually tie information that their students are learning to previous lessons are employing cognitive methods in practice. When teachers use summaries at the end of a lesson or ask their students to apply what they have learned to a novel situation, these teachers are using cognitive theory based strategies in their classrooms.

Social Learning Perspective of Learning Theory

Yet another theoretical approach to learning is called social learning theory. Social learning theory is based on the assumption that people can learn from observing other people's behaviors and consequences to those behaviors. Social learning theorists, such as Bandura, Miller, and Dollard, believe that learning can occur without a change in behavior as is required in behavioral theory. Social learning theory combines aspects of behavioral and cognitive theories in that reinforcement and punishment of behaviors as well as cognitive processes and expectations all play a role in learning.

Social learning theory applied in a classroom setting is seen when teachers make an example out of one student. Teachers often discipline one student and the other students in the class learn that the behavior that student was exhibiting is not appropriate in the classroom. These students learned by observing the behavior of the student and the consequence that student received. In the same way, teachers may reward an exemplary student and other students learn that the behavior of that student is appropriate and desirable in the classroom. It is important then, to be consistent in use of rewards and punishments in school settings because students are aware of the consequences that others have received.

Another application of social learning theory in practice is the ability of students to understand consequences without them actually happening. According to social learning theory, students can be told a consequence, either a reward or a punishment, and that knowledge of the consequence will change behavior. Unlike behavioral theory in which the individual must experience the consequence for behavior to change, social learning theory allows for instances in which students are simply warned that there will be a consequence and their subsequent behavior changes.

4 criteria for modeling to be effective:
1. attention
2. retention
3. motor reproduction
4. motivation

Teachers who use modeling as an instructional strategy are applying social learning theory in their classrooms. Students can learn and exhibit new behaviors in their repertoire by simply observing someone else perform the behavior or skill. Social learning theory prescribes four essential criteria for modeling to be effective: attention, retention, motor reproduction, and motivation.

Social learning theory also includes cognitive aspects including concepts of self-efficacy, goal setting, and self-regulation. Teachers who apply social learning theory in practice are also concerned with student beliefs about their abilities. To increase self-efficacy, teachers can make sure that students have the component skills needed to be successful at a given task. Other methods for increasing student self-efficacy include demonstrating to students that other students in their situation could also accomplish the task or by building student confidence through constructive comments.

Social learning theory applied in practice can be seen in any classroom where students observe others and then change their behavior accordingly. Models for social learning are not limited to teachers. Students are constantly able to learn from the behavior of anyone in their environment.

Students with Disabilities

Effective teachers know that all students need to be treated as individuals with specific strengths and weaknesses. Teachers who have this philosophy easily accommodate students with disabilities in their classrooms. These teachers are able to assess individual needs, regardless of a disability label, and provide accommodations to meet those needs. In addition, these teachers are able to assess individual strengths in all students and are able to use individual student strengths to encourage learning for all students. Effective teachers identify the needs of, and intervention strategies for, all students including those with disabilities.

Characteristics of Students with Disabilities

Characteristics of a disability can be seen in just about everyone. This does not mean that all people have a disability. People simply may demonstrate a characteristic that, in combination with other specific criteria, may indicate a disability. For instance, self-stimulating behavior is a characteristic of many individuals with autism. A student often taps her foot or pencil and twists her hair around her finger when thinking. These are self-stimulating behaviors. Just because she exhibits a behavior that is also characteristic of individuals who have autism, does not mean that she has autism too. Diagnostic criteria should be used to assign labels of disability. Teachers are typically not trained to use criteria to give a diagnosis or disability label. However, the characteristics of some disabilities are reviewed here so that teachers might recognize disabilities and corresponding needs of students.

Mental Retardation

Individuals with mental retardation exhibit a deficit in intellectual functioning and have limitations in at least two adaptive skills such as communication, self-care, home living, social skills, community use, self-direction, health and safety, functional academics, leisure, and work. Within that framework, individuals with mental retardation can be classified according to IQ levels from mild to profound and can be further classified using levels of support required for an individual to function as competently as possible from intermittent to pervasive. Some developmental disabilities are associated with mental retardation including individuals with Down syndrome, Fragile X syndrome, Phenylketonuria (PKU), and Tay-Sachs disease. These disabilities have additional characteristics but are all associated with mental retardation as well. Other individuals experience mental retardation due to brain damage, infection, and fetal alcohol syndrome.

Psychological and behavioral characteristics of individuals with mental retardation might include difficulty attending to tasks, trouble with memory, difficulty self-regulating behavior, and delayed or deviant language development such as speech problems. These characteristics are also associated with lower academic achievement, reduced social development, and decreased motivation.

 ## Learning Disabilities

Learning disabilities are a group of disabilities that, due to central nervous system dysfunction, impede learning in individuals with average to high IQ, by impairing listening, speaking, reading, writing, reasoning, or mathematical abilities. Causes of learning disabilities are largely unknown. Most individuals who have learning disabilities will have them for life because they are associated with central nervous system function. However, individuals can learn strategies to help compensate for their learning disabilities.

Individuals with learning disabilities might be characterized by having difficulties in academic achievement including reading, writing, oral speech production, and mathematics. Individuals with learning disabilities might also exhibit problems with perception, coordination in gross and fine motor skills, and trouble coordinating between perception and motor skills as is needed in sport activities. Other individuals with learning disabilities might demonstrate deficits in attention and/or hyperactivity. Still other individuals with learning disabilities might demonstrate difficulties in memory, cognition, or metacognition. Children with learning disabilities are also more likely to have secondary characteristics as a result of the primary characteristics listed above including low self-confidence, socialization issues, and decreased motivation in comparison to typically developing peers.

Emotional or Behavioral Disorders

Individuals who have emotional or behavioral disorders chronically exhibit behavior that is unacceptable in light of social or cultural expectations. The behavior exhibited by individuals with these disorders is highly unusual in comparison to that behavior exhibited by average peers. The IQ distribution for children with emotional or behavioral disorders tends to be lower in comparison to the normal curve. Individuals with emotional or behavioral disorders may exhibit aggression, be socially withdrawn, or both.

Various emotional and physical signs characterize mood or emotional disorders. Depression can manifest itself in an overall lack of interest in activities, constant crying, or talk of suicide. Anxiety or obsessive thoughts are another indication of a possible mood disorder. Physical signs include a disruption in eating or sleeping patterns.

Autism spectrum disorder (ASD). Autism is a term used to describe a range of disability from mild symptoms associated with Asperger Syndrome to severe and profound autism. Often times, individuals who exhibit autistic tendencies will receive a label of Autism Spectrum Disorder (ASD) or pervasive developmental delay not otherwise specified (PDD-NOS). The characteristics of individuals who receive these labels are similar in that they likely exhibit symptoms associated with autism to some degree. It is important to realize that children labeled with autism, ASD, Asperger Syndrome, and PDD-NOS will vary both between labels and within labels.

To be diagnosed with autism, an individual must exhibit delays or abnormal functioning in social interaction, language or communication, or symbolic or imaginative play before the age of three. In addition, individuals with autism or related disorders may exhibit behavioral excesses and deficits that are abnormal. Individuals may demonstrate behavioral deficits in language and communication skills such as eye contact, facial expression, body posture, and gestures. They often fail to form peer relationships and lack initiative to share interest or social reciprocity. They might exhibit deficits in imaginary play, and if they are able to create speech, they may lack the ability and/or drive to initiate or sustain conversation with others.

Individuals with autism or related disorders may exhibit behavioral excesses in socially inappropriate and stereotyped or repetitive use of language or idiosyncratic language. They also may exhibit excesses in stereotyped and restricted patterns of behavior or interest that is abnormal in intensity or focus. They may also exhibit stereotyped and repetitive motor mannerisms that may involve the entire body or just a hand or finger movement. Individuals may exhibit persistent preoccupation with parts of objects and they might attend to environmental cues that are abnormal such as identifying a person by an article of clothing rather than facial characteristics. Finally, individuals may exhibit behavioral excesses in adherence to nonfunctional routines or rituals.

It is important to remember that individuals diagnosed with autism or related disorders will vary widely in symptoms and intensity of symptoms. It is very difficult to generalize from one individual with autistic tendencies to others also diagnosed with the same disorder.

Communication Disorders

Individuals who have communication disorders demonstrate an inability to use speech or language to communicate. Some individuals with communication disorders will have trouble with speech, specifically articulation or fluency. Others will have trouble with language including comprehension, phonology, morphology, syntax, semantics, or pragmatics.

Often times, other disabilities have a communicative component. For instance, individuals who have autism, mental retardation, and hearing impairments may also have difficulty with speech and language. Children with autism specifically, by definition, will demonstrate a language delay.

Hearing Impairment

Individuals with hearing impairments can exhibit various levels of hearing loss from slight to extreme. Individuals with hearing impairments may demonstrate deficiencies in reading and writing in particular, but are likely to demonstrate deficits in all areas of academics if appropriate supports are not provided. Individuals who have hearing impairments that are raised in hearing-only environments may exhibit problems in socialization.

Teachers who work with individuals who have hearing impairments should be aware of the deaf culture. The deaf culture is an extraordinarily strong culture in which individuals with hearing impairments have formed their own cultural identity complete with social and behavioral norms. For individuals who have hearing impairments, it may benefit them to at least be aware of and have the opportunity to participate in the deaf culture. Individuals who participate in the deaf culture exhibit normal socialization patterns and benefit from a strong social and support network. Many individuals with hearing impairments, who attend college, choose to attend Gallaudet University, which is a university for deaf, hearing impaired, and normal hearing students.

Visual Impairment

Individuals with visual impairments may exhibit slight sight loss to complete blindness. Some visual problems other than blindness include myopia, hyperopia, astigmatism, glaucoma, or cataracts. Characteristics to look for in children are eye rubbing, shutting one eye or tilting their head when trying to see at a distance, excessive blinking, reading at an excessively close distance, or squinting when trying to see.

Individuals with visual impairments may have deficits in language acquisition at early ages due to a lack of visual exposure to items that children without a sight impairment experience. Furthermore, individuals with visual impairments may exhibit difficulty in mobility. Academic achievement will suffer in individuals who are visually impaired if they do not receive appropriate intervention. Individuals who are taught with appropriate instruction using accommodations, such as Braille, can achieve normal patterns of academic development. Individuals with visual impairments may experience trouble socializing if educators do not facilitate the education of peers about students who have visual impairments.

Physical Disabilities

Physical disabilities include traumatic brain injury, cerebral palsy, seizure disorder, spina bifida, muscular dystrophy, juvenile rheumatoid arthritis, fetal alcohol syndrome, and individuals who experienced a physically altering injury.

Individuals who experience physical disabilities may or may not also exhibit deficiencies in academic achievement. If deficiencies are exhibited they may be due to deficits in the individual or they may be due to inappropriate or insufficient accommodations on the part of the educational system. Individuals with physical disabilities may have trouble in social development due to the social perceptions of others or due to diminished ability to participate in social activities.

Intervention Strategies for Students with Disabilities

There are strategies to assist individuals with disabilities so they can attain educational goals. Strategies focus on areas of communication, behavior, academics, and socialization. Teachers should have an understanding of these strategies and be able to implement them appropriately in practice.

Functional Communication

Communication is essential for all human beings. Some students with disabilities are not able to communicate using oral speech as their typically developing peers can. However, there are many forms of functional communication that can be adapted to meet the individual needs of students so that they can communicate feelings, needs, and information.

Perhaps the most obvious form of communication that does not involve oral speech is the use of sign language. Sign language is useful for students who have trouble creating speech as well as for students who are deaf or hearing impaired. Children with many different disabilities use simple forms of sign language adapted to communicate their feelings, wants, and information. Other individuals with disabilities use pictures systems, symbols, or choice boards to communicate.

These students can point to a picture that represents what they want to communicate or can push a button using an augmentative communication device that has pre-recorded oral messages that the individual may need to use regularly.

Teachers of students with disabilities need to be aware of students' need to communicate. Often times, if a means of appropriate communication is not offered to a student, they will communicate using behavior, which may or may not be socially appropriate. In fact, much of behavioral therapy for individuals with disabilities involves providing these individuals with appropriate ways to communicate their needs so that they will not have to behave inappropriately to gain attention or avoid undesirable experiences. Making sure that all students are provided functional communication is an important strategy to use with individuals with disabilities.

Positive Behavior Support

Positive behavior support incorporates the use of functional assessment and positive behavioral intervention planning for individuals with disabilities. Positive behavior support is currently mandated for use with individuals with disabilities in educational settings by federal law when problem behaviors occur. The intervention strategies that result from functional assessments should be positive in that they increase adaptive skills, increase options available to the individual, and decrease problem or inappropriate behaviors.

Functional assessments should include operational definitions of behaviors. If a behavior is problematic, then aiming to decrease that behavior might be warranted. However, in the intervention, there should be a corresponding appropriate replacement or competing behavior, that serves the same function as the inappropriate behavior, that is increased as the problem behavior is decreased. Functional assessments should also include identification of antecedents, consequences, and setting events that are hypothesized to support specific problem behaviors.

Once hypotheses are created regarding the functions of behaviors and their corresponding antecedents, consequences, and setting events, a functional analysis using systematic data collection in direct observations can be used to validate hypotheses. Functional analysis involves systematically testing each variable identified as potential antecedents, consequences, or setting events that support the problem behavior to test which variables truly affect the behavior. Those variables that are confirmed through functional analysis can then be the focus of developing the behavioral intervention plan.

The behavior intervention plan should be directly and obviously linked to the outcomes of the functional assessment. Specific interventions should address the functions of behaviors and variables that affect those behaviors identified in the functional assessment. Interventions should be comprehensive and carried out in all relevant settings for consistency. Strategies typically include creating plans that alter the antecedents, consequences, and setting events to make problem behavior ineffective, inefficient, or irrelevant.

Functional Academics

Individuals with severe disabilities might benefit from accommodations to academic curriculum that focus on functional academic skills rather than abstract concepts. The focus on functional academic skills for students with severe disabilities increases the functional knowledge and skills of these students without having to teach the abstract concept and then later apply it to a real life situation as is typically the case in general education.

For instance, rather than teaching addition and subtraction as abstract concepts, students with severe disabilities may benefit more from lessons in monetary value, making change, and adding or subtracting prices. This is a functional academic skill that incorporates the same academic knowledge but in an applied and functional form that increases the student's adaptive skills and independence. Similarly, academic skills that focus on reading for students enrolled in general education might focus on functional skills such as reading street signs, bus schedules, and menus for individuals with severe disabilities. Along the same lines, lessons in science can be centered on practical application and functional skills. For teachers who work with students with severe disabilities, it is important to understand the need for real life functional applications for the academic topics they teach.

CONSISTENCY

Home, School, and Community Collaboration

A final strategy for working with individuals with disabilities is to ensure a collaboration between home, school, and the community. Teachers should take advantage of the wealth of information that parents can provide about their children. Parents are truly the experts on the topic of their child. Teachers can gain information about student behavior, likes and dislikes, and family issues from talking with parents. In addition, teachers can provide parents with information on student progress. Behavioral interventions and academic lessons are far more effective when parents and teachers work on the same goals using similar strategies in the home and school environment.

Another piece to collaboration involves the community. The community provides valuable resources for student experiences and support. Similarly, teachers can involve students in community activities that support the community as well. Reciprocal relationships between home, school, and community settings ultimately help students learn about and contribute to their community, school, and home as members in those social groups. Consistency across environments is an important strategy to support the behavior and education of individuals with disabilities.

References

Further reading of these references may enhance understanding of the competency and may also increase performance on the examination.

Eggen, P., and Kauchak, D. *Educational Psychology: Windows on Classrooms* 4th ed. Upper Saddle River, NJ: Prentice-Hall, 1999.

Greydanus, D. E., ed. *The Complete and Authoritative Guide: Caring for Your Adolescent Ages 12 to 21.* Bantam Books: American Academy of Pediatrics, 1991.

Hallahan, D. P., and Kauffman, J. M. *Exceptional Learners: Introduction to Special Education* 7th ed. Needham Heights, MA: Allyn and Bacon, 1997.

Ormond, J. E. *Human Learning* 3rd ed. Upper Saddle River, NJ: Prentice-Hall, 1999.

Ormond, J. E. *Educational Psychology: Developing Learners* 4th ed. Upper Saddle River, NJ: Prentice-Hall, 2003.

Schor, E. L., ed. *The Complete and Authoritative Guide: Caring for Your School-age Child ages 5 to 12.* Bantam Books: American Academy of Pediatrics, 1995.

Shelov, S. P., and Hannemann, R. E., eds. *The Complete and Authoritative Guide: Caring for Your Baby and Young Child Birth to Age 5* Rev. ed. American Academy of Pediatrics, 1998.

Snell, M. E., and Brown, F. *Instruction of Students with Severe Disabilities* 5th ed. Upper Saddle River, NJ: Prentice-Hall, 2000.

Taylor, R. L. *Assessment of Exceptional Students: Educational and Psychological Procedures* 4th ed. Needham Heights, MA: Allyn and Bacon, 1997.

Competency 8:
Subject Matter

Definition of Competency

The teacher has knowledge of subject matter incorporating reading and literacy strategies as they apply across the curriculum to increase learning.

- The teacher identifies appropriate corrective strategies for determining when reading comprehension is preventing the mastery of subject material.

- The teacher identifies references, materials, and technologies appropriate to the subject and the learners' abilities.

- *The teacher identifies strategies that encourage multidisciplinary studies.*

Knowledge of subject matter and helping students learn it are two sides of the same coin. On one side, Knowledge of Subject Matter is one of the fourteen standards of which teachers are required to display competence. The definition of "Knowledge of Subject Matter" and identified indicators of it are:

The Professional teacher has a basic understanding of the subjects she/he teaches and is beginning to understand that her/his subject is linked to other disciplines and can be applied in real world "integrated settings." The teacher seeks out ways and sources to expand her/his knowledge. The commitment to learning about new knowledge includes keeping abreast of sources that will enhance teaching. The teacher's repertoire of teaching skills include a variety of means to assist student acquisition of new knowledge. The teacher:

- *Communicates accurate knowledge of subject matter in a language and style appropriate to the learner and in a manner that enables students to learn.*

- *Demonstrates a breadth of subject matter knowledge that enables students to approach and to interrelate topics from a variety of perspectives, interests, and points of view. Uses her/his breadth of subject matter knowledge to interrelate topics from a variety of perspectives, interests, and points of view within the subject area.*

- *Uses the references, materials, and technologies of the subject field in developing learning activities in a manner appropriate to the developmental stage of the learner.*

- *Maintains currency in regard to changes in the subject field.*

- *Demonstrates a breadth of subject matter that enables her/him to collaborate with colleagues from other subject fields in the integration of instruction.*

- *Develops short and long term personal and professional goals relating to knowledge of subject matter.*

All of this makes a great deal of sense. It would be very difficult for a teacher to do a good job of teaching a subject area discipline in which he/she is not proficient. Even to attempt this would limit the "teacher" to presenting directly out of the textbook, in a sense, chapter-by-chapter coverage of the textbook. It would not permit spontaneous and correct responses to student questions or integrating subject areas so that students get a solid "real-world" sense of the discipline area being taught. It would not permit the teacher to probe the students' knowledge with challenging questions to lead them to understanding.

Of course, the teacher needs to make sure the subject area reading material is written at an appropriate level for the students. Even so, reading subject area material often is a very abstract activity for many students. If they do not "get it" the first time through, they are likely to quit, unless they have some strategies to help them make meaning of what they have read. To move the student into abstract thinking, the teacher will need to make use of every opportunity to provide concrete examples of the concepts being taught. Special attention must be given to introducing vocabulary in meaningful contexts and to linking new concepts with those that have been previously learned.

What really needs to happen is that the student should be able to read and understand the subject area material so that he/she can utilize its concepts in that subject area or wherever they may be useful. There are a myriad of strategies that the teacher can utilize to help maximize learning and meaning-making for the student. Of primary importance are reading and literacy strategies.

Reading Strategies

A look at strategies used by proficient readers will help the teacher make skillful choices of activities to maximize student learning in subject area instruction. Goudvis and Harvey (2000) offer the following list:

Making connections between prior knowledge and the text. Readers pay more attention when they relate to the text. Readers naturally bring their prior knowledge and experience to reading, but they comprehend better when they think about the connections they make between the text, their lives, and the larger world.

Asking questions. Questioning is the strategy that keeps readers engaged. When readers ask questions, they clarify understanding and forge ahead to make meaning. Asking questions is at the heart of thoughtful reading.

Visualizing. Active readers create visual images in their minds based on the words they read in the text. The pictures they create enhance their understanding.

Drawing inferences. Inferring is when the reader takes what is known, garners clues from the text, and thinks ahead to make a judgment, discern a theme, or speculate about what is to come.

Determining important ideas. Thoughtful readers grasp essential ideas and important information when reading. Readers must differentiate between less important ideas and key ideas that are central to the meaning of the text.

Synthesizing information. Synthesizing involves combining new information with existing knowledge to form an original idea or interpretation. Reviewing, sorting, and sifting important information can lead to new insights that change the way readers think.

Repairing understanding. If confusion disrupts meaning, readers need to stop and clarify their understanding. Readers may use a variety of strategies, to "fix up" comprehension when meaning goes awry.

As the teacher goes about instruction in a subject area, it probably goes without saying that she/he needs to determine if the reading material is at the students' level of reading mastery. If not, accommodations need to be made either in the material itself, or in the manner in which it is presented.

These strategies can be taught explicitly to students in a carefully orchestrated manner. First, the teacher should model the strategy, explain it and how to successfully apply the strategy. It will help if the teacher "thinks" aloud while modeling the strategy for students. Second, the teacher should practice the strategy with the students. He/she should scaffold the students' attempts and support their thinking, give feedback during conferring and classroom discussion. Here also, it will help if the students "think" aloud while practicing the strategy. Third, the teacher should encourage the students to apply the strategy on their own and give them regular feedback. Fourth, once the students clearly understand the strategy, they should apply it on their own in new reading situations.

As the teacher monitors understanding of subject matter he/she should become aware of student thinking as they read and detect obstacles and confusions that derail understanding. The teacher can then suggest, teach, or implement strategies to help students repair meaning when it breaks down.

Teachers need to be explicit about teaching students to be aware, to constantly check for understanding, and to use reading comprehension strategies to make meaning. To monitor and repair their understanding (Goudvis and Harvey, 2000), teachers should explicitly teach students to:

- Track their thinking through coding with sticky notes, writing, or discussion.

- Notice when they lose focus.

- Stop and go back to clarify thinking.

- Reread to enhance understanding.

- Read ahead to clarify meaning.

- Identify and articulate what is confusing or puzzling about the text.

- Recognize that all of their questions have value. There is no such thing as a stupid question.

- Develop the disposition to question the text or author.

- Think critically about the text and be willing to disagree with its information or logic.

- Match the problem with the strategy that will best solve it.

Then, depending on the situation, these strategies may be employed across the curriculum in any subject area.

In addition, the effective teacher may make use of graphic organizers such as:

- *Double entry journals* in which the student devises a two-column paper with the left column devoted to direct quotes from the text (with page number) and the right column to "thinking options" such as "This is important because," "I am confused because," "I think this means," etc.

- *Venn diagrams* (two overlapping concentric circles) in which the reader compares two items or concepts by placing specific criteria or critical attributes for one in the left circle, for the other in the right circle, and attributes or characteristics that are shared by the two in the overlapping section in the center.

• *Webs* in which the student charts out a concept or section of text in a graphic outline. The web begins with the title or concept written in the middle of the page and branches out in web fashion noting specific bits of information on the branches or strings of the web. Arrows or lines in other formats can make connections from one bit of information to another.

These and many other graphic organizers will help the student gain understanding of the text by making it visual and more concrete. As the student manipulates information in writing, he/she has a better opportunity to effectively and more concretely deal with it.

Reference Materials and Technology

An effective teacher will make use of both reference materials and technology to enhance a lesson.

Print resources will almost definitely include the use of a textbook, but there are several other print materials that should be considered in planning instruction. Among them are local, state, and national newspapers and magazines. These materials provide up-to-date coverage of numerous topics and can assist the student with making real-world connections to the content area being taught.

Audiovisual aids may be used at any point in the lesson—to introduce the lesson, explain concepts within it, or at the end as a summary. Videos and films can be stopped for discussion which tends to keep students' attention focused and assists them in learning note-taking skills. Numerous video-streaming databases are available online to the teacher and can be searched for available and appropriate material. Visual material may also include the chalkboard or whiteboard, overhead transparency projector, posters, charts, and computer screens. The effective teacher will make sure the print is clear and of a readable size and that use of different colors emphasizes relationships or differences.

The computer offers the opportunity to the teacher and the student to engage in a variety of learning experiences. The use of word processing programs, databases, and graphic arts programs can be used by the teacher to organize and present material and by the student to demonstrate learning and understanding by applying subject area knowledge in projects, reports, etc. The availability of material on the Internet offers the teacher an incredible array of sources from which to borrow and adapt material to enhance curricular objectives.

The computer can also be used as a teaching device. Computer-Assisted Instruction (CAI) has often existed as a drill and practice activity, but more recently it has taken the form of tutorials that may be used both for remedial work and also for instruction. However, tutorials should be used only to supplement, not supplant, teacher instruction.

Simulations or problem-solving programs provide learning opportunities for students which would take too long in real time, are

Computer tutorials shd be used to SUPPLEMENT NOT SUPPLANT teacher instruction

too costly or difficult, or would be impossible to experience. For example, a teacher might employ a simulation that allows students to "dissect" animals. This saves time and materials, is less messy, and accommodates students who might be reluctant to dissect real animals or learn about them. There are also several social studies simulations that allow students to invent a country and then see the effects of their political and economic decisions on the country.

The effective teacher will make use of manipulatives in numerous subject areas and with all ages of students. Manipulatives are touchable, movable materials that enhance students' understanding of a concept. They are used particularly in mathematics and science to give students a concrete way of dealing with concepts, but tangible materials are appropriate and helpful in all subject areas. Math teachers use plastic shapes in studying geometry. Number lines, place value cubes, and tessellation blocks are used to help students understand math, not only in elementary classes but also at higher levels in algebra, trigonometry, and calculus. Elementary language arts teachers use wooden letters or cut-outs to help students learn the alphabet; secondary English teachers can make parts-of-speech cards for sentence structure, frames for structured poetry, and blocks for essay structure. Science teachers are required to use many manipulatives during hands-on lab activities. Social studies and history teachers can use a wealth of cultural artifacts from countries that are being studied.

The effective teacher uses criteria to evaluate audiovisual, multimedia, and computer resources. The teacher should look for the material's congruence with lesson goals. If the material does not reinforce student outcomes, then it should not be used, no matter how flashy or well done it may be. The teacher should also consider his/her students' strengths and needs, their learning styles or preferred modalities, and their interests. Evaluation of resources should be accomplished in advance by the teacher, before purchase whenever possible. Evaluation is also conducted during student use of materials. Assessment after student use may be accomplished by considering the achievement level of the students and/or by surveys which ask for students' responses.

Multidisciplinary Studies

The effective teacher knows how to collaborate with peers to plan instruction. Collaboration may be as simple as planning and sharing ideas, or as complex as developing a multidisciplinary thematic unit in which teachers of several subject areas teach around a common theme. Teachers are responsible for finding ways to integrate learning into an interdisciplinary curriculum such that engineering students, for example, must be able to write an effective research report—good grammar and all—as well as do their calculations. Teachers need to be aware of and use strategies and techniques for coordinating the studies within a curriculum such that the outcome of a passing grade depends upon the student's effective use of skills applied—where relevant—across the curriculum. As in life, the "subjects" the teacher teaches are not used in isolation, but applied in combinations for success.

Consequently, teachers must look for methods to integrate the curriculum. They need to know the uses, benefits, and limitations of specific instructional approaches and how to use resources and special forms of instruction to enhance the learning experience.

Methods

1)

Cooperative learning is a method being used more and more in school settings. Briefly defined, this is the strategy for instruction that has students learn to work together in face-to-face situations in groups, pairs, or some other arrangement, in which one helps another without the interference of the teacher to arrive at the understanding needed for a project. Teachers should be able to apply this strategy as an alternative or adjunct to simple lecturing or reviewing textbook material, which can often be cut and dry.

2)

Sometimes teachers from different disciplines work together on a single project to accomplish many learning tasks. This is often called interdisciplinary instruction. For example, a geology teacher in a secondary school class might require a term paper on the definition and variety of metamorphic rock, and a colleague who is an English teacher might use that same paper as a term paper required of her class. This teaches the student the values of interdisciplinary writing and how writing for the discipline of geology is both similar to and different from writing a term paper in literature.

3)

Live-event learning is another strategy in which the teacher(s) can blend various subject area disciplines along with real life situations. In this example, the teacher structures an event or a field trip and takes the students to the location of the activity. For example, the teacher might take middle or high school students to a court hearing or trial, or elementary students to a dairy farm. In each example, the teacher plans ahead and helps the students to focus on learning that is connected to the curricular objectives. However, additional and often unplanned learning will also occur. The teacher needs to make careful use of debriefing techniques to uncover learning, to refocus learning, and/or to enhance connections among facets of learning in an interdisciplinary fashion.

References

Further reading of these references may enhance understanding of the competency and may also increase performance on the examination.

Behrens, Laurence, and Rosen, Leonard J. *Writing and Reading Across the Curriculum* 8th ed. New York: Longman Publishing Group, 2002.

Dockterman, David A. *Weaving Technology Into Your Teaching.* New York: Tom Snyder Productions, 2002.

Goudvis, Anne, and Harvey, Stephanie. *Strategies that Work.* Portland, Maine: Stenhouse Publishers, 2000.

Tovani, Cris. *I Read It, But I Don't Get It.* Portland, Maine: Stenhouse Publishers, 2000.

Competency 9: Learning Environments

Definition of Competency

The teacher has knowledge of strategies to create and sustain a safe, efficient, supportive learning enviroment.

- *The teacher evaluates the appropriateness of the physical environment for facilitating student learning and promoting safety.*

- *The teacher identifies a repertoire of techniques for establishing smooth, efficient, and well-paced routines.*

- The teacher identifies strategies to involve students in establishing rules and standards for behavior.

- The teacher identifies emergency procedures for student and campus safety.

Physical Environment

While there are certain physical aspects of the classroom that cannot be changed (size, shape, number of windows, type of lighting, etc.), there are others that can be. Windows can have shades or blinds which distribute light correctly and which allow for the room to be darkened for video or computer viewing. If the light switches do not allow part of the lights to remain on, sometimes schools will change the wiring system. If not, teachers can use a lamp to provide minimum lighting for monitoring students during videos or films.

Schools often schedule maintenance, such as painting and floor cleaning, during the summer. Often school administrators will accede to requests for a specific color of paint, given sufficient time for planning.

All secondary school classrooms should have a bulletin board used by the teacher and by the students. The effective teacher has plans for changing the board according to units of study. Space should be reserved for display of student work and projects, either on the bulletin board, the wall, or in the hallway. (Secondary teachers who need creative ideas can visit elementary classrooms.)

Bare walls can be depressing; however, covering the wall with too many posters can be visually distracting. Posters with sayings that promote cooperation, study skills, and content ideas should be displayed, but the same ones should not stay up all year because they will seem invisible when they become too familiar.

Most classrooms have movable desks, which allow for varied seating arrangements. If students are accustomed to sitting in rows, this is sometimes a good way to start the year. Harry K. Wong has described his method of assigning seats on the first day of school, which is to assign each desk a column and row number, then give students assignment cards as they come into the room. Another method is to put seating assignments on an overhead, visible when students enter the room. Once students are comfortable with classroom rules and procedures, the teacher can explain to students how to quickly move their desks into different formations for special activities, then return them to their original positions in the last 60 seconds of class.

The best place for the teacher's desk is often at the back of a room, so there are few barriers between the teacher and the students and between the students and the chalkboards. This encourages the teacher to walk around the classroom for better monitoring of students.

Social and Emotional Climate

The effective teacher maintains a climate that promotes the lifelong pursuit of learning. One way to do this is to practice research skills that will be helpful throughout life. All subject areas can promote the skills of searching for information to answer a question, filtering it to determine what is appropriate, and using what is helpful to solve a problem.

Here is an example. Most English teachers require some type of research project, from middle school through the senior year. Ken Macrorie's books on meaningful research can guide English teachers as they develop a project which can answer a real-life issue for students. For instance, a student who is trying to decide which college to attend could engage in database and print research on colleges that have the major characteristics he or she is interested in, conduct telephone or written interviews with school officials and current students, review school catalogs and other documents, and find magazine or journal articles that deal with the school. At the end of the process, students will have engaged in primary as well as secondary research, plus they will have an answer to a personal question.

The English teacher and any other subject area teacher can team up to collaborate on a joint research project. The resulting product satisfies both the need of the English teacher to teach research skills and the need of the subject area teacher to teach content knowledge as well as research skills. Primary research can be done through local or regional resources such as business owners, lawyers, physicians, and the general public. Research questions could include: (1) What effects do artificial sweeteners have on the human body's functioning (biology)? (2) What process is used to develop the platform of a political party (history)? (3) What happens when a business is accused of Title IX violations (business)? (4) What effects have higher medical costs had on family budgets (economics)? (5) How has the popularity of music CDs affected the music industry and businesses that sell records and tapes (music and business)?

The effective teacher also facilitates a positive social and emotional atmosphere and promotes a risk-taking environment for students. He or she sets up classroom rules and guidelines for how he or she will treat students, how students will treat him or her, and how students will treat each other. In part this means that he or she does not allow ridicule or put-downs, either from the teacher or among the students. It also means that the teacher has an accepting attitude toward student ideas, especially when the idea is not what he or she was expecting to hear. Sometimes students can invent excellent ideas that are not always clear until they are asked to explain how they arrived at them.

Students should feel free to answer and ask any questions that are relevant to the class, without fear of sarcasm or ridicule. Teachers should always avoid sarcasm. Sometimes teachers consider sarcasm to be mere teasing, but because some students often interpret it negatively, effective teachers avoid all types and levels of sarcasm.

Academic Learning Time

The effective teacher maximizes the amount of time spent for instruction. A teacher who loses five minutes at the beginning of class and five minutes at the end of class wastes ten minutes a day that could have been spent at educational activities. Ten minutes may not seem like a lot of time to lose. However, this is equivalent to a whole period a week, four classes a month, and 25 periods a year.

Academic learning time is the amount of allocated time that students spend in an activity at the appropriate level of difficulty

student
no frustration

appropriate level of difficulty

with the appropriate level of success. The appropriate level of difficulty is one which challenges students without frustrating them. Students who have typically been lower achievers need a higher rate of success than those who have typically been higher achievers.

One way to increase academic learning time is to teach students procedures so they will make transitions quickly. Another way to increase academic learning time is to have materials and resources ready for quick distribution and use. In addition, teachers can give students a time limit for a transition or an activity. In general, time limits for group work should be slightly shorter than students need, in order to encourage time on task and to prevent off-task behavior and discipline problems. It is essential for the teacher to have additional activities planned should the class finish activities sooner than anticipated. As students complete group work, they should have other group or individual activities so they can work up until the last minute before the end of class.

Student Behavior

Jaime Escalante, called "America's greatest teacher" by President Reagan and the subject of the motion picture *Stand and Deliver,* tells a story about having two students named Johnny in his class. He says that one, "good Johnny," was a dedicated and responsible student, courteous, polite, and high-achieving. The other Johnny, "bad Johnny," seldom came to class, and when he did, he created discipline problems. "Bad Johnny" wouldn't listen, wouldn't do his work, and wouldn't cooperate.

On the night of the annual open house, a very nice woman came to Mr. Escalante's classroom and introduced herself, "I am Johnny's mother." Mr. Escalante assumed she was "good Johnny's" mother. He said, "Oh, I am so glad to meet you. You must be very proud of your son. He is an exceptional student, and I am pleased to have him in my class."

The next day, "bad Johnny" came to class. After class, he approached Mr. Escalante and asked, "Hey, why did you tell my mother those things last night? No one has ever said anything like that about me." It was then that Mr. Escalante realized his mistake.

He did not admit his error to Johnny, and the strangest thing happened next. "Bad Johnny" stopped being bad. He started coming to class. He started doing his work. He started making good grades. Mr. Escalante concludes his story by saying, "I ended up with two 'good Johnnys' in my class."

This anecdote emphasizes an important aspect of teaching: Teacher perception is ultimately significant. Students may be what their teachers think them to be. What's more, students may also become what their teachers believe them to be. Teachers report that when they treat their students like responsible young adults, most students rise to the occasion.

Cognitive Development and Moral Decision Making

Of course, teachers of young children may have to contend with some different issues, but all teachers should be aware of age and maturational differences among students. Jean Piaget, whose ideas on cognitive development have greatly influenced American education, thought that children younger than eight years of age (because of their egocentric thought) were unable to take the perspective of another individual. Thus, Piaget concluded that children under the age of eight made decisions about right and wrong on the basis of how much harm was caused. For example, children might say that a child who ate two forbidden cookies was less guilty than the child who ate six forbidden cookies. Children over the age of eight, however, were able to take into consideration whether or not the individual acted purposely or accidentally. For example, a child who broke a toy by accident was not as guilty of misbehavior as the child who broke the toy on purpose. Researchers who have tested Piaget's ideas have found that children younger than age eight are able to engage in moral reasoning at much more complex levels than Piaget thought possible.

The term *standards*, when used with regard to behavior, evokes issues of right and wrong, sometimes referred to as ethical or moral decisions. With regard to moral development, teachers should be familiar with the concepts of Lawrence Kohlberg. Kohlberg, following the example of Piaget, developed a scenario to quiz children and teens. Kohlberg told a story about a man whose wife was so seriously ill that she would die without medication, yet her husband had no money to buy her medicine. After trying various legal means to get the medicine, her husband considered stealing it. Kohlberg asked if it was wrong or right to steal the drug and to explain why it was either wrong or right. Kohlberg did not evaluate whether the respondent said it was wrong or right to steal the drug; he was interested in the reasons given to justify the actions.

On the basis of the responses he received, Kohlberg proposed six stages of moral development. **Stage one, punishment and obedience**, describes children who simply follow the rules so as to escape punishment. If these children, for example kindergarten-age students, are told not to talk or they'll lose their chance to go outside for recess, they will not want to lose their playground privileges, so they will not talk. On the other hand, **stage two, individualism and change**, refers to children who follow the rules, not only to escape punishment, but also when they think there is some reward in following the rules. These children, for example older primary-grade children, seek not only to escape punishment, but also to receive a reward or benefit for their good behavior.

Kohlberg's **stage three is described as mutual interpersonal expectations and interpersonal conformity**; at this stage, children want to please the people who are important to them. Junior high students, for example, may behave in a manner that gains the approval of their peers or their idols. At **stage four, Kohlberg said that adolescents become oriented to conscience**, and they recognize the importance of established social order. Teens at this stage obey the rules unless those rules contradict higher social responsibilities. In other words, most high school students realize that rules are necessary, and they will obey most rules if the rules are based on basic social values, such as honesty, mutual respect, courtesy, and so forth.

Post-conventional morality was the term Kohlberg gave to stages five and six. At stage five, individuals recognize the importance of both individual rights and social contracts, but believe that people should generally abide by the rules to bring the greatest good to the majority. Kohlberg believes that about one-fifth of adolescents reach stage five. Therefore, Kohlberg would have expected that few high school students would be operating at this level.

Finally, Kohlberg would not have expected high school students to reach stage six, since he believed that very few individuals ever reached this stage. Stage six is characterized by universal principles of justice. Individuals at this stage believe that most rules should be obeyed because most rules are based on just principles; however, if rules violate ethical principles, then individuals have a greater obligation to follow their conscience even if that means breaking the rules. Social reformers, such as Martin Luther King, Jr., would be an example of stage six moral reasoning.

Kohlberg's theory describes the progression of children's moral reasoning from school entry at kindergarten (stage one) to graduation from high school (stages four and five, for some). Kohlberg's theory has been widely taught and applied in school settings, but not without controversy.

Some have contended that Kohlberg's theory is limited and biased because of his research techniques (getting reactions to a scenario) and because his theory was based on a study of white, middle-class males under the age of 17. Many would say that his ideas have limited application to other ethnic groups, socioeconomic groups, or females.

One theorist interested in applying Kohlberg's theory to women is Carol Gilligan, a student of Kohlberg's, who developed an alternative theory of moral development in women. Gilligan found that women, unlike the men at Kohlberg's stages five and six, tend to value caring and compassion for others above abstract, rational principles. Therefore, when women make decisions, they base their conclusions on how others will be affected by their choices and actions.

Gilligan posited that women pass through three levels of moral reasoning, although like Kohlberg, not all reach the third level. At the first level, the individual is concerned only about herself. At level two, the individual sacrifices her own interests for the sake of others.

Finally, at the third level, the individual synthesizes responsibilities to both herself and to others.

An effective teacher may want to consider the implications of these theories for the behavior of students in their classes, in particular, how students will respond to rules of behavior. Although students taking the exam will not be tested on these specific theorists, their theories are, nonetheless, a valuable resource for assessing student behavior. For example, according to Kohlberg, younger students are more concerned about punishments and rewards; older students are more concerned about reasonable rules based on principles of fairness and equality. According to Gilligan, female students may be thinking about how rules affect their friendships. To illustrate, according to these theorists, a male student might be offended by someone cheating (because cheating is wrong) and report the individual to the teacher. Female students, on the other hand, might value their friendship with the cheater more than the principle of honesty; therefore, females might be less likely to report cheating to the teacher.

Learning Styles and Personality Types

Information about learning styles and personality types essential to effective teaching can also shed light on how individuals make ethical and moral decisions. For example, research indicates that the population is fairly evenly distributed between people who make decisions based on rational, logical, and objective data—thinking types—and those who make decisions based on feelings—feeling types. Slightly more males than females are thinking types.

The feeling half of the population tends to make decisions based on how those decisions may affect others, avoiding conflict and promoting harmony; slightly more females than males are feeling types.

Most people (approximately 76 percent) are the sensing type, those who learn through sensory experiences; they are linear learners who enjoy facts and details. They like sequential organization and memory tasks. They often work slowly and methodically, taking great care to finish each project before beginning another one.

On the other hand, however, are the minority (approximately 24 percent) who are the intuitive type. This type learns not through experience, but by insight and inspiration. These students are bored by facts and details, preferring global concepts and theories. They dislike memory work. Generally, they are quick to grasp ideas and catch on to the gist of things; this means they can be disruptive because they have already learned their lesson or finished their assignment. While they generally perform well on tests, they also daydream and lose interest quickly in the things that they deem uninteresting or dull. They like to do several things at once and find it tedious to have to slow down or wait for others to finish.

Standards for Classroom Behavior

Teachers who understand these characteristics and ways of thinking, whether it is in regard to information processing or moral decision making, can use this information to establish standards for classroom behavior. Standards should reflect community values and norms and should take into consideration students' ethnicity (i.e., what language they speak at home), socioeconomic status, and religious beliefs. These factors are important when formulating a dress code, determining how to address authority figures, defining the use of appropriate language, examining interactions between males and females, or developing school safety procedures. An important part of the teacher's role is to educate the students about school policies and/or district and state policies with regard to these issues.

What are common values across cultural, ethnic, religious, and social strata? Honesty, mutual respect, consideration, and courtesy are among those virtues that have widespread acceptance. Students (and their parents) should know about standards for attendance, grades, and student behavior. Students should know how to dress for school, how to address their teachers and other school employees, and what is appropriate language for school (limiting the use of slang or vulgarities). They should know rules for turning in homework, rules for making up missed assignments, and rules for handing in work late (if it is accepted). They should know what they can and cannot bring to school (certain kinds of materials and tools). They should know what will happen if they break the rules.

Psychological research on behavior modification and reducing aggression shows that modeling acceptable and nonaggressive behaviors is more effective than catharsis and punishment. Teachers are most effective when they follow the rules and exemplify the standards of conduct themselves. Teachers who are courteous, prompt, enthusiastic, in control, patient, and organized provide examples for students through their own behavior. They send the message "Do as I do," not "Do as I say."

The Florida Department of Education states in its "Code of Ethics and the Principles of Professional Conduct" that teachers shall a) make reasonable efforts to protect students from conditions that would harm learning or mental and physical health and safety; b) not restrain students from independent action in pursuit of learning; c) not deny students' access to diverse points of view; d) not intentionally suppress or distort information regarding students' academic program; e) not expose a student to unnecessary embarrassment or disparagement; f) not violate or deny students' legal rights; g) not harass or discriminate against students on the basis of race, color, religion, sex, age, national or ethnic origin, political beliefs, marital status, handicapping condition, sexual orientation, or social and family background, and make reasonable efforts to assure that students are protected from harassment and discrimination; h) not exploit a relationship with a student for personal gain or advantage; and i) shall keep information in confidence or as required by law (Florida State Board of Education, Rule 6B-1.006, FAC). Teachers who honor this code will be modeling the appropriate standards of behavior for their students.

In addition to modeling appropriate behaviors, another effective way of treating misbehavior (that is, more effective than catharsis and punishment) is the use of incompatible responses. Effective teachers learn how to employ these responses. Some studies have even suggested that open body language (arms open, not crossed) and positive facial expressions (smiling) can be used by teachers to diffuse student anger.

Rules and the Student's Role in Decision Making

Some educational experts have suggested that standards and rules are most effective if students play a role in formulating them. This does not mean that students make all the rules, but it means that they can contribute ideas. Stephen Covey, author of the best-selling *The Seven Habits of Highly Effective People,* suggests that people who desire to be effective or successful should be proactive. He explains that being proactive means anticipating everything that can go awry before it does; teachers can think about what could go wrong in class concerning a student's conduct and be prepared if it ever happens. Of course, a teacher may not be able to predict everything that a student may attempt, but trying to analyze many possibilities may provide a teacher some level of comfort in dealing with misbehaviors. Covey also uses the term *proactive* to stress the importance of self-direction, not only for teachers, but for students, as well.

Allowing students to have a voice in establishing standards and formulating codes provides students with an excellent opportunity to exercise their problem-solving skills and critical-thinking abilities. Although one key purpose of education is often purported to be graduating students who are responsible citizens capable of participating thoughtfully in a democratic society, educational practices have had a tendency to foster dependency, passivity, and a "tell me what to think and do" complacency.

Older students especially can benefit from participating in the decision-making process. American industries and businesses have attained greater success, efficiency, and effectiveness through principles of Total Quality Management (TQM). Many TQM principles have also been applied to American education with great success.

One of the key ingredients of TQM is information sharing, so that all partners in an endeavor are aware of goals and objectives. If education is the endeavor, then applying TQM principles means that teachers and students, parents and principals, and other supporting players are all partners in the endeavor. Following TQM principles also means that if all partners have information concerning goals and objectives, then they can form a team to work cooperatively with greater efficiency and effectiveness to achieve goals and objectives.

These ideas require teachers to share authority with students, allowing students a voice in decision making. For some teachers, learning to share control with students may be difficult. Helping students to make some of their own decisions will conflict with some teachers' training, as well as their own ideas and expectations about being in charge. But the many benefits of shared decision making, already described, are worth the struggle to adjust.

Although this may not sound like the perfect classroom to every teacher, Covey describes what, for him, was his most exciting learning experience:

> As a teacher, I have come to believe that many great
> classes teeter on the very edge of chaos.... There are
> times when neither the teacher nor the student

knows for sure what's going to happen. In the beginning, there is a safe environment that enables people to be really open and to learn and to listen to each other's ideas. Then comes the brainstorming, where the spirit of evaluation is subordinated to the spirit of creativity, imagining, and intellectual networking. Then an absolutely unusual phenomenon begins to take place. The entire class is transformed with the excitement of a new thrust, a new idea, a new direction that's hard to define, yet it's almost palpable to the people involved.

Covey describes a dynamic classroom, not one in stasis; however, there are important requirements for the classroom. First, the students have to feel safe, not only safe from physical harm, but safe from mental harm—from mockery, intimidation, unfair criticisms, threats—from teachers or, especially, other classmates. These features describe a classroom where there is mutual respect and trust between teacher and students and among the students themselves.

Rules and School Safety Issues

The importance of a safe school environment for promoting good behavior has been mentioned already; however, statistics indicate that school safety is a vital concern for all educators. More than 100,000 students bring weapons to school each day. Every day, 40 students are killed or wounded with these weapons. One out of every five students is afraid to go the restroom at school for fear of victimization. In addition to student fears, more than 6,000 teachers are threatened by students each year.

Research shows that the following factors contribute to school violence and antisocial behaviors: overcrowding, poor design and use of school space, lack of disciplinary procedures, student alienation, multi-cultural insensitivity, rejection of at-risk students by teachers and peers, and anger or resentment at school routines. On the other hand, the following characteristics contribute to school safety: positive school climate and atmosphere, clear and high performance expectations for all students, practices and values that promote inclusion, student bonding to school, high levels of student participation and parent involvement in school activities, and opportunities to acquire academic skills and develop socially.

Effective teachers need to be alert to the signs of potentially violent behavior, acknowledging that signs can easily be misinterpreted and misunderstood. Warning signs should be used to get help for children, not to exclude, punish, or isolate them. Experts also emphasize that warning signs should not be seen as a checklist for identifying, labeling, or stereotyping children, and that referrals to outside agencies based on early warning signals must be kept confidential and, except for those suspected of child abuse or neglect, must have parental consent.

The American Psychological Association has identified four "accelerating factors" that increase the risk of violence. These four factors are a) early involvement with drugs and alcohol; b) easy access to weapons, especially handguns; c) association with antisocial, deviant peer-groups; and d) pervasive exposure to media violence. Longitudinal studies (studies following groups over time) have shown youth violence and delinquency to be linked with situations in which a) one or more parents have been arrested; b) the child has been the client of a child-protection agency; c) the child's family has experienced death, divorce, or another serious transition; d) the child has received special-education services; and/or e) the youth exhibits severe antisocial behavior.

Along somewhat analogous lines, the U.S. Department of Education and Department of Justice have compiled a long list of possible early warning signs. These signs include a) social withdrawal (often associated with feelings of depression, rejection, persecution, unworthiness, and lack of confidence); b) excessive feelings of isolation and being alone; c) excessive feelings of rejection; d) being a victim of violence—including physical or sexual abuse; e) feelings of being picked on and persecuted; f) low school interest and poor academic performance; g) expression of violence in writings and drawings; h) uncontrolled anger; i) patterns of impulsive and chronic hitting, intimidating, and bullying behaviors; j) history of discipline problems; k) history of violent and aggressive behaviors; l) intolerance for differences and prejudicial attitudes; m) drug use and alcohol use; n) affiliation with gangs; o) inappropriate access to, possession of, and use of firearms; and p) serious threats of violence.

In addition to these early warning signs are what the Departments of Education and Justice called imminent warning signs, requiring an immediate response. Imminent warning signs are a) serious physical fighting with peers or family members; b) serious destruction of property; c) rage for seemingly minor reasons; d) detailed threats of lethal violence; e) possession and/or use of firearms and weapons; and f) other self-injurious behaviors or threats of suicide. Immediate intervention by school authorities and possibly law enforcement officials is required if a child has presented a detailed plan to harm or kill others or is carrying a weapon, particularly a firearm, and has threatened to use it. In situations where students present other threatening behaviors, parents should be informed immediately.

Violence prevention strategies at school range from adding social-skills training to the curriculum to installing metal detectors at the entrances to buildings. Educational experts recommend that schools teach all students procedures in conflict resolution and anger management, in addition to explaining the school rules, expectations, and disciplinary policies.

The federal Gun-Free Schools Act of 1994 required every state to pass zero-tolerance laws on weapons at school or face the loss of federal funds. Every state has complied with this law and requires school districts to expel students for at least a year if they bring weapons to school.

The U.S. Department of Education and the Department of Justice have produced a joint report recommending actions to promote school safety. First, an open discussion of safety issues is essential. "Schools can reduce the risk of violence by teaching children about the dangers of firearms, as well as appropriate strategies for dealing with feelings, expressing anger in appropriate ways, and resolving conflicts. Schools also should teach children that they are responsible for their actions and that the choices they make have consequences for which they will be held accountable." Also recommended is treating students with equal respect, creating ways for students to share their concerns, and helping children to feel safe when expressing their feelings.

In review, effective and safe schools develop and enforce consistent rules that are clear, broad-based, and fair. Effective schoolwide disciplinary policies include a code of conduct, specific rules, and consequences that can accommodate student differences on a case-by-case basis when needed. School policies need to include anti-harassment and anti-violence policies and due process rights. Rules should reflect the cultural values and educational goals of the community. School staff, students, and families should be involved in the development, discussion, and implementation of fair rules, written and applied in a nondiscriminatory manner, and accommodating cultural diversity. Consequences for violating rules must be commensurate with the offenses, and negative consequences must be accompanied by positive teaching for socially appropriate behaviors. Finally, there must be zero-tolerance for illegal possession of weapons, drugs, or alcohol.

"With it"-ness in the Classroom

Teachers must be "with it" in a classroom to prevent misbehavior that will interrupt the flow of learning. The level of "with it"-ness must extend beyond the obvious events of the classroom. A teacher needs to understand the dynamics behind the actions that occur in the classroom, and then proceed accordingly.

There are many factors that influence student behavior. Young children will generally follow the rules of the classroom out of a desire to please their teachers. Misbehavior that occurs in a classroom may be the result of a conflict that is occurring elsewhere. Teachers should be aware that these conflicts can occur between peers, between students and the teacher, or as a result of events in the student's family or out-of-classroom experiences.

The goal of "with it"-ness is to prevent misconduct in the classroom. Through everyday interactions, the teacher develops a sense of an individual student's normal behavior and general mental state. The "with it" teacher also develops a sense of the relations between the students in a class and within the school. If the beginning of a conflict between individuals in a class is noticed, the "with it" teacher is able to mediate the students to a resolution that avoids the disruption of class time.

The desired behavior for the students should be well-explained and clearly displayed in a classroom. Posted rules provide a constant guide and reminder of classroom rules. Teachers can also use these displays as a reference when discussing expected behavior, either individually or with the class as a whole.

Teachers should self-monitor their interactions with the misbehaving students. Children may act out if they feel they are threatened, disliked, or treated unfairly. A "with it" teacher knows which particular students are causing the class disruption and works to curb this behavior without punishing the class as a whole. The class momentum can be disrupted either by the teacher's response to the behavior or by the teacher allowing the misbehavior to persist.

Both the individual student and the class as a whole are affected by how the teacher handles classroom misconduct. The effective approach is when the teacher compliments the positive behavior modeled by other students in the classroom, rather than individually reprimanding student misbehavior. If certain students are not properly addressing the task at hand, the teacher can say, "I like the way Glen is working in his math book" or "Belinda, I like the way you are quietly raising your hand and waiting your turn." By doing so, the teacher is reinforcing the desired behavior for the class without directly addressing and calling attention to the misbehavior. The individual student has an opportunity to monitor his or her own behavior, and class momentum is not lost.

Teachers can also guide a student toward appropriate behavior by stating the student's name, or explaining what task he or she should currently be working on. Non-verbal cues include walking toward the student, making eye contact, or gently touching the student's desk or shoulder. These techniques can be used without disrupting the flow of the classroom.

non-verbal cues don't disrupt the flow of the classrm.

Teachers must clearly voice their expectations without yelling or becoming angry. Quiet and controlled reprimands have been shown to be very effective. Maintaining control without involving punitive measures lowers the tension in the entire classroom. Students should not be made to feel uncomfortable because the teacher is angry. This is especially important when teachers are working with small groups, or when working on simultaneous tasks. Individualized instruction should not suffer when the teacher must reprimand another student. When a teacher demonstrates "with it"-ness, students do not feel that they have an opportunity to misbehave just because the teacher's attention is not focused directly on them.

Don't yell or become angry

Procedures for Learning Success

One of the most challenging and important synthesizing activities of the teaching professional is determining how to match what needs to be taught with the specifications of those who need to learn it. The successful teacher spends considerable time becoming familiar with required instructional objectives, curriculum, and texts. This should be done well in advance of the start of the school year. In addition to general knowledge about the intellectual and social developmental levels of students, the particular needs which characterize any specific group of students, including their individual learning styles, are more apparent to the teacher after the first few days and weeks of school. The effective teacher must then be organized enough to choose and sequence learning activities before the school year begins, but flexible enough to adapt these activities after becoming acquainted with the special needs and learning styles of specific students.

VERY IMPT.

There are several steps the teacher should follow to ensure success for student learning: a) know and start teaching at the proper level of the students; b) share with students learning objectives and the processes chosen to attain them; c) prepare for the successive steps in the learning process—from instruction, through guidance and support, to feedback; d) choose relatively small steps in which to progress, and include regular assessments of these progressions; e) distinguish between the learning a student can do independently and that which is best facilitated and monitored by the teacher, and choose methods appropriate to content and skills; and f) include a variety of activities and methods which appeal to the full range of student learning styles and preferences.

Organizing Activities

Instructional objectives necessitate that the skill or knowledge to be taught should be valuable on its own, or should clearly lead to something else which is valuable. When the class begins, these long-range objectives should be shared with students as part of the teacher's planned "idea scaffolding," to acknowledge learning as a mutual enterprise. Sharing these objectives is the first important learning activity because this serves as the basis for the communal task of "making sense" of the learning in progress.

Since teachers are expected to be professionally prepared to recognize the cognitive and social levels of students, a simple review of the generally accepted theories of Piaget, Erikson, and other research theorists may be necessary to recall specific characteristics appropriate to various developmental levels. Familiarity with the learning objectives and material to be mastered, as well as the level of the students, enables the teacher to choose and develop a wide range of appropriate activities and to tentatively sequence them in ways that facilitate learning.

A high school language arts teacher, for example, who wishes to convey to his or her students the excitement and value of closely reading literary texts will, at the start of the year, address this learning objective with them. The teacher may also include a personal experience of a close reading that is inspiring and revealing. He or she can then plan a series of short-term goals, such as "Students will be able to read carefully enough to gather important details of plot" and "Students will be able to read sensitively enough to notice the connotative dimensions of words and appreciate the nuances suggested by cumulative connotation." Naturally, recognizing denotative details will precede appreciating connotative dimensions. Both will precede the students' ability to identify and appreciate the author's choice of point of view.

Careful, incremental goal-setting allows for considerable flexibility in pace and methods, and leads to further valuable sequencing of strategies. For example, a variety of activities may be used to enhance close reading: the teacher may model close reading of a very short story; the teacher may assign small group work with close reading of paragraphs where one student identifies an important detail, and another student suggests its relevance to the details; the teacher can show the class an overhead color-marking of important descriptive words from one page of a short story or poem; students can work on individual in-class color-marking for the next page, followed by a group discussion of student results; the teacher can assign homework assignments to color-mark a short story or poem; and students can work on group assignments graphing elements of literary text.

Such preliminary planning is enhanced for any specific group of students by a perceptive teacher's growing awareness of individual student learning styles. Since students do not fall precisely into theoretical stages, activities must be designed for a range of developmental levels and learning styles. This includes concrete as well as abstract dimensions, opportunities for instruction by the teacher, and exploration and discovery by individual students and groups.

Once the learning enterprise is launched, the teacher's continued instruction, support, regular assessment, and feedback help maximize the potential of learning opportunities.

Outcome-Oriented Learning

Effective teachers plan carefully so that outcome-oriented activities will produce students who are self-directed learners, in group or individual environments. He or she knows how to plan so that the curriculum guides, lesson plans, actual lessons, tests, and assessments are correlated. Effective teachers plan in advance, explain the unit's goals and objectives to the students, then choose activities which will help the class reach the desired outcomes.

In outcome-oriented learning, teachers define outcomes, or what they want students to know, do, and be when they complete a required course of study. The teachers set high but realistic goals and objectives for their students, then plan instructional activities which will assist students in achieving these goals.

The key to effective outcome-oriented planning is to consider what outcomes must be achieved, then determine which teacher and student behaviors will improve the probability that students will achieve the outcomes.

Outcome-based planning starts with the end product—what must be learned or accomplished in a particular course or grade level. For example, an algebra teacher may decide that the final outcome of his or her algebra course would be that students use quadratic equations to solve problems. He or she then works "backwards" to determine prerequisite knowledge and skills students need to have in order to accomplish this outcome. By continuing to ask these questions about each set of prerequisites, the teacher finds a starting point for the subject or course, then develops goals and objectives. The outcomes should be important enough to be required of all students.

An outcome-oriented system means that students are given sufficient time and practice to acquire the knowledge and skills. It also means that teachers take into account students' various learning styles and time required for learning, and make adaptations by providing a variety of educational opportunities.

Wait Time for Questions

Students need adequate time to respond to questions. Do not allow outbursts, or choral responses, of answers to your questions. Answering questions without calling on specific students for their response generates a faction of students who are always answering the questions. In addition, providing appropriate time to think about the answer, or wait time, of 3 to 5 seconds is necessary for students to thoroughly formulate their responses. The proper way to ask a question is to first, ask the question, second, provide adequate wait time, third, call on the student, and last tell them if their response was correct. If it is correct, it is appropriate to give specific praise. However, overuse of specific praise devalues the praise mechanism within the classroom. Students who are constantly praised do not know when to really be proud of their good answers. The only time a student's name is called, followed by the question, is to bring a student back into the discussion for disciplinary reasons. Then, it is appropriate to call the name first so you are certain they are aware of the question being asked. This technique brings back a disruptive or off-task student and gives them a non-verbal message that their attention is needed.

[handwritten in margin: IMPT – disruptive or off-task]

Effective Use of Time

Idle hands generate a variety of discipline issues. The teacher should keep a steady pace throughout the entire class from the beginning of the lesson to the independent practice or homework time. If a mere minute is wasted each day, this will accumulate to well over 3 hours of lost instruction during a single year. Smooth transitions from topic to topic, class to class, and subject to subject are needed so time is not wasted, interruptions minimized, and downtime becomes non-existent.

Organizing Instruction

First, a teacher should clearly have all materials prepared and ready to go before beginning any classroom lesson. Then when class begins, the teacher can immediately start with an initiating or motivational activity that has the students working and interested from the beginning. This activity could begin with a "hook" that draws student interest, states the objective for your lesson or a review of concepts that will help lead lesson success. During this time, the teacher may choose to take attendance or complete other administrative activities that are required. Then, the teacher should use a smooth transition into the instructional part of the lesson followed by a short assessment, also referred to as a guided practice activity, that determines the student's level of understanding. Last, the closure of the lesson reminds the students of the key components of the lesson. The transition from initiating to lesson presentation to closure can be thought of as the rules to giving a good speech. First, the teacher tells the students what you are going to say (motivational hook), then the teacher tells the students (instructional section), and last, the teachers reviews what was just taught (closure).

Keep in mind that the instructional section can use a variety of approaches including a guided discovery lesson, a free exploration lesson, cooperative projects, or a teacher-directed lesson. Instructional variety has proven to be a surefire way of maintaining student interest and improving achievement. Good instruction may include providing clear directions, asking open-ended questions, addressing questions, modeling approaches, encouraging discourse, and assessing student understanding to monitor their progress and to provide them feedback. The conclusion of most lessons will have students practicing the skills they learned in class.

This momentum will ensure a smooth transition and a natural routine that will encourage learning, provide a consistent pattern that students will anticipate and assist the teacher in moving smoothly from one activity to another. Routines will help students anticipate the next move. However, varied routines help in minimizing the boredom that can exist within a regulated highly routine environment.

References

Further reading of these references may enhance understanding of the competency and may also increase performance on the examination.

Blanchard, K., and Johnson, S. *The One Minute Manager.* New York: Berkley Books, 1981.

Border, L. "Morphing: A Quintessential Human Capability." *National Teaching and Learning Forum*, Vol. 7, 1998.

Covey, Stephen. *The Seven Habits of Highly Effective People.* New York: Simon and Schuster, 1989.

Florida State Board of Education. *The Code of Ethics and the Principles of Professional Conduct of the Education Profession in Florida.* 1998.

Gilligan, C. *In a Different Voice: Psychological Theory and Women's Development.* Cambridge, Massachusetts: Harvard University Press, 1982.

Kohlberg, L. "The Psychology of Moral Development: The Nature and Validity of Moral Stages." *Essays on Moral Development* Vol. 2, 1984.

Myers, I. B. *Gifts Differing.* Palo Alto, California: Consulting Psychologists Press, 1980.

Sternberg, R. *In Search of the Human Mind.* Ft. Worth, Texas: Harcourt Brace, 1995.

U.S. Department of Education and Department of Justice. *Early Warning, Timely Response.* Washington, D.C.: U.S. Government Printing Office, 1998.

Discipline by Design, The Honor Level System.
    http://www.honorlevel.com/x83.xml

ERIC Clearinghouse on Educational Management. Trends and Issues: School Safety.
    http://www.eric.uoregon.edu/trends_issues/safety/index.html

Competency 10: Planning

Definition of Competency

The teacher has knowledge of how to plan and conduct lessons in a variety of learning environments that lead to student outcomes consistent with state and district standards.

- The teacher determines instructional long-term goals and short-term objectives appropriate to student needs.

- The teacher identifies activities that support the knowledge, skills, and attitudes to be learned in a given subject area.

- *The teacher identifies materials based on instructional objectives and student learning needs and performance levels.*

Goals

All successful teachers begin the term with a clear idea of what they expect students to learn in a given course. Establishing long-range goals for a course—goals that are age-appropriate and reflect student ability and needs—help to clarify the knowledge and skills that teachers and students will work toward during the school year.

Long-range goals can be established for the classroom by the Board of Education, by knowledgeable curriculum specialists, or by a single teacher or group of teachers. Stated in clear, concise language, these goals define the knowledge that students will achieve or the skills that they will acquire through specific instructional activities. For example, a language arts instructor might state the following long-range goals for high school students:

- The student is able to identify major American poets and authors of the twentieth century;

- The student is able to write narrative, informative, and persuasive essays;

- The student is able to properly cite research references;

- The student is able to identify important themes in literature;

- The student is able to identify with multicultural perspectives on the American experience.

After developing a list of potential goals for a course, it is necessary to evaluate those goals against the following criteria:

Importance: The resulting learning must be significant and relevant enough for students to aim for.

Instruction: Appropriate classroom activities must be able to support the learning of the stated goal.

Evaluation: Students must be able to demonstrate the achievement of the goal.

Suitability: The goal must be challenging, as well as reachable, for all students.

Importance

There are many ways to evaluate the importance of selected goals. Teachers can judge goals on the basis of whether the stated outcome is necessary to gain advanced knowledge of a particular field of study, as in the following goal: Students will memorize the letters of the alphabet or master the use of punctuation. Goals can be evaluated on the basis of whether or not their achievement will lead students to become better citizens, such as: Students will apply their knowledge of the constitution to judge a contemporary court case. Goals can also be judged on the basis of whether or not their achievement will lead students to become well-adapted members of society or competitive in the workforce, as in the following: Students will be able to demonstrate their ability to use the Internet to locate information. Finally, goals can be selected on the basis of whether or not their achievement will help prepare students for college admissions standards.

Instruction

In order to ensure that students achieve the stated goal, appropriate classroom activities must be chosen to support its learning. When students have completed these activities, they should be able to successfully demonstrate the knowledge or skills that they have achieved.

Evaluation

Through the successful completion of writing assignments, tests, projects, or activities, students must be able to demonstrate that they have achieved the stated long-range goals.

Suitability

All goals for a given course must be achievable for the entire class, while leaving room to challenge students to master new skills. In order to determine if long-range goals are appropriate, teachers can refer to a number of resources, including student files which may include the results of basic skills tests and reading level evaluations, as well as writing samples.

Identifying Student Knowledge, Skills, and Attitudes

After identifying long-range goals for a given subject, it is necessary to recognize the short-range goals that are essential to achieving the larger objective. In order to do this, teachers must be aware of the underlying skills needed to successfully achieve the stated long-range objective. For example, in order to write an essay, a language arts teacher must ensure that students are able to compose complete sentences and paragraphs, develop a coherent outline of ideas, create a thesis, write an introduction, advance the stated thesis through supporting ideas in the body paragraphs, and form a logical conclusion. If students are unable to master these basic skills, they will be unable to achieve the long-range goals of producing an essay.

Likewise, a biology teacher, whose long-range goal is for students to understand the process of photosynthesis, will identify another list of necessary skills. For example, students must know basic elements like hydrogen, oxygen, and carbon, and students must understand how these elements combine to form water (H_2O) and carbon dioxide (CO_2). Moreover, a geometry teacher would know that in order for students to find the area of a triangle or the circumference of a circle, they must know how to compose and solve basic geometric problems.

Constructing or Adapting Short-Range Objectives

Short-range objectives should be stated in simple terms and should outline identifiable behaviors and skills. When constructing short-range objectives for a course of study, teachers must make certain that each objective leads to the realization of a long-range goal and that the skill or knowledge is easily observable. For example:

- Students will be able to demonstrate an understanding of Shakespearean language;

- Students will be able to list the pros and cons of various forms of energy, including nuclear energy, natural gas, solar energy, dams, and coal;

- Students will be able to solve advanced word problems involving multiplication and division;

- Students will be able to complete a diagram outlining the processes involved in digestion; or

- Students will be able to recite a poem by a well-known twentieth-century poet.

When short-range objectives have been supplied by the Board of Education or the local school system, teachers must be able to interpret and adapt them, making certain that they are appropriate to the age and ability of their own students. For example, a high school senior might be able not only to list the positive and negative implications of nuclear fusion as an energy source, but also to write a persuasive essay, arguing for or against nuclear energy. While an elementary school student might find reciting a poem from memory to be a formidable task, he or she might be appropriately challenged by the assignment of selecting a poem and reading it aloud to the class.

Organizing and Sequencing Short-Range Objectives

As learning is achieved by moving from basic skills and knowledge to the understanding of complex ideas and functions, it is important for teachers to sequence short-range objectives according to their appropriate place in the development of higher-order thinking. For example, a history student might first be introduced to the life and achievements of Einstein through a documentary film, later studying his most famous equation for the production of energy ($E=mc^2$). Later, that student might be introduced to the top-secret Manhattan Project that involved hundreds of physicists in the race to turn Einstein's equation for energy into an atomic weapon. Still later, the disastrous results of the atomic bomb in Hiroshima and Nagasaki might be introduced through first-hand accounts from survivors. Finally, he or she might be required to study current treaties surrounding the control of nuclear proliferation. The students might conclude their course of study with a class debate on nuclear proliferation and how it promotes or threatens chances for global peace. From the study of historical events like the Manhattan Project and basic terms like nuclear proliferation to the application of this knowledge in a classroom debate, the short-range goals that guide the activities of this history class have been sequentially ordered to allow students the opportunity to gradually develop and demonstrate higher-order thinking skills.

Other examples of the sequencing of short-range objectives to build upon knowledge can be found in the very clear development of skills outlined in the study of mathematics. From the simple memorization of numbers beginning in the first grade, to the mastery of addition, subtraction, multiplication, and division studied throughout elementary school, through more complicated functions in middle school like algebra and the application of these skills in advanced word problems, to the study of geometry, trigonometry, and calculus in high school—mathematical studies are clearly delineated to build upon previously acquired skills. Without knowledge of multiplication, the idea of division would be impossible to master. Without an understanding of division, fractions would be beyond the reach of students. Inasmuch as no decent math teacher would consider asking students to give the area of a triangle without first ensuring that the students know basic algebra, all teachers must be aware of the basic skills necessary to achieve higher-order skills, and must arrange classroom activities and short-range goals in the order that best promote learning.

Choosing Educational Materials

The effective teacher continually seeks materials which help instigate and enhance student learning. In some instances, the teacher may select instructional materials from those readily available based on the appropriate age level for his or her students. In other instances, he/she will need to adapt available materials to better serve individual needs and learning styles. And in yet other instances, the teacher will need to design and develop materials specifically suited to his or her learning objectives and the needs of the students. Such acquisition, adaptation, or creation of materials will primarily be done prior to the beginning of the school year. However, some of it will need to occur while the school year is in progress, as particular learning challenges arise and as individual student needs are discovered. A considerable proportion of the time invested in locating and shaping these materials will bear dividends, since materials which prove to be well-suited to a particular unit are eligible for repeated use.

Educational Resources

The teacher uses a variety of educational resources (including people and technology) to enhance both individual and group learning. The effective teacher includes resources of all types in the curriculum planning process. He or she should be very familiar with the school library, city/county library, education service center resources, and the library of any college or university in the area. The teacher should have a list of all audiovisual aids which may be borrowed, for example, kits, films, filmstrips, videos, laser disks, and computer software. All audiovisual aids should be related to curricular objectives. Many librarians have keyed their resources to objectives in related subject areas so the teacher can incorporate them with ease into the lessons. However, resources should never be used with a class unless they have been previewed and approved by the teacher. The list of resources to be used in a lesson or unit should be included in the curriculum guide or the lesson plan for ease of use.

Planning for Resources

The effective teacher determines the appropriate place in the lesson for audiovisual aids. If the material is especially interesting and thought-provoking, he or she may use it to introduce a unit. For example, a travel video on coral reefs or snorkeling might be an excellent introduction to the study of tropical fish and plants. The same video could be used at the end of the study to see how many fish and plants the students can recognize and name. Computer software that "dissects" frogs or worms may be used after a discussion of what students already know about the animals and how their internal organs compare with those of humans. A video of a Shakespearean play could be intermixed with discussion and class reading of scenes from the play.

Videos, films, and filmstrips may be stopped for discussion. Research reveals that students comprehend better and remember longer if the teacher introduces a video or film appropriately, then stops it frequently to discuss what the students have just seen and heard. This method also helps keep students' attention focused and assists them in learning note-taking skills.

Print Resources

The most common print material is the textbook, which usually is selected by teachers on the campus from a list of books approved by the state. Textbooks are readily available, economical, and written to match state curriculum requirements. However, the adoption process is a long one, and textbooks (particularly science and history) can become out-of-date quickly; therefore, the teacher must use additional resources with recent dates.

Local, state, and national newspapers and magazines should not be overlooked. Some newspapers and magazines have special programs to help teachers use their products in the classroom for reading and writing opportunities as well as for sources of information. Local newspapers may be willing to send specialists to work with students or act as special resource persons.

A limitation of textbooks is their tendency to provide sketchy or minimal treatment of topics, partly because publishers are required to include such a broad range of topics. An ineffective teacher may use the "chapter a week" theory of "covering" a textbook. This method pays no consideration to the importance of information in each chapter or its relevance to the overall district curriculum. Neither does it promote critical thinking on the part of the teacher or the student. Students tend to believe the textbook is something to be endured and not employed as a tool for learning. The effective teacher chooses sections from the textbook that are relevant to his or her learning goals and omits the rest. He or she also supplements the sketchy treatments by using an abundance of other resources.

Visual Materials

The most available visual tools in classrooms are the chalkboard and the overhead projector. There are several principles which apply to both. The teacher must write clearly and in large letters. Overhead transparencies should never be typed on a regular typewriter because the print is too small. Computers allow type sizes of at least 18 points, which is the minimum readable size. Also, both boards and transparencies should be free of clutter. Old information should be removed before new information is added. These tools are more

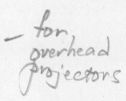 *for overhead projectors*

effective if the teacher plans ahead of time what he or she will write or draw on them. Using different colors will emphasize relationships or differences.

Posters and charts can complement lessons, but the walls should not be so cluttered that students are unable to focus on what is important for the current lesson. Posters and charts can be displayed on a rotating basis. Filmstrips, films, and videos are appealing to students because they are surrounded by visual images on television, computers, and video games. Films and filmstrips have the advantage of being projected on a large screen so all students can see clearly. Videos and computers can be connected to large displays or projected on large screens, but these projection devices are rather expensive. If the available screen is too small for large-group viewing, then the teacher might break the class into groups and have several different projects for them to do on a rotating basis.

Some of the best graphic aids will be those developed by individual students or by groups of students. Along with learning about subject area concepts, students will be learning about design and presentation of information. Students can take pictures of their products to put in a portfolio or scrapbook.

Videodisc and Interactive Video

Videodiscs provide a sturdy, compact system of storage for pictures and sound. They can store more than 50,000 separate frames of still images, up to 50 hours of digitized stereo music, or about 325 minutes of motion pictures with sound. An advantage of videodisc over videotape is that each frame can be accessed separately and quickly. The simplest level of use involves commands to play, pause, forward, or reverse. Individual frames can be accessed by inputting their number.

These programs can become interactive by linking them to a computer. The teacher can then individually access, sequence, and pace the information from the interactive system. An art teacher with a collection of pictures of the world's art treasures can choose which pictures to use and the order in which to show them, then design custom-made lessons which can be used repeatedly or easily revised. He or she might decide to develop a program on landscapes as portrayed in art during a certain period of time. By using the videodisc's reference guide, the teacher determines which pictures to use and the length of time he or she wants each displayed. He or she can develop numerous lessons from one videodisc.

More comprehensive interactive programs can use the computer to present information, access a videodisc to illustrate main points, then ask for responses from the student. A multimedia production run by the computer can include images, text, and sound from a videodisc, CD-ROM, graphics software, word processing software, and a sound effects program. Teachers can develop classroom presentations, but students can also develop learning units as part of a research or inquiry project.

The cost of a multimedia system remains relatively high, but students can use it to develop high-level thought processes, collaborative work and research skills, as well as content knowledge and understanding.

Human Resources

Parents and other members of the community can be excellent local experts from which students can learn about any subject—mathematics from bankers, art and music from artists and musicians, English from journalists, history from club or church historians or librarians, business from owners of companies. The list can be endless. Effective teachers make sure that any guest who is invited to speak or perform understands the purpose of the visit and the goals or objectives the teacher is trying to accomplish. Preparation can make the class period more focused and meaningful.

Field trips are excellent sources of information, especially about careers and current issues such as pollution control. One field trip can yield assignments in mathematics, history, science, and English, and often art, architecture, music, or health. Teachers can collaborate with each other to produce thematic assignments for the field trip or simply to coordinate the students' assignments. Often a history report can serve as an English paper as well. Data can be analyzed in math classes and presented with the aid of computers.

Planning Processes

Madeline Hunter describes a planning model which requires teacher decisions about content, teacher behavior, and student behavior. The three parts of this model overlap and are related to each other; a decision in one category influences a decision in another. **Decisions about content** are often made at the state or district level. Teachers use frameworks from the state, curriculum documents developed by the district, and materials from district-chosen textbooks as bases for planning lessons.

A teacher using this model would make decisions about content, including goals and objectives for a lesson or unit, length of lesson or unit, emphasis of lesson, textbooks, and additional resource materials. **Decisions about his or her own behavior** include teaching strategies, accommodations for various learning styles, types of activities, sizes of groups, uses of technology and other resources, and room arrangements. **Decisions about students' behavior** include individual or group responses, format of responses, ways students will demonstrate learning, and products of activities.

Robert Gagné outlined nine external events which are important in planning an appropriate sequence of instruction. They are:

- gaining attention;

- informing students of the lesson objectives;

- stimulating recall of previous learning;

- presenting stimuli with distinctive features;

- guiding learning;

- eliciting student performance;

- providing informative feedback;

- assessing student performance;

- and enhancing the retention and transfer of learning.

The term "lesson cycle" has been applied to processes of lesson planning developed by a variety of people because the process repeats itself continually. These planning processes usually include the development of objectives and a focus for attention, a design for instructional input, constant monitoring of student understanding, provision for rehearsal and practice of knowledge, and opportunities for enrichment or follow-up.

Teachers choose objectives for a lesson from a curriculum guide, or develop their own from their knowledge of their subject area and the needs of students. These objectives should be clearly communicated to the students in terms of what they will learn (not activities they will do) during the lesson. In a deductive lesson, these objectives are explained to students at the beginning; in an inductive lesson, objectives are clarified at the end of the lesson. Teachers develop a focus or introduction to the lesson (called an anticipatory set by Hunter) which should hook the students' interest and focus attention toward the upcoming activities. Instruction may take a variety of forms. The teacher provides instructional activities which will produce the desired outcomes in the students. A wide variety of instructional methods may be used for input, from mastery lectures or labs to cooperative learning or several different types of inductive strategies. The teacher is constantly monitoring student behavior, checking for understanding, and modifying the instruction as necessary.

After or during instructional input, the students rehearse or apply what they have learned. In guided practice, the teacher watches carefully to make sure students have grasped the material correctly. Because the teacher is on hand to assess student responses, he or she is able to provide correction or additional input if necessary. During independent practice, students work independently. At the end of each lesson (or at the end of the class), the teacher or students summarize or review what has been learned. An additional feature is enrichment, which should be for all students, not only the faster ones. Enrichment means that students either delve deeper into a subject they have been studying, or broaden their understanding of the general topic. For example, students who have been studying the stock market could research the history of its development, or they could study the market in other countries.

Lesson cycles are repeated for additional blocks of content. A lesson may last anywhere from a few minutes to several days; it is not limited by the period or the bell.

Teaching Methods

lecture – a deductive method

Teaching methods can be divided into two categories: deductive and inductive. **Deductive methods** are those in which teachers present material through mastery lecture, or students teach each other through presentations. In deductive lessons, the generalizations or rules are taught from the beginning, then examples and elaboration are developed which support the generalizations or rules. Deductive thinking often requires students to make assessments based on specific criteria which they or others develop.

Inductive methods are those in which teachers encourage students to study, research, and analyze data they collect, then develop generalizations and rules based on their findings. During inductive lessons, a hypothesis or concept is introduced at the beginning, but generalizations are developed later in the lesson and are based on inferences from data.

Deductive Methods

The lecture is a deductive method, whereby information is presented to students by the teacher. New teachers are especially attuned to lecture because that is the usual mode of instruction in college classes. An advantage of lecture is that large amounts of information can be presented in an efficient manner; however, effective teachers avoid dumping loads of information through lectures. Mastery lectures should be short, usually no more than 10 or 15 minutes at a time, and constantly interrupted with questions to and from students. Questions during a lecture tend to be lower-level ones, where the teacher is building a foundation of knowledge for students to use in later activities. The effective teacher, however, uses higher-level questions even during lectures.

Information sessions must also be supplemented with an array of visual materials that will appeal to visual learners as well as auditory ones. Putting words or outlines on the board or a transparency is very helpful; however, this is still basically a verbal strategy. Drawings, diagrams, cartoons, pictures, caricatures, and graphs are visual aids for lectures. Teacher drawings need not be highly artistic, merely memorable. Often a rough or humorous sketch will be more firmly etched in students' minds than elaborate drawings. Using a very simple sketch provides a better means of teaching the critical attributes than a complicated one. The major points stand out in a simple sketch; details can be added once students understand the basic concepts. For example, a very simple sketch of the shapes of the snouts of alligators and crocodiles can fix the difference in students' memory; identification from pictures then becomes easier.

Teachers should also be careful to include instruction on how to take notes while listening to a speaker, a skill that will be useful during every student's career, whether listening to instructions from a supervisor or a speaker at meetings and conferences. One way a teacher can do this is to show students notes or an outline from the mini-lecture he or she is about to present, or to write notes or an outline on the board or overhead while the teacher is presenting the information. This activity requires careful planning by the teacher and will result in a more organized lecture. This type of structure is especially helpful for sequential learners, those who like organization. It will also help learners develop organizational skills. A web, map, or cluster is a more right-brained method of connecting important points in a lecture or a chapter. The effective teacher will use both systems and teach both to students, so they have a choice of strategies.

Inductive Methods

Inquiry or discovery lessons are inductive in nature. Inquiry lessons start with a thought-provoking question for which students are interested in finding an explanation. The question can be followed by brainstorming a list of what the students already know about the topic, then categorizing the information. The categories can then be used as topics for group or individual research. Deductive presentations by students of their research can follow.

Some advantages of inductive lessons are that they generally require higher-level thinking by both teacher and students, and they usually result in higher student motivation, interest, and retention. They are also more interesting to the teacher, who deals with the same concepts year after year. Disadvantages include the need for additional preparation by the teacher, the need for access to a large number of resources, and additional time for students to research the concepts. The teacher spends a great amount of time in planning the lessons, then acts as facilitator during classes.

Generally, the greater the amount of planning and prediction by the teacher, the greater the success of the students. This does not mean that the activity must be tightly structured or set in concrete, but the effective teacher tries to predict student responses and his or her reactions to them. The need for purchasing additional resources has been moderated by computerized bibliographic services, interlibrary loan, and CD-ROMs with all types of information. Because inductive, research-oriented units require more class time, subject-area teachers must work together to determine what concepts are essential for students to understand; other nonessential concepts are omitted.

An English teacher wishing to introduce an inductive study of *Julius Caesar* might ask students what would happen if a group of United States senators and representatives banded together to kill the current president and take control of the government. After brainstorming ideas about causes and effects of the assassination, students could categorize the ideas (political, irrational, economic, etc.), then work in cooperative groups to develop their predictions about each area. Groups could also research the assassinations of Lincoln, McKinley, and Kennedy, then study *Julius Caesar* for comparison of motives and effects. A culminating activity could be to write a scenario of what might happen in an assassination of the current president. English and history teachers who want to team-teach could develop this project together.

A computer science teacher could ask students if they think there will ever be a computer that is smarter than a human being. This would lead to a definition of terms, investigation into human intelligence, artificial intelligence, computer languages, and films such as *2001: A Space Odyssey*, along with demonstrations of computer programs related to artificial intelligence.

Books such as *The Timetables of History* or *The People's Chronology* can be used as a reference for history, English, science, business, and the arts. Students can analyze ten-year periods to discover what was happening in Western Europe and the Americas, then look for connections. Is literature connected to political events? Do art and music reflect current events? What effects do scientific discoveries have on economics? Does the U.S. "Black Friday" of October 28, 1929, have any relationship to the "Black Friday" in Germany in 1927? What predictions does William Beveridge make in his 1942 "Report on Social Security"? A major class project could be to extend a section of the timetables to include African and Asian events. Over a period of several years, this could become a valuable resource for the school.

A science teacher has numerous opportunities for using inductive approaches; in fact, he or she could develop his or her complete curriculum around problems to solve. He or she could ask students to brainstorm a list of everything they can think of that runs by electrical power, then to predict what the world might be like today if electricity had not yet been discovered, or if it had not been discovered until 1950. Would there have been any world wars? Atomic weapons? Movies? Pollution? Their study could include effects on the people in the time it was discovered (including violent reactions), resulting devices which use electricity, ecological issues, possible future uses of electrical power, etc.

Science teachers could also lead a discussion of ethical issues in science during a study of cell biology. What would happen if biochemists discover how to clone people, and a dangerous criminal steals the formula and clones himself or warlike leaders of nations? What effects might this have on law and order, peace and war? Should there be laws to stop scientific experiments of certain types?

Teachers of mathematics could introduce a lesson on place value or number systems by asking students how mathematics might be different if people had eight or twelve fingers instead of ten. Students could then investigate number systems and even invent one of their own.

Art or music teachers could show a selection of paintings or play several recordings and ask students in what decade they were created. Students must explain their reasons for giving a particular date. Research could lead to discussion on what paintings or music of a particular decade had in common, their countries of origin, the influence of religion on art or music, and whether political events influence art and music. They could also be asked to predict what art will look like or how music will sound in the year 2050. Students could do projects based on how someone in the year 2050 might write about current art or music. Content area teachers can team with an art teacher to discuss mathematics in art and music, the influence of historical events on the arts, poems, or plays related to the art or music world, or the science of sound. Art or music students could develop original projects as part of subject-area class assignments.

Business teachers might ask students what kind of business they would like to own if money were no object. Students would need to explain their reasons, then research the business they chose. The class could brainstorm questions for study, then categorize them to determine general areas of research. Students who choose the same business could work together; resource people from the business community could visit the class to explain business concepts, answer questions, and predict what business will be like in 10, 20, or 50 years.

Cooperative Strategies

Cooperative learning lessons may be developed as deductive or inductive. Deductive activities include practice and review of information through games or tournaments and presentations made by the teacher or by students. Inductive activities include research, analysis, and synthesis of information.

Discussion Strategies

Discussions are often thought of as unstructured talk by students sitting around in a circle, answering the basic question, "What do you think about _____?" However, profitable discussions are carefully planned, with specific objectives leading to understanding of specific concepts.

Discussion lessons may be deductive or inductive, depending on the emphasis. Deductive lessons will be more structured, often with clear answers which the teacher expects and leads the students to provide. Inductive lessons will be less structured, but very well planned. Teachers ask open-ended questions and accept a variety of answers which are well supported by information or inferences from the text. The effective teacher plans a variety of questions, with learner outcomes in mind, and leads the discussion without dominating it. He or she also will make certain that all students participate and have an opportunity to contribute. Students may also plan and lead discussions, with careful assistance from the teacher.

An English teacher may plan a discussion of *Our Town*. All students write a variety of questions, e.g., based on levels of Bloom's taxonomy. Half the class discusses among themselves the questions presented by the other half of the class; roles change for the last half of the period or the next class period. The teacher's main role is to facilitate and make sure students follow the guidelines.

An important advantage, which is also a disadvantage, is the amount of time required by genuine discussion. The advantage is that all students have opportunities to contribute to learning and, therefore, feel a greater sense of ownership; the disadvantage is that productive discussion takes a great deal of time.

Teaching Styles

Just as students have learning styles, teachers also have learning styles as well as teaching styles. Since teachers, naturally, prefer their own learning style (a learning style is a set of preferences), they may teach according to their personal way of learning. Many teachers end up teaching the way they were taught when they were students—whether or not their own teachers were using effective methods!

When a teacher becomes aware of his or her own learning and teaching styles, then the teacher has the freedom of choice. The teacher can choose the most effective methods to reach all the students in class. Thus, it is worthwhile for each teacher to learn more about his or her learning and teaching styles.

This section focuses on giving directions so that students can complete instructional activities. Directions are an important part of the information that teachers dispense to their students, and it is important to develop strategies and techniques for giving good directions.

A teacher may give some thought to his or her basic approach to teaching. Is the teacher a sympathetic and friendly teacher, or a realistic, pragmatic, and practical teacher? On the other hand, the teacher may be more logical, intellectual, and knowledge-oriented, or curious and imaginative. Out of a teacher's basic approach to teaching comes the teacher's values. For example, Silver and Hanson describe four categories of teachers: a) nurturers who value interaction and collaboration and tend to stress role-playing, teamwork or team games, group projects, and so forth; b) trainers who value knowledge and skills and stress drills, observations, demonstrations, and time on task; c) intellectuals who value logic and critical thinking and who stress inquiry, concept development, problem-solving, and analysis; and d) facilitators who value creative expression and flexibility and who stress inductive learning, divergent thinking, hypothesis formation, and metaphoric expression. It follows that these different categories of teachers will choose different instructional activities to achieve educational objectives held in common by all teachers.

With regard to giving directions, however, some teachers will choose to be more directive, giving more commands and orders and allowing less room for the student to make choices concerning activities and behaviors, whereas other teachers will choose to be less directive, giving few commands and allowing students to make more choices for themselves. These are differences in teaching style. These differences reflect the different values and priorities of the teachers and should be considered equally valid; no one style, in general, is superior to another. Nonetheless, there are times when most teachers will find that they must be open to adopting the most effective teaching style for accomplishing the objectives at hand. In other words, sometimes teachers adopt a strategy that is not their natural preference in order to be more effective.

To illustrate this point further, consider the tools a carpenter may have in a toolbox. A hammer is not necessarily a better tool than a saw or a screwdriver. However, there are some tasks that may require a hammer and neither a saw nor a screwdriver can do the job or perform the task as well as a hammer. Likewise, teachers have natural preferences or styles, but, if they understand the characteristics of their own style, they can select the tools or approaches that will allow them to be most effective.

This information about teaching styles explains the importance of giving directions effectively and efficiently and meeting the many needs of diverse learners. Even as some teachers may be directive and others less directive or nondirective, so there are some students who demand detailed, step-by-step, precise, and definite directions; that is their learning style. Likewise, there are some students who prefer to make more decisions for themselves, and they need very general directions, preferring to fill in the details for themselves. For example, the teacher may tell the class, "I want you to write a five-paragraph essay about anything you choose." Some students will pick up their pens and begin to write. Other students may ask, "What should we write about?" Those students would benefit by the teacher simply saying, "If I were you, I might write about ..." and providing some suggestions.

Directions

left-brain → analytic, sequential, linear, step-by-step learners
right-brain → global, random, nonlinear

Every teacher knows that some students are more easily motivated than others. Some students receive directions and they busily get to work. Other students resist. Some students ask, "Why are we doing this?" Such a question should not be thought impertinent or obstreperous. Students who ask this question really need to know why. Unless they can see some personal benefit or reasonable justification for the activity, they will resist. Taking the time to explain the nature of the activity and just why it is important and what it will lead to next is well worth the investment when it comes to the dividend of seeing a motivated student perform at his or her best.

Some studies suggest that analytic, left-brain students need step-by-step, sequential directions. They need to begin at the beginning, proceed methodically, step by step through the information, and finally derive the conclusion. On the other hand, global, right-brain learners need to hear the conclusion first; they need to know the goal or outcome before they begin. Instead of progressing step-by-step, global learners work in random, sporadic patterns; analytic types might even call it haphazard. However, the nonlinear approach works for global learners.

An effective teacher will attempt to accommodate the needs of all students in class. This is one reason effective teachers give verbal announcements, send home written reminders, put signs on the wall and in the hall, write messages on the board, and direct students to take notes. The more ways the teacher can find to communicate the information, the more likely the message will get through.

Sometimes the teacher is most effective when starting directions by saying, "This is what we are going to do today in order to …" and then telling what the objective of the learning activity is. This will satisfy the needs of the global learners. Then, the teacher can say, "Now the way we are going to do this is, first, …" and then give the steps, one by one. This way the teacher can address the needs of the sequential learners. Teachers who are aware of preferences in teaching and learning styles can give more successful directions.

Objectives

In addition to giving students general directions and specific instructions about academic tasks and instructional activities, teachers need to announce and explain objectives. Teachers also need to announce all formal tests or assessments, giving students and their parents complete and accurate information.

The more information a teacher can provide about a test, the better the student can prepare for and perform on the test. Teachers need to tell students when they will have to take the test. Just announcing the test topic or the chapters to be covered on the test is insufficient. Teachers need to thoroughly describe the test: How many questions will be on the test, how much time will students have to answer the questions, what kind of questions—multiple-choice, fill-in-the-blank, true or false, matching, or essay? All of these questions should be answered so that conscientious students can adequately prepare for each test. The point value of each question or of each section of the test should be made clear.

To help those students who may be more sensitive or prone to test anxiety, the teacher should also be careful in making speculative or prejudicial comments about tests. The teacher who says, "Oh, this test is really going to be hard," may cause some students to panic and suffer increased anxiety about their test performance.

When teaching a lesson, an effective teacher gives clear, complete, and concise instructions, making certain that students understand why they are doing the lesson (the objectives). When preparing students for a test, an effective teacher provides complete and thorough details concerning the test, making sure that students have had an opportunity to acquire the skills or knowledge the test will measure.

Performance Standards

In addition, effective teachers describe performance standards so that there is no mystery about what a student must do in order to be successful. Performance standards are the criteria against which success is measured. For example, if grades are awarded, what makes a paper an "A" paper versus a "B" paper or a "C" paper? What must a student do in order to score 95 percent on the test versus 75 percent? Students should know what constitutes above-average, average, and below-average performance. Criteria should be discussed and explained. The value of every assignment should be discussed at the time it is assigned. At the beginning of the academic year, teachers should thoroughly explain the grading scale.

Students should also have opportunities to learn about their performance and how their performance compares to the established standards. They should be provided with information to help them improve their performance. Students need to know what it is that they must do in order to demonstrate proficiency. Teachers of younger children need to take special care to communicate objectives, assessment information, and information about performance standards to parents who often are eager to work with their children to help them achieve school success.

Supplies

Informing students about the materials needed for learning and how to use those materials is also an important part of teaching. At the beginning of the school year, teachers and school districts should provide students and their parents with a list of the routine materials that will be needed: pencils, pens, notebook paper, notebooks, crayons, scissors, and so forth.

If the teacher needs to bring special materials to class, he or she will probably find it helpful to include a list of materials needed on the lesson plan. If students need special materials, in addition to their routine school supplies, the teacher should give them a list to take home to give their parents or send a message to the parents.

Students usually have a great deal on their minds, so they need frequent reminders to bring special supplies to class. If students need a dictionary in order to complete the day's lesson, they must know in advance to bring their dictionaries or they will end up wasting a day of precious instruction and time on task.

When a student uses a tool for the first time (the dictionary, for example), the teacher should spend time carefully introducing the tool and explaining its use. With the dictionary, the effective teacher will talk about how the dictionary is organized (alphabetical order), its standard features (pronunciation keys, etymologies, definitions, sentence examples), and special features (appendices with biographies, geographical information, tables, and so forth).

Most experienced teachers have learned firsthand the costs of assumptions. A teacher should not assume that a student knows how to use a calculator, computer, or even a ruler. The teacher, paying attention to details to meet the special needs of all students in the class, should carefully explain how tools or materials will be used.

Classroom Assessment

Teachers spend a great deal of their time explaining and giving directions. To some, that seems to be what teaching is all about. But, despite all the effort that teachers expend and all the expertise they develop in explaining and instructing, some students ignore instructions. Some experts even suggest that some students' learning styles intentionally skip the directions or avoid instructions. For these reasons, teachers must check to make sure that students do understand the directions and are, in fact, following instructions.

"Does everyone understand? Are there any questions?" are probably two of the most misused and unproductive questions that teachers ask. Seldom does the student who does not understand ask a question. There are better ways to check comprehension.

The teacher can give the students a chance to get started on the work and then check each student's progress. Sometimes a teacher may want to call on a student to ask a specific question or to "say back" an important piece of information.

Angelo and Cross, authors of *Classroom Assessment Techniques*, recommend classroom assessment techniques as being most effective at checking comprehension. They further recommend that classroom assessment can a) increase students' active involvement in learning; b) promote students' metacognitive development; c) foster student cooperation and a sense of community in the classroom; d) increase student satisfaction with learning; and e) may even improve students' performance.

A simple classroom assessment technique is to ask students to write a summary of the information or instructions given. The teacher can then quickly read the summaries to determine if there have been misunderstandings or incomplete understanding.

The teacher could give the students a feedback form, asking the students questions about the test they took (Did you think it was a fair test? Did you enjoy one part more than another? What kind of test do you prefer? Why?) or a reading they have completed (How well did you read this? How useful was this reading assignment in helping you understand the topic? How well did you understand the reading?). Asking students to do something (write or talk or draw) to demonstrate that they have understood instructions is a much more effective method of checking comprehension than simply asking what has become to many students (and maybe even some teachers) nothing more than a rhetorical question, "Do you understand?"

Practice to Promote Retention and Learning

It is obvious that in virtually any human activity we learn by practice. Whether we are trying to learn to play tennis or to speak a second language, we quickly realize how much we need to practice in order to make progress in the new skill. And yet, it is sometimes easy for teachers to neglect the importance of practice because they themselves are so familiar with the material they teach. It is so clear and plain to them that they forget what is was like to learn it as new and different. However, it became clear and plain only through long familiarity and practice.

Students need not only to understand a lesson; they need practice in using and applying their new knowledge. A child may "learn" one day that $4 \times 25 = 100$, but may not fully master that knowledge until he or she has several times given or received four quarters for a dollar. He or she may learn that valiant means brave, but the child may not remember the meaning or use the word until he or she has seen or heard it used many times.

The practice a teacher provides must be appropriate— that is, it must promote the objective established by the teacher or the prescribed curriculum. For example, if the objective is for students to be able to locate specific states on a map of the United States, practice in spelling the names of the states is inappropriate for that particular objective. The student must have practice in trying to do the very thing that is expected. To take another example, if the objective is to enable students to carry on simple conversations in Spanish, they must practice listening to and speaking Spanish; practice in reading Spanish would not be appropriate for that objective.

Varying Practice Activities

Numerous studies have shown that variety in teaching methods and styles promotes student achievement and helps maintain attention.

The nature of practice activities, therefore, should be varied. At one time, the teacher may have the students respond in unison; at another time, the teacher may have students work in pairs, where they ask one another questions; still another time, he or she may call on individuals or have all the students do written exercises at their seats.

Perhaps the most common of all practice activities is recitation, whereby the teacher poses questions to the class and calls on individuals to answer. Once a pupil has answered, the teacher responds to the answer and either calls on another pupil in the event that the question has been answered incorrectly, or goes on to another question if the student's answer is correct.

There are, however, many alternatives to recitation that teachers can and should use:

- demonstrations by the teacher of a student,

- oral reports,

- slides,

- movies,

- television,

- radio, and

- recordings.

Small group activities, such as the following, can all help provide practice in newly learned material:

- debates,

- role-playing sessions,

- panel discussions,

- project construction, and

- discussions of test answers.

duration of practice depends

— on difficulty of subject matter

— on ability of learner

The duration of practice should be varied according to the difficulty of the material. Grammatical concepts of subject-verb-object may need considerable repetition and practice exercises, while the concept of size (large/small) may need only brief practice before it is mastered.

The duration of practice should vary also according to the ability of the learner. Some students will catch on right away to the idea of subject-verb-object; others will need considerable practice with it. Teachers need to determine which students are "getting it" quickly and which ones need to spend more time learning the material so that they grasp it fully. This may mean that the teacher gives most of the class a new activity while he or she works individually or in small groups with those who require help and practice.

One of the teacher's weightiest responsibilities is to pay close attention to the progress of individual students, providing more practice for those who have not yet mastered the material and introducing new or related challenges to those who have mastered it.

Reinforce Retention of Specific Information

A geography teacher is trying to help his/her students learn the names and locations of the major regions and countries in Africa. He or she can ask the students individually to come up to the map and point to Egypt or South Africa. The teacher can also ask individuals to name the country or the region to which he/she points. Or, the teacher can have the whole class call out the names of the countries and regions as he/she points to them in turn. If the teacher uses a variety of these methods, he/she is more likely to keep students' attention longer, and hence increase the learning that takes place in that session.

Varying the method is important for another reason—each method has its own benefits. Individual student responses give the spotlight to particular students, increasing their involvement in the class and developing their ability and comfort in speaking in a group. Group response ensures that everyone is involved. Of course, the teacher should watch for the student who is not responding and encourage him or her to participate.

In calling on and responding to individual students in class, teachers must be especially mindful of personal biases to which everyone is susceptible. Do you tend to call on boys more than girls, or vice versa? Do you tend to call only on those who raise their hands? Should you ignore "call-outs"? The last question has no easy answer. If a student who is usually nonparticipatory calls out an answer on one occasion, it may be better to reward that student's willingness to participate by acknowledging the response. On the other hand, if a student frequently calls out without raising his/her hand, it is probably better to ignore the response until the student raises his/her hand and waits to be recognized.

Provide a Variety of Activities to Promote Retention

Repetition is the mother of learning. Unfortunately, it can also be the father of boredom. To prevent practice exercises from becoming monotonous and unproductive, the teacher needs to vary the kinds of repetitive practice.

If, for example, students are to learn 20 new vocabulary words, the teacher may use some or all of the following practice activities:

- fill in the blanks in sentences with the appropriate vocabulary words,

- create your own sentences using the vocabulary words,

- match the vocabulary words to synonyms or antonyms,

- match the vocabulary words to definitions,

- find the vocabulary words in a word-search puzzle,

- complete a crossword puzzle whose answers are the vocabulary words, and

- write a brief story of speech using the vocabulary words.

To practice material that has been explained by the teacher and discussed in class, students can work in pairs or small groups, asking questions of one another. In foreign language classes, for example, students can practice simple conversations in pairs, using newly learned words and phrases.

In mathematics classes, practice need not be limited to homework assignments of number problems and word problems. If, for example, students are learning to add fractions, they might be asked to make up their own word problems using real-life situations, exchanging problems with their classmates, and solving one another's problems. Such an activity not only gives the students practice in adding fractions, it also engages their imaginations since they have to think about situations in their own lives where fractions are used and need to be added.

Assist Students During Seatwork

One common and potentially effective way to give students practice in the material is to assign them seatwork—reading, writing, or some other individual activity done by the student at his or her desk. It is estimated that elementary school students spend 300-400 hours a year doing seatwork in language arts alone. It is obviously important, then, that seatwork be well designed and appropriate to the learning goal and the learner, and that the teacher explain clearly:

- what is to be done,

- how to do it, and

- what the student should learn from doing it.

Unfortunately, many teachers neglect the last two instructions, telling the students only what they are to do.

With seatwork, the teacher's job is to make sure that individual students are

- staying on task,

- understanding what they are doing (not just going through the motions), and

- receiving help when they need it.

The teacher should be especially watchful for low achievers who often do poorly on seatwork assignments, answering questions without really understanding the material. For example, a student may perform arithmetic operations with the numbers in word problems without having any idea what particular operation (addition, subtraction, multiplication, or division) is called for.

The teacher can prevent children from wasting time by carefully overseeing what they are doing in their workbooks or on their activity sheets. Also, since these practice materials often fail to require higher levels of comprehension, such as reasoning and drawing conclusions, the teacher would be well advised to use them sparingly.

For seatwork, some good alternatives to workbooks and worksheets are the following:

- silent reading,

- answering open-ended questions,

- writing an alternate ending to a story, and

- writing an ending for another student's story.

Sometimes it is good to have students work together on seatwork. You may want to have them debate an issue in a story, compare endings that they have written, and so forth.

Practice Activities Promote Long-Term Retention

One way to vary practice exercises is to alternate between massed and distributed activities. A massed activity is a single activity done by the whole class; a distributed activity is one that is divided into a number of parts, each part assigned to a different group or individual.

Let us suppose, for example, that you have been teaching your class about the elements of a story: plot, character, setting, theme, conflict, and so on. You could have the whole class first do a massed activity—all pupils write out in their own words what is meant by plot, character, setting, etc. Once they have done that, you could have them do a distributed activity by dividing the class into as many groups as there are elements of a story. Each group would be assigned a story element and would describe that element in a story they have recently read. Group A would describe the plot of the story, Group B would name and describe the main characters, and so forth.

Once all the groups have completed their work, a spokesperson for each group could read to the whole class the description that group wrote. This last activity would combine massed and distributed activities: the whole class is listening, but each group is reporting on a different story element.

The combination of massed and distributed activities promotes long-term retention through repetition (several activities all about the elements of a story) and variation (individual, small-group, and whole-class activities). The teacher who limits him- or herself to either massed or distributed activities is less likely to achieve the same degree of understanding and retention as the teacher who avails him- or herself of both methods.

Reviewing Material

Sandra Morris has spent several weeks teaching a Native American unit in her seventh-grade social studies class. She begins each class meeting with, "Yesterday we talked about ..." or "What did we discuss yesterday?" Ms. Morris knows that this summary of previous material is an essential step in creating transitions between units or lessons. Students need specific reminders of what had been covered previously in class in order to better understand the present material.

Giving students background to new material is a way to help them add meaning to text and ideas. For example, an instructor who teaches the elements of a short story over a period of time will review and rehearse previously studied stories before introducing a new one. Integrating new material with material previously presented in class helps students make sense of new material and view learning as a series of building blocks, not skills in isolation.

Ms. Morris says to her literature class, "Yesterday we studied the significance of authorial tone and style in Poe's *Tell-Tale Heart*, and today we're looking at characterization. Can you give me an example of how Poe uses tone to describe a character? How would you define tone?" Here the instructor requires students to mesh what they studied previously with the current story element. Each time they receive a new mental image, they have an opportunity to place it into a meaningful context.

It also helps students to review previously learned material in order to remember it better and for a longer period of time. They take notes and learn items, not just to put them away and look at them only at test time, but in order to remind themselves on a daily basis what has been learned before. Without such review, students tend to ignore and certainly forget material until the test, and do not appreciate the importance of careful rehearsal.

Reviews can go beyond oral discussion. Students may write index card summaries of previously learned material, lists of ideas, and outlines of key concepts which can be submitted to the instructor, who determines if material is being recalled and understood. Students can act as surrogate teachers, taking the lead role in conducting a five-minute review at the beginning of each class, quizzing one another on central concepts and major ideas from former lessons.

Taking time to review material teaches students an important lesson about learning—that it is imperative to master old ideas before tackling new ones. Teachers in a rush to cover content, or students in a hurry to process it, lose sight of the need to have deep understanding about each piece of information as it appears in the course. Delving into the previous lesson helps students gain insights into the material at hand. A student can ask him- or herself, "What have we already learned that applies in this case? and "How do old scenarios fit the ones at hand?"

Every discipline lends itself to review of certain procedures and knowledge. Summarizing ideas helps students to practice convergent thinking and synthesis, requiring them to place their learning into a meaningful context. If the class has just studied the causes of the Civil War, the teacher takes time to ask the class to recount those causes before moving to effects. If the class has just learned binary equations, the instructor takes time to practice with the class before moving to other problems.

The individual members of the class must be involved and engaged in the summary of previous material; the instructor should not just spoon-feed the class a recap of the material. Students learn to take responsibility for their own learning as they move from one piece of the educational puzzle to another. Each step reinforces previous knowledge, and the rehearsal, whether oral or written, assists students in recalling facts at test time.

Recapping Significant Points

As essential as reviewing previous lessons, recapping significant points of a discussion before moving to a new concept or problem is equally important. As varying perspectives are given in discussions, students may lose sight of the key points. Asking students to summarize what they have just heard is an excellent way to determine if ideas are being understood. Students may have missed the major concept or tenet, and multiple interpretations become evident in oral sharing.

Here are some questions that can be utilized to recap points in a discussion before moving on, depending on the discipline or subject:

1. Do the author's ideas make sense? Why or why not?

2. If you had to put the main idea into one sentence, what would you say?

3. Where do you note the difference between fact and opinion here?

4. How can you relate this reading or exercise to your own experiences?

5. What information have you gained that will help you perform a new task?

6. What questions does this article raise?

7. Can you find the supporting details for the main argument here?

8. Based on what you know so far, what can you predict about what will happen next?

9. How would you describe the major events of this historical period thus far?

10. What relationships do you find between early information and present information?

11. Can you give examples of the main points discussed here?

12. Who might disagree with the major ideas here, and why?

Asking students to list in writing what they have learned so far, then orally reviewing it is a quick and effective way to determine if ideas are being understood. Students need time to process and integrate information, with instructors emphasizing depth over coverage.

Thesis, Antithesis, and Synthesis

to recap class discussion and material

Thesis, antithesis, and synthesis are effective ways to recap class discussion and material. **Thesis** refers to the central message, claim, or point, which students can be directed to find. **Antithesis** addresses the opposing claims and arguments to the central message. **Synthesis** is a blend of these two ideas, convergent thinking used to find a common ground between thesis and antithesis. How can we bridge the gap between these oppositional viewpoints? Pointing out conflicts and gaps in concepts helps students to reconcile ideas and commit to a perspective of their own.

Recapping Discussion and Reviewing Subject Matter

Recapping discussion and reviewing subject matter helps to reinforce retention of ideas and concepts. Students may not realize the importance of stopping to reflect on what they are learning until the skill is taught to them. The desire to cover content often overshadows the importance of mastering major points one at a time. Each piece of information must be placed in perspective, with the instructor's assistance, and related to the material before and after it.

Instructors who help students to recap major points of a discussion may promote these skills:

1. Use examples and illustrations to support ideas

2. Use oral sharing to gain information, explain ideas or experiences, and seek answers

3. Demonstrate proficiency in constructing meaning from text

4. Relate materials to own background and interests

5. Organize and group related ideas

6. Evaluate the validity of information

7. Recognize persuasive text

8. Sequence information

9. Read for information to use in performing a task

10. Read to confirm predictions about text

11. Identify personal preferences in espousing ideas and opinions

12.   Participate in group discussions about central and opposing ideas

13.   Check for wholeness or clarity of ideas

14.   Describe, analyze, and generalize a wide variety of concepts

15.   Identify patterns in logic and arguments

16.   Make inferences based on available information

17.   Collect, organize, and interpret data in midstream

18.   Analyze the likelihood of events occurring

19.   Apply major points to real-world problems

20.   Make decisions on how to proceed

Recapping and reviewing gives students an opportunity to self-correct, retell, question, and predict, based on the information available.

End of the Lesson Recap

Equally essential to student review of main points during discussions is the end-of-lesson recap, or summary of subject matter. Closure should be brought to each lesson as it concludes, and before another is initiated. Putting a frame on the picture is an important part of learning; recalling key concepts and filling in any gaps of information is vital. Instruments such as self-quizzes may help students to discover how much they have remembered and understand what they have learned.

At the end of the lesson, the teacher or the students can develop ten questions related to the material. If students cannot answer these questions, they know that more study and time are required. Questions can be used as a way to discuss and rehearse the material as well. Misunderstandings and misinterpretations become apparent in classroom oral sharing.

Journal Writing

Journal writing is another way for students to review material at the end of a lesson or unit. What is the most important or meaningful idea learned here? What is the author's central purpose? Journal writing can be shared among class members for responses and read aloud for discussion. This kind of writing helps students to focus on key ideas, while reflecting in prose narrative style on a summary of the lesson.

Cooperative Learning

Cooperative learning can play an integral role in providing review opportunities, with each team member assigned a portion of the material on which to give the group a review. Taking different parts of a chapter or dividing the unit into themes, group members are responsible for listing the key points. The entire cooperative group creates a list for the class, and lists are compared across groups for the one that most effectively covers the material. The class draws conclusions concerning the ideas based on cooperative efforts.

Some other skills that can be built by students through careful end-of-lesson review include these:

1. Develop an understanding of terms and definitions

2. Examine one's own value positions in relation to the material

3. Develop the skills and understandings needed to perform tasks related to the material

4. Suggest changes and improvements in ideas and concepts

5. Defend ideas with specific examples and statistics

6. Explain ways in which the material might relate to a real-world context

7. Summarize the philosophical positions inherent in the material

8. Evaluate ways ideas relate to other disciplines or subjects

9. Explore models and applications of the material

10. Relate concepts and issues to the surrounding cultural, historical, philosophical, and political circumstances

11. Compare and contrast major ideas

12. Communicate effectively about interpretations of issues

13. Predict how variables and events will interact and make projections based on current evidence

14. Research case studies as examples of available information

15. Consider the consequences of studied events and behaviors

16. Examine patterns of thoughts

17. Develop questions based on the material that lead to new understandings

18. Determine the difference between theory and fact

19. Analyze written statements for validity

20. Look for discrepancies and conflicting points of view

Weekly and Monthly Reviews

To ensure retention of material, students should also be engaged in weekly and monthly reviews of subject matter. Like end-of-lesson summaries, weekly reviews must address key points and organize concepts.

For example, if an instructor has taught students about technology terms for a week, before introducing new terms, time should be taken to ensure understanding of the current vocabulary. Similar techniques, such as self-quizzes, graded quizzes given by the instructor, journal writing, cooperative learning activities, and oral review of the material can be used.

A technology instructor might conduct a review by stating, "We have covered several computer terms this week. In the next ten minutes, I want you to write as many of these terms as you recall from memory, with their definition beside each one." Students can then compare their results with class notes and discuss any questions related to material with the instructor and peers. Without such a review, neither instructors nor students would have an opportunity to synthesize knowledge or discover gaps in learning.

Weekly reviews help instructors determine if students are making responsible use of information and knowledge. Can students place isolated facts into a meaningful context? Can they relate them to real-world problems and applications? Are all terms and definitions clear? It is essential that students have clear understandings and mastery, if possible, of current material, before they move on to any new ideas.

Along with weekly reviews of subject matter, effective instructors spend time at the end of each month to look back at what has been learned and accomplished. This monthly review reinforces concepts and gives students assistance in retaining material. Monthly reviews must cover the scope and sequence of all major ideas and give students an overview and sense of completeness. Are there any issues or topics not understood by the class as a whole? Where is understanding weak? The review reveals such gaps in the knowledge base.

Students should take an active role in the monthly summary, bringing all applicable notes and materials. Instructors can ask students to list three or four major themes or concepts they discover in their notes. Emphasis should be placed on unifying concepts: Students should ask themselves which ideas stand at the center of the information, which are central to developing others, and which are missing or unclear?

Another approach to monthly reviews is to require students to write possible test questions that cover the material. Students examine the material in terms of what is fundamental or key. Test questions can be shared with the class, who can attempt to answer them in writing, and then discuss their responses. Writing test questions helps students to sort out and prioritize information, as well as synthesize and analyze ideas. The teacher, the textbook, and experts in the discipline must be brought together at this point to provide an effective overview of material.

Does any of the new knowledge make other information obsolete? Do any new facts replace previous ones? Reviews provide an opportunity for field testing the worthiness of ideas. Extensive understanding of concepts may not occur until the learner places knowledge in an overview, that is, in an overall perspective. Coherence and interrelatedness of ideas become apparent when one focuses on the process of knowing how to arrive at different forms of knowledge.

Overall, in conducting reviews of subject matter, instructors must pay close attention to a summary of the previous lesson at the beginning of the new one; a recap of the significant points of discussion before moving on to a new topic; and a weekly or monthly review of lessons to ensure long-term retention. In going over what has been learned, teachers need to ensure that knowledge is placed into a meaningful context.

Reviews can be oral, written, and even completed by technological means. Students may use e-mail to answer teacher questions about material, to form study groups around organizing questions, and to communicate about the central point of each lesson. It is the educator's responsibility to reinforce that each idea and skill should be mastered before a new one is integrated into the learning experience.

What is the student's responsibility in review of material? A central obligation of the student is to bring all necessary notes, text, and materials to the review session and to keep current on topics and issues introduced in the course. Through the review experience, students can discover gaps and discrepancies in their comprehension and absorption of ideas, themes, and facts.

Oral and written summaries of what has been learned give shape to the course design and help students differentiate the end from the beginning. They visualize the overall course concept and achieve a global view through synthesis and convergence of major themes. The summary brings a wholeness to the material, taking seemingly isolated bits of information and tying them together with a common thread. What are the similarities and differences in these concepts? How does this issue contrast with that one? Review brings a unity and coherence to the scope and range of ideas presented in the class.

Review also reinforces the notion of organization and sequence, placing ideas into a meaningful time frame and order. As each part of a lesson is introduced during the week or month, students do not always see how the parts make up the whole or fit together. In summarizing items from the course, the learner amasses the wealth of facts and opinions learned and makes sense of them, fitting them into a useful pattern.

From class goals to objectives to assessment, each instructor has certain aims for each course. If time is not given to focusing on main concepts before new ones are introduced, students do not have an opportunity to process and inculcate what they have learned. Learning is looking back as well as looking ahead. Students who rush through material or attempt to process it too quickly miss the dual experiences of reflection and introspection. Material must apply to their real-world, ill-defined problems in such a way that it guides them in effective decision-making.

Involving students in effective review of material is fundamental to learning, comprehension, and retention of ideas.

Learning is looking back as well as looking ahead.

References

Further reading of these references may enhance understanding of the competency and may also increase performance on the examination.

Angelo, T. A. and Cross, K. P. *Classroom Assessment Techniques*. San Francisco: Jossey-Bass, 1993.

Dunn, R. "Using Learning Styles Information to Enhance Teaching Effectiveness" Paper presented at the Learning Styles Institute, Lubbock, Texas, June 5-9, 1993.

Lawrence, G. *People Types and Tiger Stripes*. Gainesville, Florida: Center for Applications of Psychological Type, 1993.

Silver, H. F. and Hanson, J. R. *Learning Styles and Strategies*. Princeton, New Jersey: The Thoughtful Educational Press, 1980.

Competency 11: The Role of the Teacher

Definition of Competency

The teacher has knowledge of collaborative strategies for working with various educational professionals, parents, and other appropriate participants in the continuous improvement of educational experiences of students.

- The teacher identifies student behavior indicating possible emotional distress, substance abuse, neglect or abuse, and suicidal tendencies.

- The teacher identifies school and community resources and collaborative procedures to meet the intellectual, personal, and social needs of all students.

- *The teacher identifies the rights, legal responsibilities, and procedures for reporting incidences of abuse or neglect or other signs of distress.*

- *The teacher applies knowledge of the content of, and the procedures for, maintaining permanent student records.*

- *The teacher identifies the role of teachers collaborative teams (e.g., IEP, 504, AIP, and Child Study).*

The Teacher's Role in Classroom Management

One experienced teacher of seventh- and eighth-grade students has suggested the following guidelines for teachers in managing their classes:

- Let students have input whenever you can, and when you cannot, let them think they are giving input;

- Listen to students; they have surprising insights and viewpoints;

- Be consistent with expectations and consequences;

- Do not make exceptions to school rules, even if you do not agree with them;

- Do not correct or reprimand a student in front of a class. Quickly establish that your classroom is a safe place and can be a fun place, but that disrespect for learning, others, or property will not be tolerated and there will be no further warnings;

- Do not begin teaching until everyone is ready to learn;

- Do consult with colleagues and administrators for advice;

- Make sure that students know their rights and their responsibilities.

Blanchard and Johnson, the authors of *The One Minute Manager,* a best-selling book for those wanting to achieve success, describe one-minute goal-setting as: a) deciding on goals; b) identifying what good behaviors are; c) writing out goals; d) reading and re-reading goals; e) reviewing goals every day; and f) determining if behaviors match goals. This list is applicable to the classroom teacher who needs to decide on behavioral goals and identify behaviors both expected and unacceptable.

Another good technique offered by these authors is the "one-minute praise," method by which they encourage catching people (in this case, students) doing something right. Blanchard and Johnson suggest to praise people immediately, telling them what they did right. In applying this principle to students, the teacher would tell students how he or she feels about their behavior and how it has helped others in class and helped the success of the class. The teacher would stop for a moment after the praise to let the student feel good about the praise. Finally, the teacher would encourage the student to continue behaving in this manner, shaking hands with the student.

Likewise, the one-minute reprimand could also be useful. However, the teacher should reprimand the student after class, avoiding interruptions to a lesson whenever possible. Specifically, the teacher should tell the student what was done wrong. After correcting the student, the teacher should stop and let the student think about the situation for a moment. Then, the teacher should shake hands with the student and remind the student that he or she is valued and affirmed as a person, even though his or her behavior was inappropriate. It is important to distinguish between the individual student (who deserves respect) and the individual's actions (which may be disrespectful and/or unacceptable).

As final advice, Blanchard and Johnson admonish, "When it's over, it's over." After correcting the student, the teacher should not harbor a grudge or ill-will toward the student or dwell on the infraction, but move on to the next task at hand. The authors conclude their book by stating, "Goals begin behaviors, [sic] Consequences maintain behaviors."

When teachers discipline students, they would do well to remember that the word *discipline* comes from the Latin word for teaching. The whole point of disciplining a student should be to teach the student what is right and correct, not to embarrass, humiliate, or shame a student.

Teachers should make sure that students understand the rules and that they understand the consequences for breaking the rules. Teachers, like parents, should carefully choose their battles.

They should not make rules that they do not want to enforce. Consequences for breaking rules should be certain and swift. Consequences should be appropriate in scope and severity to the infraction.

Budd Churchward, creator of *The Honor Level System: Discipline by Design,* describes a system of discipline with four stages. Step one is a reminder. He explains that a reminder is not a reprimand. A reminder can be directed at an individual or the entire class. Churchward stresses that many students will learn quickly to respond to reminders, but he points out, "Some teachers may complain that they should not have to remind children over and over. We remind the children because they *are* children."

Step two is a reprimand, approaching a student and issuing a verbal or written reprimand. Verbal warnings are not given across the room, but delivered personally to the student. The teacher comes close to the student and tells him or her what to do; the student is asked to identify the next step (step three). Written warnings, however, are described as being even more effective. The teacher approaches the student and gives the student an infraction slip. The teacher has checked an item on the slip and tells the student that if no further problem occurs, the student can throw the slip away at the end of the class or period. If the misbehavior continues, the slip will be collected and turned in (to the principal's office). Churchward emphasizes that it is important that the child have possession of the slip and know that he or she is in control of the slip and what happens to it next (fostering and encouraging internal locus of control, or a feeling of being in charge, being self-directed, or proactive, as Covey would say).

Step three is collecting the infraction slip. If the student is approached again, he or she is reminded that a warning already has been issued. If the student received a verbal warning, an infraction slip now is sent to the office. If the student has the infraction slip, it is taken up. The student is then asked to identify the next step.

The fourth and final step, is to send the offender to the office, removing the student from class. Churchward advises that if the first three steps are followed faithfully, the last step is rarely required. However, if things do go this far, he insists that the teacher can stay calm and unemotional, perhaps saying something such as, "Tomorrow we will try again. I'm sure that we can work this out."

Churchward recommends that these steps be posted in several places in the classroom, as well as posting three to five selected classroom rules important to teaching. The list should be short and stated in a positive way. For example, instead of writing, "Students will not ask for repeated directions," the teacher should write, "Students will follow directions the first time they are given." By taking time to go over the rules and the steps with students, they will know that they can always look on the wall if the teacher asks them what the next step will be. Churchward says it is important to let students know that they may be asked to identify the next step if they get in trouble; also, students should know that the teacher has the right to skip steps in extreme cases if there are certain behaviors that cannot be tolerated. Teachers should be specific about the behaviors that are not tolerated and give students exact examples of what is meant.

Some other practices, which may encourage good classroom behaviors, are a) monitoring; b) low-key interventions; c) "I" messages; and d) positive teaching. Briefly, monitoring refers to walking around the room to monitor what students are doing. After a teacher gives an assignment, he or she should wait a few minutes to give students time to get started and then should move around the

[handwritten margin notes: Encourage good classroom behaviors, monitoring, low-key interventions, "I" messages, positive teaching]

room, checking to make sure that all students have begun their work. Thus, the teacher can also give individualized instruction as needed. Students who are not working may be motivated to begin as they see the teacher approaching. The teacher should not interrupt the class during monitoring, but should use a quiet voice to show personal attention.

Low-key interventions are quiet and calm. Effective teachers are careful that students are not rewarded for misbehavior by becoming the focus of attention. By being proactive, teachers have anticipated problems before they occur. When teachers correct misbehaving students, the teachers are inconspicuous, making sure not to distract others in the class. When they lecture, effective teachers know to frequently mention students by name to bring the students' attention back to class.

"I" messages are an effective communication technique, whatever the situation; however, they can be used with particular success in the classroom. The message begins with the word "I" and contains a message about feelings. For example, a teacher might say, "I am very frustrated about the way you are ignoring instruction. When you talk while I am talking, I have to stop teaching and that is very frustrating."

Finally, positive discipline refers to the use of language to express what the teacher wants instead of the things that students cannot do. Instead of saying, "No fighting," a teacher can say, "Settle conflicts using your words." Taking a positive approach with language also means using lots of praise. An effective teacher is quick to praise students for their good behavior, using lots of smiles and positive body language, as well as laudatory words.

Effective teachers are careful that students aren't rewarded for misbehavior by becoming the focus of attention

Classroom Behavior

The effective teacher realizes that having an interesting, carefully planned curriculum is one of the best ways to promote desired student behavior and to prevent most discipline problems. Teachers should maintain a system of classroom rules, consequences, and rewards to guide students toward proper classroom behavior with the goal of keeping them engaged and on-task. Inevitably, students will misbehave and test the techniques and procedures that teachers use to guide students back on-task. Some students will not respond to the standard procedures used by the effective teacher. If a student continues to misbehave frequently or in a disturbing manner, the effective teacher observes the student with the intent of determining if any external influences are causing the misbehavior that may require additional intervention from the student's teacher and family.

When under stress, students may be inclined to act out or to behave differently for the duration of the stress-inducing event. Students may react to events in the classroom or in their homes in a manner that violates the established policies of the classroom. For example, nervousness caused by a test or a school play audition may cause a student to speak out of turn or appear skittish. The loss of a loved one may cause a student to become depressed. Such behaviors are normal reactions to stress. However, teachers must pay attention to these situations and observe if the misbehavior occurs for an extended period of time. Unusual and/or aggressive student behavior may indicate that the student is suffering from severe emotional distress. Teachers must be careful to note the frequency, duration, and intensity of the student's misconduct.

Atypical behaviors, such as lying, stealing, and fighting, should be recorded if they transpire frequently. The teacher should attempt to determine the motivation behind the behavior. Is the child lying to avoid a reprimand? Is the student telling false stories to hide feelings of insecurity? Does the student cry during a particular subject, or at random moments during the school day? These are some of the many questions the teacher needs to consider.

Misbehaving may be a sign that a student is losing control of his or her actions and is looking for help. The role of the teacher in these situations is to help determine if the student is acting out as a reaction to a particular issue, or if there is a deeper emotional problem. Some students may require various forms of therapy to treat the emotional disturbances that cause the misbehavior. Therapy can also be used to examine the possibilities of a more severe cause for the student's behavior.

If concerned that a student is suffering from emotional stress, the teacher should contact, and then remain in constant discussion with, the student's parents. It is particularly important in these situations to establish an open dialogue with the student's family to facilitate the student's treatment. When combined, the parents and teacher will be able to provide important and unique insights into the student's situation.

School professionals are another valuable resource for advice, assistance, and support when dealing with students' emotional disturbances. Guidance counselors, school psychiatrists, and other specialists are able to aid in the counseling of these students and make recommendations for the parents and teacher. Together, with the student's family, these professionals may develop or recommend a particular program or therapy for treatment.

When working with a class of students with emotional disorders, the management of the classroom must be flexible to aid in the student's development. While the goal of any management system is to prevent misbehavior, the teacher must be prepared to provide an area or opportunity for the student to regain control, should an emotional episode occur.

Teachers should also be aware that drug therapy is often used as a form of treatment. Prescribed by medical doctors, the drug treatments that are available can help students gain independence from their disorder. However, these drugs treat the symptoms, rather than the cause of the disorder, and can have severe side effects. Drug treatments should not be taken lightly. Their use should also be closely monitored by the classroom teacher and the school nurse.

Behavior Patterns

Established behavior patterns that teachers must be aware of include neurotic disorders, psychotic disorders, and autism.

(1) Neurotic Disorders *a. depression b. anxiety or obsessive thoughts*

Neurotic disorders, or neuroses, are characterized by various emotional and physical signs. Depression can manifest itself in an overall lack of interest in activities, constant crying, or talk of suicide. Anxiety or obsessive thoughts are another indication of a possible neurotic disorder. Physical signs include a disruption in eating or sleeping patterns, headaches, nausea and stomach pain, or diarrhea. These difficulties need to be addressed by the teacher as a cause for serious concern and treatment.

② Psychotic Disorders   — *Schizophrenia*

Psychotic disorders, such as schizophrenia, are serious emotional disorders. These disorders are rare in young children and difficult to diagnose. One of the warning signs for this disorder is a student who experiences a complete break from the reality of his or her surroundings. Schizophrenics may have difficulty expressing themselves, resulting in unusual speech patterns or even muteness. Schizophrenics, who are more likely to be boys than girls, may also exhibit facial expressions that are either markedly absent of emotion or overly active.

③ Early Infantile Autism   *emotional disorder so can be found in all ranges of intelligence*

Infantile autism is a serious emotional disorder that appears in early childhood. It is characterized by withdrawn behavior and delayed or absent language and communication skills.

Symptoms of autism can appear in children between four and eighteen months of age. Autistic children will usually distance themselves from others and may be unable to experience empathy. In addition, they often cannot distinguish or appreciate humor. These symptoms are frequently misdiagnosed as mental retardation, hearing/ auditory impairment, or brain damage.

Autistic children may have a preoccupation with particular objects, or may perform particular activities repeatedly. While autistic children can range in all levels of intelligence, some children can be extremely skilled in particular and focused areas, such as music or math.

Treatment for autistic children may involve therapy, drugs, or residential living. However, only five percent of autistic children become socially well-adjusted adults.

Recognizing Substance Abuse

Dr. Elaine M. Johnson, Director of the Center for Substance Abuse Prevention, recently wrote, "...We must prevent substance abuse if we really hope to reduce crime, violence, school failure, teen pregnancy, unemployment, homelessness, HIV/AIDS, diminished productivity and competitiveness, highway death, and escalating health care costs." The risks to society of substance abuse are encapsulated in this single statement.

Substance abuse prevention focuses on the promotion of healthy, constructive lifestyles for individuals without the use of drugs. Prevention reduces the risk of danger in society and fosters a safer environment. Successful prevention programs have led to reductions in traffic fatalities, violence, HIV/AIDS and other sexually transmitted diseases, rape, teen pregnancy, child abuse, cancer and heart disease, injuries and trauma, and many other problems associated with drug abuse.

The backbone of substance abuse prevention is education. Every professional educator should be aware of the behaviors and characteristics that indicate a tendency toward the use of drugs and/or alcohol and the physical and behavioral signs indicating that students are under the influence of drugs and/or alcohol. Moreover, teachers must be able to make immediate referrals when any student is suspected of using drugs and/or alcohol in order to protect other students and to secure assistance for the abuser. Finally, teachers must be equipped to provide accurate information to students concerning substance abuse.

Behaviors that Indicate a Tendency Toward Substance Abuse

Drug and alcohol problems can affect anyone, regardless of age, sex, race, marital status, place of residence, income level, or lifestyle. However, certain risk factors for substance abuse have been identified. Risk factors are those characteristics that occur statistically more often for those who develop alcohol and drug problems, either as adolescents or as adults, than for those who do not develop substance abuse problems. Recent research studies have identified a number of such factors, including individual, familial, and social/cultural characteristics.

Individual Characteristics

Studies have shown that certain personality characteristics or traits are associated with problems of substance abuse. These personality characteristics include the following: a) aggressiveness; b) aggressiveness combined with shyness; c) decreased social inhibition; d) emotional problems; e) inability to

STUDENTS WHO ARE AT RISK ACADEMICALLY
ARE ALSO SUSCEPTIBLE TO SUBSTANCE ABUSE
PROBLEMS.

Chapter **12**   *FTCE - Review*

express feelings appropriately; f) hypersensitivity; g) inability to cope with stress; h) problems with relationships; i) cognitive problems; j) low self-esteem; k) difficult temperament; and i) overreaction.

Other important personal factors are whether the individual is the child of an alcoholic or abuser of other drugs, whether there is less than two years between the child and older/younger siblings, and whether the child has any birth defects, including possible neurological and neurochemical dysfunctions. The presence of physical disabilities, physical or mental health problems, and learning disabilities can also add to the student's vulnerability to substance abuse. In many ways, students who are at risk academically are also susceptible to substance abuse problems.

factors in adolescents

In adolescence, other factors emerge that are statistically related to problems with substance abuse. These factors are a) school failure and attrition (dropping out); b) delinquency; c) violence; d) early, unprotected sexual activity; e) teen pregnancy/parenthood; f) unemployment or underemployment; g) mental health problems; and h) suicidal tendencies. Teachers should be alert to these factors as they may be symptomatic of a number of negative adolescent behaviors and experiences, including: a) a failure to bond with society through family, school, or community; b) rebellion and nonconformity; c) resistance to authority; d) a strong need for independence; e) cultural alienation; f) feelings of failure and a fragile ego; g) lack of self-confidence and low self-esteem; and h) the inability to form positive, close relationships and/or an increased vulnerability to negative peer pressure.

Family Characteristics

Many family characteristics are also associated with substance abuse among youth. First, and perhaps most important, is the alcohol or other drug dependency of a parent or both parents. This characteristic might be linked with another significant factor—parental abuse and neglect of children. Antisocial and/or mentally ill parents are also factors that put children at risk for drug and/or alcohol abuse. In addition, high levels of family stress (including financial strain), large, overcrowded family conditions, family unemployment or under-employment, and parents with little education or socially isolated parents are also risk factors. Single parents without family or other support, family instability, a high level of marital and family conflict or violence, and parental absenteeism due to separation, divorce, or death can also increase children's vulnerability. Finally, other important factors to consider are the lack of family rituals, inadequate parenting, little child-to-parent interaction, and frequent family moves. These factors describe children without affiliation or a sense of identity with their families or community. All of these family factors can present risks for substance abuse.

[handwritten margin note: describe children w/o affiliation or a sense of identity w/ their families or community]

Social and Cultural Characteristics

Living in an economically depressed area with high unemployment, inadequate housing, a high crime rate, and a prevalence of illegal drug use are social characteristics that can put an individual at risk of substance abuse. Cultural risk factors include minority status involving racial discrimination, differing generational levels of assimilation, low levels of education, and low achievement expectations from society at large.

[handwritten note: VERY IMPT. TO NOTE:]

While these are recognized as risk factors, they are only indicators of the potential for substance abuse. Although these factors can be helpful in identifying children who are at risk or vulnerable to developing substance abuse problems and useful to teachers in helping them develop prevention education strategies, they are not necessarily predictive of an individual's proclivity to drug or alcohol abuse. Some children who are exposed to very adverse conditions grow up to be healthy, productive, and well-functioning adults. Yet, if teachers recognize these risk factors in some of their students, there are certain things that teachers possibly can do to increase the chances that the youngster or adolescent will resist the lures of illegal and dangerous alcohol and drug abuse.

Experts suggest that children have a better chance to grow up as healthy adults if they can learn to do one thing well that is valued by themselves, their friends, or their community. Teachers certainly can help assure that students achieve this goal by teaching them the crucial reading, writing, and math skills that will enable them to become independent learners. By presenting lessons that require the development of effective communication and critical thinking skills, teachers can help students acquire important life skills.

Other important strategies for educators to consider are listed below:

- Require children to be helpful as they grow up;

- Help children learn how to ask for help themselves (develop assertiveness skills);

- Help children elicit positive responses from others in their environment (enable children to develop a sense of community in their classrooms and to work collaboratively and/or in cooperation);

- Assist children in developing a healthy distance from their dysfunctional families so that the family is not their sole frame of reference;

- Encourage children to form bonds with the school and to identify with the school as an important and integral part of the community.

Finally, the teacher can be a caring adult who provides students with consistent caring responses and messages. Researchers have identified this as a crucial element in preventing substance abuse among children exposed to multiple risk factors.

Physical and Behavioral Characteristics of Students Under the Influence of Drugs

Sometimes it can be difficult to tell if someone is using illegal drugs or alcohol. Usually, people who abuse drugs or alcohol (including young people) go to great lengths to keep their behavior a secret. They deny and/or try to hide the problem. However, there are warning signs that can indicate if someone is using drugs or drinking too much alcohol.

Some of the signs that substance abuse is a problem include: a) lying about things; b) avoiding people who are longtime friends or associates; c) giving up activities that once brought pleasure and positive feedback (ranging from failing to turn in homework assignments to giving up extracurricular activities such as sports, drama, band, and so forth); d) getting into legal trouble; e) taking risks (including sexual risks and driving under the influence of alcohol and/or drugs); f) feeling run-down, hopeless, depressed, even suicidal; g) suspension from school for an alcohol- or drug-related incident; and h) missing work or having poor performance.

Teachers should be alert to these signs in their students' behavior at school. When students stop coming to class, stop doing their work (or start performing poorly), avoid making eye contact with the teacher, have slurred speech, smell of alcohol or drugs (such as marijuana), complain of headaches, nausea, or dizziness, fall asleep in class and/or have constant difficulty in staying awake and participating in class activities—a teacher's suspicions should be awakened. These examples, in and of themselves, are insufficient to confirm a substance abuse problem, but in combination and when displayed with consistency over time, they are strong indicators. Teachers should record their observations, keeping written reports of the behavioral changes they witness. Moreover, they should report their suspicions to the appropriate school authorities.

The Use of Referrals

Schools should adopt zero tolerance policies for guns and drugs. For safer schools and a higher quality of education, schools should provide effective anti-drug and substance prevention programs, including programs that teach responsible decision making, mentoring, mediation, and other activities aimed at changing unsafe, harmful, or destructive behaviors.

Teachers should report suspicious behaviors to the appropriate school authorities. Florida State Law requires that school personnel "report to the principal or the principal's designee any suspected unlawful use, possession, or sale by a student of any

controlled substance, any alcoholic beverage, or model glue."
The law further states that:

> School personnel are exempt from civil liability when
> reporting in good faith to the proper school authority
> such suspected unlawful use, possession or sale by
> a student. Only a principal or the principal's designee
> is authorized to contact a parent or legal guardian of
> a student regarding this situation. (Florida State Law,
> Chapter 232.277, Item 1)

Teachers should not delay in taking action, since substance abuse has
the potential for great harm. Authorities can investigate and verify or
allay the teacher's concerns.

In addition to school resources, students with substance
abuse problems can find help in a number of community resources.
These community resources can include community drug hotlines,
community treatment centers and emergency health care clinics, local
health departments, Alcoholics Anonymous, Narcotics Anonymous, Al-
Anon and Alateen, and hospitals.

Teaching about the Dangers of Substance Abuse

Teachers will find a number of helpful resources for
teaching students about the dangers of substance abuse and for

promoting prevention by contacting different agencies or organizations, including those listed below:

American Council for Drug Education

164 West 74th Street

New York, NY 10023

(800) 488-DRUG
http://www.acde.org

The National Center on Addiction and Substance Abuse at Columbia University

633 Third Avenue, 19th Floor

New York, NY 10017-6706

(212) 841-5200
http://www.casacolumbia.org

National Clearinghouse for Alcohol and Drug Information

11420 Rockville Pike

Rockville, MD 20852

(800) 729-6686
http://www.ncadi.samhsa.gov

In addition, the Internet offers a number of sites with useful information. The Substance Abuse and Mental Health Services Administration (http://www.samhsa.gov/index.apsx) and the National Institute on Drug Abuse (http://www.nida.nih.gov/) have excellent web sites with links to updated statistics, reports, and educational materials.

Prevention education promotes healthy and constructive lifestyles that discourage drug abuse and fosters the development of social environments that facilitate and support drug-free lifestyles. Successful prevention means that underage youth, pregnant women, and others at high risk do not use alcohol, tobacco, or other drugs. Education for prevention does work. Research studies show that in 1979, 37 percent of all adolescents aged 12–17 drank alcohol in the past month; by 1992, that number dropped to 16 percent. The incidence of cirrhosis of the liver, a product of alcohol abuse, has dropped significantly, and 14,000 lives have been saved that would have been lost in alcohol-related traffic fatalities, with credit given to minimum drinking age laws. Teachers play an important role in drug and alcohol education and abuse prevention.

Recognizing Abuse and Neglect

During an observation, you see that the teacher is getting nowhere with Belinda, the child who sits in the third row, center, of the classroom. No matter how many times her teacher, Mr. Smith, smiles at her, she flinches. If he waves his hands while illustrating a point, she flinches. If he raises his voice to ask for quiet, she flinches. He's taken the few extra minutes he finds in his teaching day to sit with her independently, but she does not seem to want this. Is it his fault? Is it the child's? Maybe there's another question to ask: Is it the fault of another who may be abusing or neglecting her?

Despite all the media attention given to child abuse and neglect, many teachers still believe that it cannot happen to their students. They may think, "This is a nice neighborhood," or "Most of these students have both a mother and father living at home with them," or "The children are too outspoken to allow that to happen." However, abuse and neglect happen to children all the time, possibly even to some of your students.

abused = overstimulated
neglected = understimulated

Symptoms of Abuse

abused child → chronic shock
↓ result of increased hormones & electrical impulses

Contemporary research has led scientists to believe that modifications of both the chemistry of the brain and a child's neurological structure may be caused during abuse and, worse yet, that these effects are permanent. The child suffers from chronic shock, which is a result of increased hormones and electrical impulses. Each time the child is abused, a modification in the child's brain and its systems occurs. It is the stress accompanying the abuse that causes the child to become hypersensitized to the abuse; this hypersensitizing then causes brain and body modification.

This process may also explain why Belinda involuntarily flinches when her teacher smiles at her—she may believe he is singling her out and, based on her experience, not necessarily in a positive way. When he makes sudden motions with his hands—as is done when striking a person—or raises his voice, which may also be a precursor to rage, Belinda associates these behaviors with patterns of abuse. The effects of child abuse may not be as evident when dealing with an older child (possibly as a result of being told he or she "asked for it" or being threatened with dire consequences if he or she tells), but may be clearer in the child's peer interactions. At times, the teacher may become overly sensitive and may see child abuse/neglect in every bruise and mood change. But, through practice and by discussing suspicions with other teachers, one can become adept at recognizing signs that suggest child abuse.

neglected child wants to be left alone

While the abused child may be angry, "wired," unruly, and/or belligerent (in a word, "overstimulated"), the neglected child acts differently. All he or she may want is to be left alone. Common symptoms of neglect include being unsociable, sedate, withdrawn—all of which point to understimulation. It is thought that this behavior is taught at home during periods of neglect. The child's affect has been changed by the neglect, but the range is wide, varying from almost flat—registering no emotion—to anger. While poor attention, tears, violence, and languid behavior may be indicators of either abuse or neglect, the children usually have feelings of hopelessness and cannot adequately control their thoughts. Students either become obsessed by the neglect or refuse to acknowledge that the neglect is really happening.

Darnell looks like he is not getting enough to eat, yet he eats everything—including the other children's leftovers at lunch—but remains underweight. He is a loner who seems shy and always looks rundown. He seems oblivious to his appearance, but the teacher notices he is often absent due to colds and other minor ailments. What the teacher may not know is that these are symptoms of neglect; it is poor nutrition that causes these illnesses. It is important for the teacher to see that Darnell's immunizations are up-to-date since he is so susceptible to illness. Darnell's sad affect may be another clue to the neglect he has experienced.

Visible Signs of Abuse

There are visible signs of child abuse. Among those are red welts on the body that are caused by being hit. This may be proof that the child is being abused and teachers must report the evidence. It is also one of the ways teachers separate the real abuse cases from those which are unfounded. While marks from the hand, fist, or belt are usually recognized, other marks in geometric shapes—eating utensils, paddles, coat hangers, and extension cords—can signify child abuse. If, for example, a boy in your class has unrecognizable bruises on his arms and legs, they could be the result of whippings; furthermore, if he constantly has bruises on his neck and head and always tells you they are from falling, be prepared to report suspicion of child abuse—this could be the result of hitting, possibly even choking. Teachers need a basis for their reports, so they must notice capillary ruptures.(reddened areas) in any bruise, which indicate a strong hit. If a bruise is shaded on its outer borders, it may still be a result of hitting—just a softer hit. It may help to establish the charge of abuse if the teacher also reports the size and shape of the bruises, since they may indicate what was used to create such bruises. Teachers should be alert to any suspicious marks or signs of abuse and neglect.

Teachers must be aware of children who are prematurely interested in sex acts. Children who are prepubertal and act in a sexual manner have been taught, by example, to act this way. They are possible victims of sexual abuse. For example, young children who have been known to masturbate in the classroom or to attempt to foist sexual behavior on their classmates are simply not sexually developed nor mature enough to understand the consequences of their actions. A sudden show of promiscuity may follow molestation. Kissing, usually seen as a positive interaction between parent and child, if done in a sexual manner, is also abuse, as are leers and sexual stares. Parents are not the only ones to commit sexual abuse of children; grandparents, family friends, and siblings may also be the perpetrators of criminal abuse.

How to Report Suspicions of Abuse

teachers must not interview child, let a professional who's trained, handle it

Teachers may want to comfort the child after he or she admits to being sexually abused. However, they must be careful not to interview the child, but to wait for the professional who is trained to deal with abuse. Otherwise, teachers may inadvertently delay or even damage the possibility of a conviction and potentially cause more harm to the child. As a state-licensed teacher, educators must report suspicion of child abuse/neglect.

Summary

The role of the teacher includes knowing the student's abilities and conferring this to the student. Proper feedback during class, on homework, and on assessments will provide students with the assessment information they need to perform to the best of their ability.

Outside support is a vital asset to any teacher and should be solicited. As Hillary Clinton has said, "It takes a village to raise a child." The community should be involved in the educational process. Parent Teacher Associations, School Improvement Teams, Colleague Networking Teams, and community volunteers can all work together to ensure a safe, nurturing climate where all students can bloom to their full potential.

In addition, the teacher should become a vital part of the community outside the school system. Students who see their teachers actively involved in their communities gain a respect for their teachers and perceive their teachers as a positive role model in their lives.

References

Further reading of these references may enhance understanding of the competency and may also increase performance on the examination.

Breaking New Ground for Youth at Risk: Program Summaries. OSAP Technical Report 1 BK 163, 1990.

Florida State Law, Chapter 232.277.

Johnson, Elaine M. *Making Prevention Work.* Center for Substance Abuse Prevention, Rockville, MD: NCADI, 1998.

National Clearinghouse for Alcohol and Drug Information. *Straight Facts About Drugs and Alcohol,* Rockville, MD: NCADI, 1998.

Competency 12: Technology

Definition of Competency

The teacher has knowledge of strategies for the implementation of technology in the teaching and learning process.

- The teacher identifies appropriate software to prepare materials, deliver instruction, assess student achievement, and manage classroom tasks.

- The teacher identifies appropriate classroom procedures for student use of available technology.

- The teacher identifies appropriate policies and procedures for the safe and ethical use of the Internet, networks, and other electronic media.

- The teacher identifies strategies for instructing students in the use of search techniques, the evaluation of data collected, and the preparation of presentations.

Educational Technology in the Primary Classroom

Technology is an important part of the world and, therefore, must be an important part of the educational environment. Students should be exposed as early as possible to computer literacy so that they will be prepared for a technologically advanced society. Appropriate software can be used to meet content standards and curriculum goals. Teachers must be able to integrate their existing curriculum to meet these standards. Students must be versed in computer curriculum to prepare them for their future.

Classroom Management and Technology

There are a variety of classroom settings that can be utilized with regard to computers. Some schools may have only one computer per classroom, while others may have a computer lab. The majority of teachers and students have access to at least one computer in the class.

The teacher should take the time to learn how to use appropriate educational media, computer applications, and the wide range of instructional technology that is available for today's classroom. Evaluating and selecting the appropriate technology, whether it be a computer, calculator, or additional device, can actually enhance the instructional experience and promote better management of student data. Teachers should work collaboratively with instructional specialists to familiarize themselves with the variety of technical resources available that help improve instructional design and improve student learning. To assist in this endeavor, school districts should provide ample opportunity for professional development. Instructional programs should include courses that help familiarize the student with the variety of technical aspects necessary in today's culture.

PROF'L. DEVT. of TEACHERS

The teacher must use a variety of innovative methods to ensure that the students to have quality computer time whenever possible. The computer can be used as an audiovisual tool. New lessons can be presented by the teacher to the students using the computer as an electronic blackboard. It can also be used as a technology center, where students can research subjects, take tutorial lessons, and learn word-processing skills. The students, as well, can use the computer for visual and oral presentations when multimedia projects are presented to the class.

Because of limited computer time, most work has to be completed before arriving at the computer. The school version of most software includes excellent ideas for setting up a station and gives seatwork activities for that specific program. Students can print out the graphics and keep them in a folder to be used while working at their desk. They can prepare their entire project before working at the computer.

BANK OF COMPUTERS - 3 or more

If a teacher is working with a bank of computers (three or more), assigning small groups is the best method of classroom management. Many primary classrooms already use centers and small group activities as part of the classroom management system. The computer center can be used as one of these learning centers. Themes can be used for the students to research science topics, for example. Reference books, multimedia encyclopedias, and posters can be placed in the center. The students can then exhibit their work on a bulletin board that is part of the computer center. Name checklists can be used so the students are aware of their turn to work at the computer. While a group of students is at the computer, the other students are also at work at other workstations in the class. Students can then rotate with the rest of the class after a certain time allotment.

In some schools, a media center is used so that there is a place for teachers, as well as students, to access computers. In most cases teachers bring their classes into the center at a scheduled time every week. Some administrators prefer this type of arrangement because every student is assured of computer time and it is less costly than supplying computers in every classroom. Each child is given a disk to save his or her work. The disk is then placed in a specific classroom file so that the child has easy access to his or her disk each time he or she enters the center. Usually a computer technician or computer teacher, an assistant, and the classroom teacher are in the center. When the child needs assistance, one suggestion is for the student to place a red cube on top of the computer. The teacher can then scan the room for those children requiring aid. Children can use a green cube to indicate that they have completed their project and are now ready to explore selected computer programs on their own.

Integrating Computers in Instruction

In any classroom environment, one of the major teaching problems is student motivation. Students have a natural motivation to use computers. The more they are exposed to computers, the more they want to learn. A teacher must also exhibit a sense of excitement toward computers. Computers in the classroom offer opportunity for a direct integration with the curriculum.

Planning for a computer-based lesson is similar to planning for a traditional lesson. The traditional format generally includes: topic, materials, goals and objectives, procedures, and assessment. Once a topic and objective are chosen, then it is necessary to find the materials and resources available to help meet these objectives. Technology is not always the best resource. Sometimes the traditional book, pencil, and paper is the best mode. Many times a marriage of the two (tradition and technology) is needed.

Educational Technology in the Secondary Classroom

Computer Software Tools

There are several software tools which are extremely useful for teachers and students. Word processing allows teachers and students to write, edit, and polish assignments and reports. Most programs have a spelling-checker or even a grammar-checker to enhance written products. Students can use word processors to write term papers or reports of their research for all subject areas. Many word processors allow writers to put the text into columns so that students can produce newsletters with headlines of varying sizes. For example, an English class could write a series of reviews of Shakespeare's plays or sonnets, add information about Shakespeare and his times, then collect everything into a newsletter as a class project. There are also desktop publishing programs which allow text and graphics to be integrated to produce publications, such as a class newsletter and school newspapers and yearbooks.

Databases are like electronic file cards; they allow students to input data, then retrieve it in various ways and arrangements. History students can input data about various countries, e.g., population, population growth rate, infant mortality rate, average income, and average education levels. They then manipulate the database to call out information in a variety of ways. The most important step in learning about databases is dealing with huge quantities of information. Students need to learn how to analyze and interpret the data they see in order to discover connections between isolated facts and figures and how to eliminate inappropriate information.

On-line databases are essential tools for research. Students can access databases related to English, history, science— any number of subject areas. Most programs allow electronic mail (e-mail) so that students can communicate over the computer with people from around the world. There are also massive bibliographic databases which help students and teachers to find the resources they need. Many of the print materials can then be borrowed through interlibrary loan. The use of electronic systems can geometrically increase the materials available to students.

Spreadsheets are similar to teacher grade books. Rows and columns of numbers can be linked to produce totals and averages. Formulas can connect information in one cell (the intersection of a row and column) to another cell. Teachers often keep grade books on a spreadsheet because of the ease in updating information. Once formulas are in place, teachers can enter grades and have completely up-to-date averages for all students. Students can use spreadsheets to collect and analyze numerical data which can be sorted in various orders. Some spreadsheet programs also include a chart function so that teachers can display class averages on a bar chart to provide a visual comparison of the classes' performance. Students can enter population figures from various countries, then draw various types of graphs, bars, columns, scatters, histograms, and pies to convey information. This type of graphic information can also be used in multimedia presentations. There are also various stand-alone graph and chart software packages.

Graphics or paint programs allow users to draw freehand to produce any type of picture or use tools to produce boxes, circles, or other shapes. These programs can illustrate classroom presentations or individual research projects. Many word processing programs have some graphic elements.

Computer-Assisted Instruction

drill & practice
① interesting but generally low-level in nature

Many early uses of computers tended to be drill-and-practice, where students practiced simple skills such as mathematics operations. Many elaborate systems of practice and testing were developed with management systems so that teachers could keep track of how well the students were progressing. This type of software is useful for skills that students need to practice. An advantage is immediate feedback so students know if they chose the correct answer. Many of these programs have a game format to make the practice more interesting. A disadvantage is their generally low-level nature.

2) tutorials = include explanation + info.

Tutorials are a step above drill-and-practice programs because they also include explanations and information. A student is asked to make a response, then the program branches to the most appropriate section based on the student's answer. Tutorials are often used for remedial work, but are also useful for instruction in English as a second language. Improved graphics and sound allow nonspeakers of English to listen to correct pronunciation while viewing pictures of words. Tutorials are used to supplement, not supplant, teacher instruction.

3) simulations or problem-solving programs

Simulations or problem-solving programs provide opportunities for students to have experiences which would take too long to experience in real-time, would be too costly or difficult to experience, or would be impossible to experience. For example, one of the most popular early simulations allowed students to see if they could survive the Oregon Trail. Users made several choices about food, ammunition, and supplies, then the computer moved them along the trail until they reached their goal or died along the way. There are several simulations which allow students to "dissect" animals. This saves time and materials, is less messy, and allows students who might be reluctant to dissect real animals to learn about them. Other software might explore the effects of weightlessness on plant growth, a situation which would be impossible to set up in the classroom lab. There are several social studies simulations which allow students to do things like invent a country, then see the effects of their political and economic decisions on the country.

Selection and Evaluation Criteria

The effective teacher uses criteria to evaluate audiovisual, multimedia, and computer resources. The first thing to look for is congruence with lesson goals. If the software does not reinforce student outcomes, then it should not be used, no matter how flashy or

1. congruence w/ lesson goals
2. students' strengths & needs, learning styles, interests

well-done it is. A checklist for instructional computer software could include appropriate sequence of instruction, meaningful student interaction with the software, learner control of screens and pacing, and motivation. Other factors should be considered, such as the ability to control sound and save progress, effective use of color, clarity of text and graphics on the screen, and potential as an individual or group assignment.

Students' needs determined through formal or informal assessment

In addition to congruence with curriculum goals, the teacher needs to consider his/her students' strengths and needs, their learning styles or preferred modalities, and their interests. Students' needs can be determined through formal or informal assessment. Most standardized tests include an indication of which objectives the student did not master. Mastering these objectives can be assisted with computer or multimedia aids.

Learning styles may be assessed with a variety of instruments and models, including those developed by Rita Dunn and Anthony Gregorc. Students with highly visual learning modes will benefit from audiovisuals. Student interests may be revealed by a questionnaire, either purchased or developed by the district or teacher. A knowledge of student interests will help the teacher provide resources to suit individual needs. The effective teacher can design activity choices which relate to class goals but also to student interests.

Evaluation of resources should be accomplished in advance by the teacher, before purchase whenever possible. Evaluation is also conducted during student use of materials. Assessment after student use may be by considering achievement level of the students and/or by surveys which ask for students' responses.

Copyright Laws for Computer Programs

Computer technology is becoming a larger focus of the classroom. In addition to being part of the curriculum, computers are frequently used by educators as aids in storing information and developing lesson materials.

Computer software programs fall under the domain of copyright law. Computer programs, such as a word processing program or a graphic design program, are defined as "a set of statements or instructions to be used directly in a computer in order to bring about a certain result" (P.L. 96-517, Section 117).

Backups, or copies of a computer program, are frequently created in case the original disk containing the computer program becomes damaged. Such copies are not considered infringements of the copyright law as long as the following is true:

a. The new copy or adaptation must be created in order to be able to use the program in conjunction with the machine and is used in no other manner.

b. The new copy or adaptation must be for archival purpose only and all archival copies must be destroyed in the event that continued possession of the computer program should cease to be rightful.

c.   Any copies prepared or adapted may not be leased, sold, or otherwise transferred without the authorization of the copyright owner.

Copies of a computer program cannot be shared or borrowed. The same original disk should not be used to install a program on more than one machine unless the owner has a license to do so from the computer software company. If unsure about the licensing status of a computer program, the teacher can check with the media specialist or school administrator.

Teachers are role models for their community; it is important that all educators be aware of these laws and be in complete compliance.

References

Further reading of these references may enhance understanding of the competency and may also increase performance on the examination.

Armstrong, Sara. *Edutopia: Success Stories for Learning in the Digital Age.* Hoboken, NJ: Jossey-Bass, 2002.

Collier, Catherine, and Lebaron, John F. *Technology in Its Place: Successful Technology Infusion in Schools.* Hoboken, NJ: Jossey-Bass, 2001.

Kallick, Bena, and Wilson, James M. *Information Technology in Schools: Creating Practical Knowledge to Improve Student Performance.* Hoboken, NJ: Jossey-Bass, 2000.

Papert, Seymour. *The Children's Machine: Rethinking School in the Age of the Computer.* New York: Basic Books, 1994.

Competency 13: Foundations of Education

Definition of Competency

The teacher has knowledge of the history of education and its philosophical and sociological foundations.

- The teacher applies historical, philosophical, and sociological perspectives to contemporary issues in American education.

- The teacher distinguishes between different societal norms and values their effects on educational policy and classroom practice.

• *The teacher identifies contemporary philosophical views on education that influence teaching.*

It has been said that those who are ignorant of history are doomed to repeat it. Therefore, unless we, as professional educators, wish to replicate errors of the past, we need to become conversant with the history of education so that we can apply its lessons to the present and to the future.

Similarly, it is important that we study and understand the philosophical and sociological foundations of education so that we can apply them to contemporary issues facing American education today.

This chapter focuses on a review of the history of American education as well as on an overview of the philosophical and sociological foundations of education. Knowledge of these three segments of the basic roots of education in our society enables teachers to incorporate the wisdom gained from educational history into their own teaching, formulate and act upon a personal philosophy of education, and inculcate sociological understandings into the effective and efficient management of their classrooms.

A Brief History of the Foundations of American Education

Some of the components of American education have roots that extend as far back as early Greek and Roman times.

Socrates (469-399 B.C.), Plato (427-347 B.C.), and Aristotle (384-322 B.C.) were the Greeks whose contributions have had the greatest impact on Western thought. The methods they employed are still popular today.

Socrates developed what we now know as the **Socratic Method** based on the use of questioning to reveal universal truths. Teachers were employed to ask questions that would allow students to find the truth within themselves. Today, scholars and critics of education, such as Mortimer Adler, consider the Socratic Method a cornerstone of a truly educated populace.

Plato was an advocate of universal education so that humankind could use its intellect to reveal the universal concepts of truth, goodness, justice, and beauty. In Plato's "Myth of the Cave", light represents knowledge and truth and education the means by which man is able to discard a shadowy existence by leaving the cave and experiencing salvation from ignorance. Plato pondered the question, "What is the good life?" Moreover, he concluded that education is a necessity of a good society.

Aristotle, through his scientific writings, has influenced education for hundreds of years. He spent twenty years in Plato's Academy in Athens, and Plato had a great influence upon him. However, he did reject Plato's notion of idealism. Aristotle was a realist who believed, unlike Plato, that human thought is entirely dependent upon information received through our senses. He agreed with Plato that education should be controlled by the state and that it represented preparation for "the good life".

In addition to the contributions of Plato, Socrates, and Aristotle, the Greeks also developed the concepts of the liberal arts and vocational education. The liberal arts were necessary preparation for aristocratic men so that they would be equipped to govern. On the contrary, peasants needed to learn various occupations and trades that were taught through practical tasks and manual labor.

Some of Rome's contributions to American education are bilingual education and private education. From the second century B.C. to the fall of the empire, Roman education consisted of three bilingual levels. The primary school that was the first level or *ludus*, taught young boys, and a few girls, from aristocratic families, the alphabet, reading, writing, and counting. This schooling was low in cost and concurrently, low in status. For this reason, many aristocratic families chose to have their young sons tutored at home rather than send them to the *ludus*. This practice began a marked distinction between public (group) and private (individual) instruction, which continued in the United States until the middle of the nineteenth century.

The second level or *grammaticus* was usually in the home of the teacher. Boys from the ages of twelve to sixteen learned Latin grammar and read Roman poets and dramatists. They were also required to learn Greek by reading the Greek classics. The *grammaticus* was more costly than the *ludus*, and therefore afforded higher status. However, because of its higher cost, fewer families were able to send their sons to this second level.

At the age of sixteen, the sons of the most aristocratic families served a yearlong apprenticeship in the *tirocinium fori*. This third level consisted of tutelage by a "distinguished man" (sometimes the boy's own father) in the duties, manners, and attitudes of senators.

Toward the end of the Roman Empire, the system of formal education had lost much of its vitality. Christians, such as St. Augustine, advocated more emphasis on deeds than on words. He promoted the study of great orations rather than of rhetoric and grammar. He maintained that nothing could be learned under compulsion and that scholars should learn by questioning to aid comprehension rather than just accept the answers provided by intellectuals. Preservation of the culture was a main emphasis of the final years of the empire. Therefore, memorization and imitation were the primary methods of instruction during this time.

During the Middle Ages, Saint Thomas Aquinas (1225-1274) a Christian philosopher, espoused scholasticism, defined as logical reasoning through the examination of opinions and issues by raising questions to decide their validity. Therefore, Aquinas is credited with applying Aristotelian logic to Christian theology, thus justifying both faith and reason. Prior to Aquinas, the two were thought to be incompatible. Aquinas held that anything that is incomprehensible intellectually must be accepted on faith.

It was during the Renaissance (1330-1500) that the teaching methods advocated by early scholars came under review. The Dutch philosopher Desiderius Erasmus (1466-1536) was the first humanistic scholar. He supported a return to the classical studies of Greece and Rome. He made a clear distinction between innate abilities and learning and recognized that children are not born with equal abilities in all areas of study. Therefore, he suggested that it was necessary to develop individual methods of instruction.

Martin Luther (1483-1546), credited with the establishment of universal education regardless of class, was a religious reformer. Luther believed that the state and not the church should found schools. He advocated expanding the curriculum beyond religion and suggested the inclusion of science, mathematics, logic, and rhetoric.

John Calvin (1509-1564), a Protestant reformer, suggested that education was a joint responsibility shared by the church, the state, and the home.

John Amos Comenius (1592-1670), is thought of as the first modern educator because he developed teaching methods requiring the use of the senses to assist the intellect. He authored the first children's book, *Orbis Pictus (The Visible World in Pictures),* where he used pictures as an instructional tool. He also advocated universal education, including the education of women.

In France, Jean Jacques Rousseau (1712-1778) developed his educational philosophy, naturalism. He favored a return to nature and emphasized the role of the environment in developing the individual. He proposed that knowledge is based on the senses, natural feelings, and perceptions rather than on books and a prescribed curriculum.

Rousseau influenced Pestalozzi (1746-1827). He favored the use of real, concrete objects to teach young children before advancing to concepts that are more abstract. Pestalozzi advised that teachers should work from the simple to the complex, and the known to the unknown in sequential steps adjusted to the individual differences in children. He departed from the belief that children were born in sin and believed instead that their environment shaped them. Therefore, he advocated a loving, understanding, and patient school setting, with compassion for the poor and disadvantaged, and teaching methods that used real objects and appealed to the senses.

According to Pestalozzi, the teacher was one of the most important people in a community and, therefore, must be someone with integrity, understanding, and intelligence. He believed that the state was responsible for the education of teachers and that this would

[handwritten margin note: John Amos Comenius - 1st modern educator & developed teaching methods requiring use of the senses to assist the intellect]

Peztalozzi
founded 1st schools for teacher training in Prussia

underscore the importance of the profession. Pestalozzi established the first schools exclusively for the training of teachers in Prussia.

Johann Friedrich Herbart (1776-1841) visited Pestalozzi in Switzerland. He believed that education was a process. He affirmed that teaching was a science that could be learned rather than an inborn gift that only some possessed.

Herbart founded a pedagogical seminary and demonstration school where he experimented with educational methods. He proposed that there are five steps in the teaching process: preparation, where the teacher reviews previously learned materials; presentation, in which new material is taught; association, where the new material is systematically related to what was previously learned; generalization, in which specific examples are used to illustrate the concept being taught; and application, during which students are tested on their understanding of the material.

Froebel - *founder of the modern Kindergarten*

Friedrich Wilhelm Froebel (1782-1852) was a German philosopher and educator, and the founder of the modern kindergarten. Froebel emphasized the importance of children's play, not as preparation for adult life, but as an important and necessary stage of life itself. He used songs, stories, games, "gifts", and "occupations" to foster self-development, self-activity, and socialization in children. "Gifts" were solid objects such as bells, cubes, and cylinders that he used to show children relationships. "Occupations" were manipulatives such as clay, paper, or mud.

These philosophers, theologians, and educators had a powerful influence on colonial education. Today, they still exert an observable influence on American education.

In the schools of colonial America, modeled after the schools in Great Britain, there was no attempt to make education equally accessible to all. Reading instruction was provided to peasant children so that they could read the Bible, but they were not exposed to the classics. Upper class boys were educated so that they could pass the entrance exams for Harvard College, and other colleges and universities. The English colonists held the belief that women belonged at home, so girls were trained at home to become mothers and homemakers.

Massachusetts enacted the first compulsory education law (1642). The law did not establish schools, but required that parents make certain that their children could read and understand the laws and the religion of their community. In 1647, the Massachusetts General Court passed the Old Deluder Satan Law. The law required that schools be set up so that children could be taught religion and church values. Through this religious education, they would be protected from that "old deluder, Satan".

The colonial schools were subject centered and taught the alphabet, the Lord's Prayer, reading, writing, and counting. Boys from non-aristocratic families were often apprenticed in a trade of their choice by the middle to end of elementary school.

Most elementary schools lacked textbooks and they employed untrained teachers. Lecture and recitation were the primary methods of instruction. There were no official requirements for becoming a teacher.

4 Types of School in New England

There were four basic types of schools in the New England colonies. The first, the Latin Grammar School, was a secondary school for young men. It was a college preparatory school. The second, the Dame School, was located in a private home where several children gathered and the woman or dame of the house was the teacher. The third, the Town School, was established to afford elementary education to all of the children of New England. The fourth, District Schools, enrolled children from a larger area than the Town School, and enrolled children living on farms and in villages away from the central town. Each district employed its own schoolmaster and determined its own school year. Untrained teachers provided only basic education in the alphabet, reading, writing, and religion.

In the Southern colonies, private tutors most often educated the sons of the wealthy plantation owners. As was the case in New England, the girls were taught how to manage a household, but were not literate.

Beginning in 1619, African slaves were imported to work the plantations. It was believed that they would be less submissive if educated, so most were never taught to read or write. To preserve this illiteracy, the Southern states made teaching a slave to read or write a criminal act.

Schools in the Middle Atlantic colonies differed from those of the New England and Southern colonies. Most notably, the population of the Middle Atlantic colonies was heterogeneous in terms of religion, ethnicity, and language. The desire of these colonists to retain their cultural heritage made the establishment of a single school system impossible. Home tutoring was not practical because of the population density in this part of the country. As a result, several distinctly different types of schools flourished in this area.

TYPES OF SCHOOLS IN MIDDLE ATLANTIC AREA

Between 1720 and 1740, Pennsylvania established parochial schools. These schools received support from religious organizations. Private schools, receiving no public funding, began in Virginia during this same period.

There was a need for skilled workers for the commercial endeavors of the Middle Atlantic colonies. To satisfy this need, businesses and trades developed private venture training schools, thereby becoming the first vocational schools.

Those who followed Quaker beliefs abandoned corporal punishment and established their own schools. These schools were open to all including African children. There was a fee charged to attend these schools, but the children of the poor attended free.

During the period following the American Revolution (1776-1830), the nation's leaders sought ways of uniting the varied factions of colonists into one strong democracy. They thought the schools were the vehicle best suited to this purpose.

There were few changes in the curriculum of the elementary schools during the post revolutionary period, but new textbooks, namely *Ray's Arithmetic* (1834) and *McGuffey's Reader* (1836) made the teaching of math and reading an easier task. These texts were valued not only for their subject matter content, but because they combined subject with lessons in virtue, hard work, and resolve.

The secondary schools of the period substituted practical classes for the classics and focused on the solution of everyday problems.

The political leaders of the time, Benjamin Franklin, Thomas Jefferson, and Noah Webster advocated education that would promote republicanism. This belief, founded on the work of John Locke (1632-1704), was based on the principle that government arises from the consent of the governed. Education was seen as the mechanism that could impart the knowledge, skills, and values needed for a democratic government.

Benjamin Franklin, who was an esteemed political leader, philosopher, and scientist, developed the structure of the modern high school. He felt that focusing on Latin and Greek was impractical for a democratic populace. Instead, he proposed the study of English, oratory, commerce and politics, applied mathematics, history, foreign languages, and vocational training.

Thomas Jefferson (1743-1826) advocated equal educational opportunity. He proposed three years of free elementary education for all white children in Virginia. In addition, Virginia provided gifted males, who could not afford secondary school, a scholarship for an additional three years.

Noah Webster (1758-1843) focused on developing an American language to aid in creating a national identity. He wrote *American Spelling* (1783) in which he created a system of phonics used to differentiate American from British English. Later editions of this text, known as the *Blue-Backed Speller*, and his *American Dictionary of the English Language* (1828) replaced the *New England Primer* in American schools. His system of phonics is still in use today to teach reading.

The period in American history known as **the Age of the Common Man** (1812 to 1865), saw changes in politics, society, and economics. The presidency of Andrew Jackson (1829-1937) elected by the common man, brought about a system of state education offices, an increase in the number of women entering schools, and most of what we know as the public school system of today. Compulsory education laws were passed, high schools were opened, and normal schools were begun for the specific purpose of educating teachers.

In 1852, Massachusetts was the first state to pass a compulsory education law. It required that all children between the ages of eight and fourteen attend school at least twelve weeks per year.

Throughout the remainder of the nineteenth century and into the early twentieth century, other states passed and strengthened such laws by extending the age limits and increasing the school year.

In 1866, Massachusetts passed the Child Labor Law, which required that no child under ten be employed and that no child under fourteen be employed unless he had attended an approved public or private school for at least six months in the year prior to his employment. This law helped to promote the movement toward public schools.

In the early nineteenth century, there was a need for educated workers to operate increasingly complex machinery in industry. Educators and businessmen united publicly to support education for all children.

In the early 1800s, Robert Owen (1771-1858) developed infant schools in Scotland, housing children from two to six whose mothers worked in factories. This concept spread to America and formed the basis of the modern day care.

In 1805 in New York City, the first monitorial school in the United States was established. Such schools were based on the work of Joseph Lancaster (1778-1838) who believed that master teachers could train advanced students to teach beginning students. This method, according to Lancaster, was effective, efficient, and inexpensive. The introduction of ability grouping made teaching easier.

During the nineteenth century, the value of the classical grammar school came into question. The needs of the children of immigrants and of an industrial economy were not being served. The academy replaced the Latin grammar school, closely following the model suggested by Benjamin Franklin. Most academies were private so they did not reach the large numbers of immigrant workers.

[handwritten: high school replaces academies - urbanization industrialization]

High schools began to replace academies during the 1870s due to increases in urbanization and industrialization. Despite the need to train workers whose formal education would end with high school, the majority of the high school curriculum was for the limited number preparing for college.

[handwritten: Mann - Mass. State Board]

Horace Mann (1796-1859) became secretary of the Massachusetts State Board of Education in 1837. During the twelve years that he held this office, he advocated for better school buildings, responsible local school boards and the need for greater intellectual development. He proposed free circulating libraries in every school district, the future employment of women at wages equal to those of men, and the need to develop teacher-training institutions.

[handwritten: Barnard - Conn. State Board] *[handwritten: - increased teacher salary + improved teacher educ.]*

Henry Barnard (1811-1900) was secretary of the Connecticut Board of Education, commissioner of public schools in Rhode Island, the first U.S. Commissioner of Education, and chancellor of the University of Wisconsin. He established the *Connecticut Common School Journal* (1839) and the *American Journal of Education* (1848). He used these journals to spread his educational theories to teachers and to the public. Among his many ideals regarding education, were the overwhelming importance of the English language, improved teacher education, and increased teacher salaries. His work prompted the establishment of the first federal office of education in 1867, which has now evolved into the Department of Education.

[handwritten: First Federal Office of Educ.]

The progressive movement began in the 1890s, with reformers such as Jane Addams (1860-1935) and John Dewey (1859-1952). These educators believed that education could solve societal problems and could help the poor to succeed despite their low station

[handwritten: Jane Addams, John Dewey]

in life. Children, viewed like products of a factory, were raw material to be processed. Those who could not be processed would be dropped out of the production line, thus the origin of the term "drop out".

Addams founded Hull House in Chicago where the urban poor could benefit from lessons in childcare, the use of a gymnasium, a theater, a playground, an art gallery, and a museum.

[handwritten: Dewey Curr. based on children's experiences]

Dewey believed that children should follow a curriculum based on their experiences, and that schools should reflect society and try to find ways to improve it by encouraging students to take part in democratic processes while in school.

In the early nineteenth century, the population of the United States was becoming increasingly more diverse due to immigration. The curriculum of the Latin grammar school was not appropriate for the children of immigrants. The National Education Association supported a subject-centered curriculum, but teachers were beginning to find fault with this approach. In 1918, the NEA issued the *Seven Cardinal Principles*. This report stated that all students should be prepared in seven undertakings: health, the ability to perform fundamental processes, attain a worthy home life, a vocation, civics, worthy use of leisure time, and ethics. The NEA commission that issued this report stated that the previous curriculum served a minority rather than the majority.

This departure from the prior curriculum attempted to individualize education by offering various options to students. It did not address the needs of the poor, minority students, or women. The advent of World War I prevented the implementation of these recommendations. Despite that, this was the beginning of schools with different options for different students.

The Great Depression of the 1930s caused economic hardship for the public schools. Many rural schools were forced to close, while others operated with fewer teachers, larger classes, and outdated materials. Many young men left school to enter the job market and to assist their struggling families, while others, who could not find jobs, entered secondary schools in record numbers.

World War II was the beginning of economic recovery and promoted science, math, and physics, all required for success in the technological post-war society. When the Soviet Union launched Sputnik, in 1957, the United States began to question the quality of its public schools. In 1958, Congress passed the National Defense Education Act. This legislation provided federal aid to improve instruction in science, math, and foreign languages.

Attempts to offer equal educational opportunities dominated American education from the 1950s to the 1970s. It was during this period that increased opportunities for a diverse population became a focus of public education.

Studies of public school funding during this time showed major inequities between spending on the education of whites as compared with that of blacks. The ruling of the Supreme Court in *Plessy v. Ferguson* (1896) which upheld the principle of "separate but equal" was proving untenable. Equal educational opportunities were not afforded to students, segregated by race, educated in unequal facilities, by unequally educated teachers, and with unequal materials. In recognition of these inequities, the Supreme Court, in *Brown v. Board of Education of Topeka, Kansas (1954),* ruled that "separate is not equal." In handing down its opinion, the Court stated that "Separate but equal has no place ... Separate educational facilities are inherently unequal and violate the equal protection clause of the Fourteenth Amendment." The majority opinion also addressed the psychological effect of segregation on minority children by stating that such separation "generates a feeling of inferiority as to their status in the community that may affect their hearts and minds in a way unlikely to be undone."

School segregation did not end with the *Brown* decision. Local authorities, supervised by federal district judges, were to implement the Court's desegregation decision, but many such authorities and judges opposed desegregation and, therefore, refused to enforce the Court's rulings. Minority students attending "desegregated" schools found themselves placed in tracks with other minority students or in vocational tracks, without access to college preparatory courses, academic prerequisites, or gifted and talented programs.

In the 1960s, researchers found that schools were as segregated as they had been prior to the *Brown* decision. Schools used **de facto segregation** to ensure that integration would not occur. Minority students, usually placed on the lowest track in kindergarten, and with very few exceptions, remained there until they graduated from high school, or dropped out. Federal judges ruling in cases claiming the continued existence of a segregated school system found that the education offered children in the lowest track was inferior to that available to students in average or upper tracks.

President Lyndon B. Johnson instituted a "War on Poverty." This program included legislation specifically targeting education as a means to overcome a life of poverty. Among these new laws was the Economic Opportunity Act of 1964. This bill created the Job Corps enabling men and women between the ages of sixteen and twenty-one to work in conservation camps and training centers. It included funding for work training and Volunteers in Service to America. The latter, modeled after John F. Kennedy's Peace Corps, provided community service projects for impoverished communities. Additionally, it funded work-study programs for college students, community action programs designed to promote employment opportunities, adult literacy programs, loans for low-income families, programs for migrant workers, and incentives for new businesses in poverty areas.

The result of one of the community action programs was Head Start. This program, designed as a comprehensive approach to the development of four- and five-year-olds from low-income families, was multifaceted and addressed physical and mental health as well as intellectual development.

Initial research studies on the outcomes of the Head Start program yielded conflicting results. Some found little or no differences between impoverished children who participated in the program and those who did not. The original summer-only program was deemed ineffective in all areas and the yearlong program only minimally effective in achieving cognitive gains. Despite these findings, Head Start children were beginning to demonstrate school readiness at grade one nearing the national norms.

Some later studies revealed benefits accruing to Head Start children in cognitive development and in the ability to get and hold a job later in life, while other studies found an absence of both cognitive and socioemotional gains. These studies, with negative findings, showed that Head Start children lost the apparent short-term gains in intelligence scores and learning skills within two years of school.

Despite these conflicting results, Head Start continues to enjoy significant congressional support and funding.

Elem. &
Secondary
Educ.
as
Title I

In 1965, Congress passed the Elementary and Secondary Education Act. Title I of this legislation provided greater levels of funding for disadvantaged students than for others. Today, Chapter I, as it is now known, provides local schools with federal aid for programs, projects, equipment, and facilities all intended to diminish the developmental level disparity between those who are economically disadvantaged and those who are not.

Title VII of the Elementary and Secondary Education Act, added in 1974, provides the federal government with the legal authority to guarantee that no student be discriminated against because of race or ethnicity.

Title IX (1975) of the ESEA, prohibits schools from discriminating against men and women in admission policies and classes based on gender. This legislation required schools to establish women's athletic teams in interscholastic, intercollegiate, or intramural sports. While the bill did not require equal expenditures for women's and men's sports, it did prohibit sexual discrimination in employment, recruitment, leaves of absence, pay, fringe benefits, tuition, training, and sabbatical leaves. This was the first time in American history that federal legislation specifically targeted the education of women.

In 1978, Congress passed the Bilingual Education Act that provided federal funds to states with a high percentage of non-English-speaking students, to assist with the development of bilingual programs, to provide materials and equipment needed for those programs, and to provide pre-service teacher training in bilingual education. These programs have proven controversial in both intent and outcome. There is disagreement about the length of such programs as well as over whether they increase or decrease student achievement when students enter English-speaking programs.

In 1975, with the passage of the Education for All Handicapped Children Act, the federal government recognized the need to provide for mentally, physically, and learning disabled students. The bill mandated that schools provide free and appropriate education for all such children. The 1986 amendments to this legislation extended these services to infants, toddlers, and preschoolers.

During the 1970s, 1980s, and 1990s, federal funds for education were severely cut. President Nixon vetoed three compensatory education and desegregation programs, questioning whether previous "War on Poverty" legislation had resulted in improved educational programs for the poor. President Reagan's administration saw a further eroding of federal funding for education. Without federal funds, it became financially impossible to implement many portions of the Elementary and Secondary Education Act and the Civil Rights Act.

President Clinton's administration saw a return to federal funding for compensatory education in the 1990s. In 1994, Congress increased funding for Head Start, bilingual education, and Chapter I. President George H. W. Bush instituted America 2000, renamed Goals 2000 during Clinton's administration. The features of this plan included school readiness; increased high school graduation rates; demonstration of competency in English, math, science, foreign language, civics and government, economics, the arts, history and geography; adult literacy enabling competition in a global economy and the exercise of the rights and responsibilities of citizenship; schools free of drugs, violence, firearms, and alcohol; and programs for teachers to continue to improve their skills.

President George W. Bush has continued to favor educational reform and has emphasized increased standards at all levels of education, including teacher education itself.

References

Further reading of these references may enhance understanding of the competency and may also increase performance on the examination.

Blake, N., Smeyers, P., Smith, R., and Standish, P., eds. *The Blackwell Guide to the Philosophy of Education.* Maiden, MA: Blackwell Publishers Ltd., 2003.

Glasser, W. *Schools Without Failure.* New York: Harper & Row, 1969.

Lawton, D. and Gordon, P. *A History of Western Educational Ideas.* London: Wobum Press, 2002.

Reed, A. J. S.; Bergemann, V.E.; and Olson, M. W. *In the Classroom: An Introduction to Education.* Boston: McGraw-Hill, 1998.

Competency 14: ESOL (English for Speakers of Other Languages)

Definition of Competency

The teacher has knowledge of specific approaches, methods, and strategies appropriate for students with limited English proficiency (ESOL).

- The teacher identifies characteristics of first and second language acquisition.

- The teacher identifies ESOL approaches, methods, and strategies (e.g., materials adaptation, alternative assessment, and strategy documentation) appropriate for instruction.

- *The teacher identifies and applies cognitive approaches, multisensory ESOL strategies, and instructional practices that build upon students' abilities and promote self-worth.*

English for Speakers of Other Languages (ESOL)

The English for Speakers of Other Languages (ESOL) programs came about as a response to the Multicultural Education Training and Advocacy (META) Project. The META Project, established in the summer of 1989, was composed of eight plaintiffs who informed the state education agency of its intent to sue on behalf of underserved students with Limited English Proficiency (LEP). They based the suit on the state's failure to establish statewide standards and guidelines for the provision of services to LEP students. META and the state negotiated an agreement (called the Consent Decree) that prescribed the following four-part remedy (for more details visit the following website: http://www.firn.edu/doe/omsle/cdpage2.htm):

1. Identifying, assessing, and monitoring the progress of language minority students.

2. Providing LEP students with access to teachers trained to meet their needs;

3. Requiring teachers to obtain appropriate training and certification; and

4. Evaluating program effectiveness.

The Consent Decree is the State of Florida's framework for compliance with the federal and state laws and jurisprudence regarding the education of LEP students. In practical terms, it requires all teachers working with any LEP student to participate in courses and training related to teaching ESOL students, and earn formal bilingual or ESOL credentials.

The following questions are administered to students to determine if they qualify as LEP and require ESOL services. They are part of a document called the Home Language Survey:

to determine if a student qualified as LEP & requires ESOL services

a.   Is a language other than English used in the home?

b.   Did the student have a first language other than English?

c.   Does the student most frequently speak a language other than English?

Important Definitions of ESOL Terms

The following is a list of important definitions of basic ESOL terms (Willig, & Lee, 1996):

1.   **Basic ESOL:** This includes instruction in English/ Language Arts (whether self-contained or inclusive).

2.   **Basic Interpersonal Communicative Skills (BICS):** This term refers to the aspect of language proficiency strongly

social lang. - not highly correlated w/ literacy & academics

associated with basic communicative, oral fluency. BICS are not highly correlated with literacy and academic achievement. It is often referred to as the social language.

3.   **Basic Subject Area:** This includes language instruction as related to computer literacy, mathematics, science, and social studies.

4.   **Cognitive/Academic Language Proficiency (CALP):** This term refers to the aspects of language proficiency strongly related to literacy and academic achievement. CALP is more difficult to acquire than Basic Interpersonal Communicative Skills, and often referred to as the **academic language**.

Academic Lang. opposite of BICS Basic Interpersonal Communicator skill

5.   **Comprehensive Input (CI):** This is language that is understandable and meaningful to second language students. CI is the language that the student already knows, plus a range of new language that is made understandable by the use of certain strategies.

6.   **Home or native language:** When used in reference to an individual with limited English proficiency, it means the language normally used by such individual, or in the case of a student, the language normally used by the parents of the student.

7.   **Limited English Proficient (LEP) Basis of Entry** – A one character code indicating the student's basis for entry into the ESOL program:

a.   Aural/Oral (**A**);

b.   Reading and Writing (**R**);

c.   LEP Committee (**L**); or

d.   Temporarily placed in a program based on a "Yes" response to Home Language Survey questions b or c (**T**).

Note: LEP is also used to refer to Language Enriched Pupil

8.   **LEP Committee:** A committee composed of ESOL teacher(s), home language teacher (if any) and administrator or designee, plus guidance counselors, social workers, school psychologists, or other educators as appropriate for the situation. Parents are also invited to attend any committee meetings.

9.   **LEP student:** A student who meets the following descriptions:

a.   Was *not* born in the U.S. and whose native language is other than English; or

b.   Was born in the U.S. but who comes from a home in which a language other than English is most relied upon for communication; or

c.   Is an American Indian or Alaskan Native who comes from a home in which a language other than English has had a significant impact on his or her level of English Language Proficiency; and

d. Who, as a result of the above, has sufficient difficulty speaking, reading, writing, or understanding the English language which denies him or her the opportunity to learn successfully in classrooms in which the language of instruction is English.

10. **LEP Student Plan:** A written document(s) that identifies the student's name, instruction by program (including programs other than ESOL provided), amount of instructional time or schedule, date of LEP identification, assessment data used to classify or reclassify the student as LEP, date of exit and assessment data used to classify the student as English proficient. The plan may be included in or attached to a student's existing plan, IEP (Individual Education Plan), or may be a separate document for a given student or students. If the plan covers more than one student, each student will have an individual copy of the plan maintained in the student's file.

11. **Other Subject Areas:** This includes any instruction other than Basic ESOL or Basic subject areas.

12. **Potentially English Proficient (PEP):** This is an alternative term for LEP (limited-English-proficient). Although LEP is the term used in all legislation, many educators object to its focus on students' limitations. PEP is one of the results of such efforts.

Limited English Proficiency Codes

The State of Florida uses a coding system to identify the various levels of proficiency of Limited English Proficiency (LEP) students. This coding system is provided to teachers on their class rolls so they are able to identify the various proficiency levels of the students in their class (Willig, & Lee, 1996):

- **LF** = A former LEP student who exited the ESOL program and is being monitored for a two-year period.

- **LN** = A student identified as LEP who is not being served in an ESOL program.

- **LP** = A student who is in the 4th–12th grade, tested as fully proficient in English on an Aural/Oral Test and is LEP pending the Reading and Writing assessment or the student is in K–12th grade, answered "yes" on the Home Language Survey to the question "Is a language other than English spoken in the Home?" and is pending aural/oral assessment.

- **LY** = Student identified as LEP who is being served in an approved ESOL program.

- **LZ** = A student who exited the ESOL program and was monitored for a two-year period. Once a student completes the two-year post-reclassification monitoring period, they are re-coded LZ and remain so for the remainder of their school career.

- **ZZ** = Not applicable. Non-LEP student who is not limited English proficient. The student responded in the negative to all three required Home Language Survey Questions.

Identification of Potential LEP Students

The following steps are used in the identification of potential LEP students:

1. Parent completes Home Language Survey and answers "yes" to any of three Home Language Survey questions.

2. Student must be tested for LEP eligibility.

3. Home school personnel checks screen 15 on the state computer system to determine if student has been identified as an LEP student at a prior school.

4. If student has not been tested for LEP eligibility, testing must occur within 20 school days at the home school by the program assistant.

5. Student will receive ESOL services pending testing results.

6.   Results of the test will determine whether the student is eligible or ineligible for ESOL bilingual services.

7.   Test results are returned to school's principal or principal designee.

8.   If student is ineligible, then the home school carries out one of the following activities:

      a.   Notifies parent in writing of results and rights.

      b.   Student remains in basic program.

      c.   Original notification form is sent to parents.

      d.   Copies of program forms are filed in the student's cumulative folder.

9.   If student is eligible, then the home school carries out the following activities:

      a.   Notifies parent in writing of results using notification form.

      b.   Shares information in writing about basic ESOL and home language programs as well as the need for services and parental rights, as required by the META consent decree.

      c.   Serves the student in the ESOL or Bilingual Program.

      d.   Develops an LEP Plan upon program entry.

e.   Files copies of program forms in the student's cumulative folder.

f.   Updates screen 15 on the state computer system.

10.   If the parents question the services, then the LEP committee is convened to present available options for student. The LEP Committee makes recommendations. Parents may appeal the decision at an administrative hearing.

ESOL Program Models in Florida Schools

The following is a list of the ESOL program models in the Florida School System (Willig, & Lee, 1996):

- **ESOL pull-out:** Elementary or secondary LEP students leave their regular classroom to go to an ESOL resource classroom for at least one class period per day.

- **ESOL classroom:** Elementary level LEP students spend most of the school day in a self-contained ESOL classroom.

- **Sheltered content classes:** Secondary level LEP students are taught by subject matter teachers in classes designed specifically for their needs.

- **Inclusion classrooms:** Elementary or secondary LEP students are served in mainstream content classrooms where ESOL strategies are being used, where materials are adapted, and/or where an ESOL teacher or paraprofessional assistance is available.

- **Bilingual or home language instruction:** Elementary or secondary LEP students spend at least part of the school day being taught using the home language.

The ESOL teacher should work very closely and collaborate with the regular classroom teacher(s) to ensure that the students' needs are being met.

Considerations and Teaching Strategies for ESOL Students

The ESOL program should aim to support students' successful learning outcomes within all curriculum areas and enhance overall literacy. The ESOL program should include general teaching and learning approaches that involve students' integrated and organized use of the skills of listening, speaking, reading, and writing. Also, these programs should include *specific language skills* that are taught to meet students' needs and learning styles, and *unit topics* that are selected to provide the appropriate cultural and motivational context for learning language and structure.

When teaching ESOL students, it is important to recognize that many have been introduced to English in their native countries or homes. Nevertheless, they do not speak it fluently and confidently, have not read English literature widely, and are not accustomed to writing their assignments in English.

Considerations When Teaching ESOL Students

Consider these facts when teaching ESOL students (Badia, 1996; and Willig, & Lee, 1996):

1. Children who speak another language may not know how to pronounce certain sounds in English. For example, most Spanish speakers have difficulty with the sound of "th" and most English vowels. This could affect their writing skills as well as their understanding and comprehension of mathematics, science, and social studies.

2. Children from certain countries, such as Saudi Arabia or Korea, will not know the Roman alphabet and will have to learn it.

3. Even when a student's native language uses the Roman alphabet, the sound-symbol correspondence will not always be the same. For example, a Spanish "j" is pronounced like an English "h".

4. ESOL student's decoding skills may be inadequate.

5. ESOL student's experiential/cultural background is different and may cause a lack of comprehension of such topics as Halloween and Thanksgiving in a reading selection.

6. The student might be hesitant to participate in oral discussions because of his/her insecure feelings about his/her lack of oral language.

Teaching Strategies and Principles for ESOL Students

1. Create a **relaxed learning environment**, and provide a lot of **positive reinforcement**.

2. **Acquisition vs. Learning:** Language acquisition is described in some cases as a subconscious process. In other words, as the learner is acquiring the second language, he or she is not aware of what is taking place. On the other hand, learning a second language is a more conscious process. "In communicative-based instruction, language can be acquired in a natural way instead of being learned more formally through the explicit instruction of grammatical rules (Badia, 1996, p. 20). Some aspects of Language Acquisition vs. Learning (Willig, & Lee, 1996):

   Second Language *Acquisition* is:

   • Similar to first language acquisition

   • "Picking up" a language

   • May not be in conscious awareness

- Implicit knowledge

- Errors accepted

- Formal teaching does not necessarily help

Second Language *Learning* is:

- Formal Knowledge of a Language

- Knowing about a language

- Deliberate and conscious effort

- Explicit knowledge

- Errors corrected

- Formal teaching helps

3. **The Natural Approach (NA):** According to this approach, students acquire new vocabulary through experiences and associations with the words, because the words are used in meaningful ways and contexts (Krashen, 1985). "Extended listening experiences include physical response activities, use of vivid pictures to illustrate concepts, and active involvement of the students through physical contact with the pictures and objects being discussed—by means of choice-making, yes-no questions, and game situations" (Badia, 1996, p. 61).

   This approach is a topic-centered language program designed to develop basic communication skills

[handwritten margin note: acquire — instead of learning the lang.]

taking into account the student's natural processes of acquiring language.

The following are the four **developmental stages** identified for this approach (Willig, & Lee, 1996):

- **First Stage: Pre-production:** Focuses on listening comprehension and involves non-verbal responses from the student.

- **Second Stage: Early production:** Focuses on expanding receptive vocabulary and initial production of language.

- **Third Stage: Speech Emergence:** Focuses on the student's ability to speak in simple sentences.

- **Fourth Stage: Intermediate Fluency:** It focuses on student's ability to engage in discourse.

According to Badia (1996, p. 61), the major aspects of this approach are the following:

- Meaningful communication is the main goal in language acquisition.

- Students are directed to acquire the language instead of just learning it.

- Affective factors are key to language instruction.

- Learning of vocabulary in context is essential for comprehension and speech production.

assists students who left ESOL to go to "mainstream" lang. arts curriculum

4. **The Cognitive Academic Language Learning Approach (CALLA):** This approach assists in the students' transition from a language arts program in which content is made comprehensible through the use of ESOL strategies (Chamot & O'Malley, 1994). It is used to help students handle "mainstream" language arts curriculum with success and understand and retain content area material while they increase their English language skills (Badia, 1996). According to Badia (1996, p. 62), the major aspects of this approach are the following:

    *   **Content:** The content of a lesson is determined by the grade-level curriculum in science, mathematics, social studies, etc.

    *   **Language:** Students acquire the language functions use in content classes, such as describing, classifying, explaining, etc. At this point, the student must also learn the language arts content and some of the specialized vocabulary of each content area, such as: the phonology of the English language, syntax, lexicon, technical terms, etc.

    *   **Strategy:** Learning strategies should emphasize critical and creative thinking skills, such as problem solving, extrapolating, inferencing, etc. These learning activities are essential to mainstream success.

5. **Whole Language Approach:** In this approach, linguistic, cognitive, and early literacy skills are presented to the students using an integrated fashion. The four language

skills of listening, speaking, reading, and writing are used (Goodman, Goodman & Hood, 1989). It also incorporates elements from several instructional strategies to develop reading and writing skills, in particular the Language Experience strategy (Badia, 1996). According to Badia (1996, p. 62), the major aspects of this approach are:

Whole language is:

- Language kept "whole"

- Student-centered

- Literature-based/Content-based

- Context rich

- Writing rich

Whole Language is not:

- Phonics taught in isolation

- Teacher-centered

- Vocabulary-controlled, syntax controlled, high interest/low vocabulary texts

- Content deprived

- A focus on form over content

6. **Language Experience Approach (LEA):** The main goal of this approach is to have students achieve language development in response to first-hand and multi-sensorial experiences. (Badia, 1996). It is used to teach reading, writing, and other content areas to create a context for both cognitive and linguistic growth. It uses students' available repertoires, ideas, and language. The students are encouraged to be active participants, rather than passive learners. The steps for developing this approach are (Dixon & Nessel, 1983):

Step 1: Providing the Experience / Motivation

Step 2: Facilitating Language Production

Step 3: Creating a Personal View Representation

Step 4: Retelling Events / Reactions

Step 5: Writing Students' Statements

Step 6: Reading

Step 7: Writing

Step 8: Follow Up with Activities

7. Teach **vocabulary, concepts and/or skills within the context** of other vocabulary/material already presented, through the use of **high interest activities.** Help students **relate words and meanings to concepts** (i.e., contextually), by using demonstrations or "acting out" the meaning of words, providing antonyms and synonyms,

and using cuing strategies. Using a multi-sensory approach to support vocabulary/material being presented can help capitalize on students' various learning modalities: concrete referents (visuals, props, realia, multimedia and manipulatives) maps, charts, study guides, labels, graphic organizers, summaries, filmstrips, illustrations, pictures graphs, diagrams, videos, audiotapes, lower-level text, and/or demonstrations. "Memory anchors" should be created to help students recall the meaning of words and concepts (Badia, 1996).

Hands-on manipulatives should also be incorporated. These can include anything from Cuisenaire rods for mathematics to microscopes for science to globes for social studies. **Realia** include real-life objects that enable students to make connections to their own lives. Examples of realia include bank deposit slips and check registers for a unit on banking, or nutrition labels from food products for a health unit. **Pictures** include photographs and illustrations depicting nearly any object, process, or topic; and magazines, commercial photos and hand drawings that provide visual support for a wide variety of content and vocabulary concepts. **Visuals** can include overhead transparencies, models, graphs, charts, timelines, maps, props, and bulletin board displays. Students with diverse abilities often have difficulty processing an inordinate amount of auditory information and have an advantage with visual clues. A wide variety of **multimedia materials** are available to enhance teaching and learning. These range from simple cassette recordings to videos to interactive CD-ROMs to an increasing number of resources available on the Internet.

8. Make regular use of **context clues**: gestures, facial expressions, and body language.

9. Preview **reading content**. Encourage students to use dictionaries in English and their native language (specially for science content).

10. Use the **key words approach** to teaching vocabulary. Have students keep a collection of cards with their own personal selection of vocabulary words. These cards could be divided into curriculum areas.

11. Encourage **sustained silent reading** (SSR) and **reading for pleasure** in a variety of topics so the students can see models of different types of writing.

12. Reinforce objectives using **games** and **fun learning activities**.

13. Arrange seating so that students will **sit** and **work in groups**. If possible, group students who are less proficient in English with the native speakers for peer teaching purposes. Provide frequent daily reading in small groups.

14. Help students **distinguish** between the application of punctuation rules and grammatical structures for their first language and the English language. This is especially difficult for ESOL students who are literate in their native language.

15. If a student's English reading and writing proficiency is limited, then emphasize a **more extensive use of oral language** for instruction.

16. Expose students to **different examples of writing** in order to help them become more competent and productive writers.

17. Engage students in **varied types** of writing practice.

18. Demonstrate the **actual writing process**. Model the thinking process for students and help them build thinking strategies and higher order thinking skills.

19. Use **relevant materials** and topics that fit into and relate to the students' lives.

20. Allow students to work in **pairs** or **small groups** to accomplish learning or assessment tasks, and discuss topics, word problems, science experiments and/or materials. Pairing or grouping students provides for more communication and sharing of ideas. When working in group activities, you should not group all the low-level students together (use heterogeneous grouping instead). In some cases, peer tutoring could be effective.

21. Accept errors as part of the learning process. **Error correction** should be minimal. More time should be spent attending to students' messages than the specifics by which the messages are transmitted.

22. Use **modified language** when needed to make the English language and the intended content more accessible and

comprehensible to the students (linguistic modifications within a naturalistic setting) (Willig, & Lee, 1996):

Characteristics of modified language:

- controlled sentence length and complexity,

- controlled standardized vocabulary,

- moderate speech rate (not artificially slow), and

- restatement, paraphrasing, explanation, demonstration, expansion and repetition of the ideas for clarification.

23. **Explain new terms and processes as thoroughly as possible** when you introduce them to the class. ESOL students are often more successful in mathematics content because mathematic symbols are the same or similar in their first language, but word problems written in English are usually hard to read and understand for them. This is partly because the vocabulary used in mathematics is highly specialized and specific, is not used regularly in day to day activities, contains unique items, involves cultural differences in the type of instruction the students have received in their native countries, contains few clues to meaning, and has grammatical structures that, in many cases, are different from regular English language usage. You should not assume that mathematics notation symbols and computational formats are the same from country to country. Similarly, science content is especially difficult for ESOL students.

24. Relate and apply mathematics and scientific problems and vocabulary to **students' prior knowledge**, **background information**, and **real-life situations**. Involve students in the problems by asking appropriate questions at their individual levels of language acquisition.

25. Wherever possible and appropriate, use manipulatives and visual aids to make problems **concrete instead of abstract**. Avoid dealing with abstract concepts unless the concepts have first been experienced concretely.

26. Encourage drawing to **translate** and **visualize** word problems, stories, experiments, procedures and/or processes. Select predictable pattern and illustrated books. Ask thought-provoking questions throughout the story.

27. **Rewrite** and/or **role-play** word problems, stories, experiments, procedures and/or processes in simple English. For example, have the class work together to make a grocery store, have groups role-play the word problem situation while orally explaining the problem solving steps taken, and/or have learning centers arranged throughout the classroom.

28. Have students give an **oral explanation** of his/her thinking, leading to the solution of the problem.

29. Have students write original stories and word problems to **exchange** with classmates.

30.   Write terms, symbols, formulae, problems, and other important information on the board to provide **visual reinforcement** and provide a **contextual framework**. Review previously learned information on a daily basis.

31.   **Clearly** explain directions and procedures for activities.

32.   **Repeat** key terms or words to look for. **Read** and **re-read** students' favorites and provide follow-up activities in varied formats.

33.   Encourage students to follow these **guidelines** when solving word problems (similarly for science, use inquiry, the discovery approach and/or the scientific process to develop critical thinking skills):

    a.   Understand the question.

    b.   Find the needed information.

    c.   Choose a plan or strategy.

    d.   Solve the problem.

    e.   Check the answer.

34.   Promote a non-threatening socio-cultural **learning community** where students feel safe, are willing to take learning risks and make mistakes, and are respected by the teacher and peers.

35. Wherever possible, use **cooperative learning strategies**. The following are some possible alternatives for students to use:

    a. Read each problem or story aloud to friends.

    b. Paraphrase or explain their personal understanding, solution plan and/or possible solution of the problem or story.

    c. Ask friends to explain their understanding of the problem or story.

    d. Brainstorm for alternative understandings, strategies, solutions or plans and test them against their own ideas.

36. **Scaffolding:** ESOL students should be provided with "scaffolded" steps of learning that allow for consolidation and success. The notion of "scaffolding" was developed by researchers in an attempt to describe the ways in which adults support and elaborate on children's early language development. Just as scaffolds on a building support a new construction, adults' interventions during learning activities assist children's attempts at effective communication and language development (Cazden, 1983; Ninio & Bruner, 1976).

    Vygotsky (1978) states that students' learning is enhanced when teachers or other individuals provide scaffolding for less-experienced students. Teachers can scaffold LEP students' experiences by carefully planning demonstrations that model how to follow steps and directions needed to complete tasks, and that include supplementary materials. Teachers can also demonstrate and/or model language, like how to give an oral presentation. Students can then practice these steps in groups or alone, with the teacher or other experienced individuals nearby to assist as needed.

37. **Familiar contexts** and **authentic learning situations** should be used wherever possible; however, the introduction of richer vocabulary and new learning experiences to challenge students should be considered when appropriate.

38. Speaking a language other than English and the possibility of proficiency in more than one language should be seen as **enrichment**, and celebrated as an **asset** for the students and community in general, not as a deficit to be remedied. In other words, students should be encouraged to become bilingual. This is with the understanding that mastery of more that one language encourages cross-cultural relationships and enhances "problem-solving skills, creativity, and general cognitive development" (Schultz, 1998, p. 6). Furthermore, Cummins (1981), Collier (1992, & 1995), and Collier and Thomas (1997) have indicated that one of the primary factors in determining success in acquiring another language is the strength of the person's first language. This is another reason why students' should be encouraged to continue to develop cognitive and academic proficiency in their first language.

39. **Total Physical Response (TPR)**: TPR, developed by the psychologist James Asher, is a systematized approach

that greatly enhances the amount of language input that can be handled by beginning LEP students. According to Asher (1982), this strategy should place little or no pressure on the student to speak. The seven steps for TPR activities are (ESCORT, 1998):

a.   **Setting up:** The teacher sets up a situation in which students follow a set of commands using actions (for example, props) and acts out a series of events (for example, shopping for groceries, taking the school bus, or preparing a sandwich).

b.   **Demonstration**: The teacher or student demonstrates the series of actions. The other students are expected to pay attention but not to talk or repeat the actions.

c.   **Group live action:** The group acts out the series of actions as the teacher or student gives commands. This step may be repeated several times.

d.   **Written copy:** The series of commands is placed on a chart paper or on the blackboard for students to read and copy.

e.   **Oral repetition and questions:** Repeat each line after the teacher or student being careful with difficult words and pronunciation features (for example, soap/soup or cheap/sheep). Students have the opportunity to ask questions.

f.   **Student demonstration:** Students play the roles of reader of the series and performer of the actions.

g.   **Pairs:** Students work in small groups (two or three) telling or reading the series and listening and responding physically (for example: Stand up, sit down, raise one hand, put your hand down, raise two hands, put your hands down, touch your nose, touch your ear, etc.)

40.   **SQ4R** is an acronym for survey, question, read, reflect, recite, and review (Tomas & Robinson, 1972). It is a systematic approach for studying instructional texts, and encourages students to scan a text before reading, paying attention to headings and subheadings to look for major topics. Before reading the material, the headings of the text are used by the students to invent questions using the *wh-* words: who, what, why, where, when. After reading the material, students reflect on what has been read, try to relate the material to information already known, put major ideas into focus, and, finally, carry out an active review with the material that has not been learned (Diaz-Rico & Weed, 1995).

Principles of Second-Language Acquisition

[handwritten margin note: reflect to try to relate material to information already known & put major ideas into focus]

[handwritten margin note: students shd. be flexible users of a lang.]

ESOL programs should be grounded in the principles of second-language acquisition research and those developed in recent years. Language acquisition describes the process by which students become flexible users of a given language. A person may use a language effectively with very few if any references to rules of usage and grammar, or other linguistic principles. In other words, instruction in linguistic principles might teach us about a language, but might not help the students become flexible users of this language (Nunan, 1995). ESOL students should have the opportunity to work in mainstream classes to learn English *through* content rather than *as* content, and acquired language through thinking, clarifying and communicating across all areas of the curriculum.

Four Levels of Attention to Language and Literacy Skills (Badia, 1996; Jameson, 1998; Tomas & Robinson, 1972; Willig & Lee, 1996)**:**

1. **Comprehensive Strategies/Processes**

   • **DRTA** (Directed Reading/Thinking Activity) or **DRLTA** (Directed Reading/Listening/Thinking Activity): This teacher directed strategy helps students when reading a story or chapter from a book. The teacher models the process of creating and correcting predictions as the story progresses to strengthen comprehension. The steps are establish background, allow for oral or silent reading and study, and follow-up activities.

   • **SQ3R** (survey, question, read, recite and review) or **SQ4R** (survey, question, read, reflect, recite and review)

   • **The Writing Process:** This approach is a formalized and structured application of a process to the act of writing (Badia, 1996). This process requires the drafting, editing and publishing of a totally original, authentic and student-centered writing assignment. The following are the steps involved in this process (Badia, 1996, p. 88):

Step 1: Pre-Writing

Step 2: Writing a Draft or Drafts

Step 3: Review (Responding to the Draft or Drafts)

Step 4: Rewriting (after Reviewing the Response or Responses)

Step 5: Editing (Final Draft)

Step 6: Publication (Final Presentation)

2.   **Focused Strategies**

- **Graphic Organizers:** They help students improve organizational skills, and provide a visual, holistic representation of facts and concepts and their relationships within an organized framework. The ability to organize information and ideas is fundamental to effective thinking.

- **Think-Alouds:** This method allows the teacher and students to problem solve together. The teacher may pose a question aloud to students and the teacher, group of students, or entire class could respond utilizing unison response.

- **Cooperative Learning Strategies:** They can work well and enhance learning for all students; however, the language interactions they produce make them especially effective for limited English proficient students. The cooperative learning strategies allow and encourage students to use language for interaction to solve real problems, thus speeding up the acquisition of the English language.

3. **Language Structures**

   - Sentence Patterns

   - Frame Sentences

   - **Chunks:** Use "chunks" of language in meaningful, appropriate, and playful context (for example, pop songs and read aloud poems)

   - Sentence Starters

4. **Academic Vocabulary**

   - **Demonstrations with Vocabulary:** The teacher or student models a word, sentence or action.

   - **Semantic Webs:** Students learn how to perceive relationships and integrate information and concepts within the context of a main idea or topic

   - Personal Dictionaries

Language Developmental Stages

(adapted from Willig & Lee, 1996, Empowering Teachers, Section 5)

Stage 1: Pre-production:

- Students are totally new to English

- Generally lasts one to three months

Sample Student Behaviors:

- Points to other non-verbal responses

- Active listeners

- Responds to commands

- May be reluctant to speak

- Understands more than can produce

Sample Teacher Behaviors:

- Gestures

- Language focuses on conveying meanings and vocabulary development

- Repetition

- Does not force students to speak

Questioning Techniques:

- Point to . . .

- Find the . . .

- Put the _____ next to the _____.

- Is this a _____?

- Who wants the _____?

- Who has the _____?

Stage 2: Early Production:

- Students are "low beginners"

- Generally lasts several weeks

Sample Student Behaviors:

- One or two word utterances

- Short phrases

Sample Teacher Behaviors:

- Asks questions that can be answered by yes/no and either/or responses

- Models correct responses

- Ensures a supportive, low anxiety environment

- Does not overtly call attention to grammatical errors

- Asks short answer WH– questions

Questioning Techniques:

- Yes/no (Is the light on?)

- Either/or (Is this a screwdriver or a hammer?)

- One word response (What utensil am I holding in my hand?)

- General questions which encourage lists of words (What do you see on the board?)

- Two-word response (Where did he go? To work.)

Stage 3: Speech Emergence:

- Students are "beginners"

- May last several weeks or months

Sample Student Behaviors:

- Participates in small group activities

- Demonstrates comprehension in a variety of ways

- Speaks in short phrases and sentences

- Begins to use language more freely

Sample Teacher Behaviors:

- Focuses content on key concepts

- Provides frequent comprehension checks

- Uses expanded vocabulary

- Asks open-ended questions that stimulate language production

Questioning Techniques:

- Why?

- How?

- How is this like that?

- Tell me about it . . .

Talk about . . .

- Describe

- How could you change this part?

Stage 4: Intermediate Fluency:

- Students are "high beginners," intermediate, or advanced

- May require several years to achieve native-like fluency in academic settings

Sample Student Behaviors:

- Participates in reading and writing activities to acquire new information

- May experience difficulties in abstract, cognitively demanding subjects at school, especially when a high degree of literacy is required

Sample Teacher Behaviors:

- Fosters conceptual development and expanded literacy through content

- Continues to make lessons comprehensible and interactive

- Teaches thinking and study skills

- Continues to be alert to individual differences in language and culture

Questioning Techniques:

- What would you recommend/suggest?

- How do you think this story will end?

- What is the story mainly about?

- What is your opinion on this matter?

- Describe/compare

- How are these similar/different?

- What would happen if . . . ?

- Which do you prefer? Why?

- Create . . .

Quadrants of Language and Learning

James Cummins (1981), a leader in the field of second-language acquisition, makes a distinction between social language and academic language.

takes 2 yrs. to acquire social lang.

Basic Interpersonal Communication Skills (BICS), referred to as social language, deals with the here-and-now language that is context embedded, supported by the use of illustrations, realia, demonstrations, and so forth. Studies have shown that second language learners acquire social language in approximately two years. **Cognitive Academic Language Proficiency Skills** (CALP), known as the academic language, is the language of school tasks, which is more abstract and decontextualized. Academic language is harder to acquire because it is context-reduced with little or no context clues. It takes second-language learners five to seven years to become proficient in the academic language.

takes 5 to 7 yrs.

Cummins's Quadrants (1982) helps teachers plan appropriate tasks and identifies strategies to help LEP students at varying proficiency levels move from social language (**Quadrant A**) to academic language (**Quadrant D**). Each of the quadrants is determined by how much contextual support accompanies the language presented, and how cognitively demanding the language is.

Classification of Language and Content Activities Within Cummins's (1982) Quadrants

Quadrant A: Non-academic or Cognitively Undemanding (Easy)/Context-Embedded (with Clues):

Activities:

- Developing a survival vocabulary

- Following demonstrated directions

- Playing simple games

- Engaging in face-to-face interactions

- Participating in art, music, and physical education

Example: Maria, take this glass and fill it with water. The concepts in this command are the least demanding. The context is experiential and related to concrete items. "Hands-on" types of activities are examples of this area. This is considered the easiest area of language (West Virginia Department of Education, 2003).

Quadrant B: Academic or Cognitively Demanding (Hard)/Context-Embedded (With Clues):

Activities:

- Participating in hands-on science and mathematics activities

- Making maps, models, charts, and graphs

- Solving math computational problems

- Making brief oral presentations

- Understanding academic presentations through the use of visuals, demonstrations, active participation, realia, etc.

- Understanding written texts through discussion, illustrations, and visuals

- Writing academic reports with the aid of outlines, structures, etc.

Example: Find and name the rivers on these two maps. The concepts included here are academically demanding. The context is rich in printed materials, pictures, models, demonstrations, and realia (West Virginia Department of Education, 2003).

School District of Indian River County
1990 25th Street
Vero Beach, FL 32960
(561) 564-3000

Quadrant A
Low Non-Academic
High Context-Embedded

Quadrant B
Academic/Cognitively Demanding
Context Embedded

Quadrant C: Non-academic or Cognitively Undemanding Context-Reduced (Without Clues):

Activities:

* Engaging in predictable telephone conversations

* Reading and writing personal purposes: notes, lists, sketches, etc.

Example: Juan, write the days of the week on this piece of paper. These concepts tend to be somewhat mentally demanding. The context is low and somewhat abstract (West Virginia Department of Education, 2003).

Quadrant D: Cognitively Demanding (Hard)/Context-Reduced (Without Clues):

– lecture is one activity

Activities:

different from Quadrant B for it's context reduced (w/o clues)

* Understanding academic presentations without visuals or demonstrations: lectures

* Making formal oral presentations

* Solving math word problems without illustrations

* Writing compositions, essays, and research reports in content areas

* Reading for information in content areas

* Taking standardized achievement tests

Example: Explain the theory of gravity. The concepts involved in this situation are academically demanding. The context is low, not concrete, and more abstract than before. This is the most difficult area of language (West Virginia Department of Education, 2003).

Assessment

The following are descriptions of different types of assessments used to assess students in the classroom (Badia, 1996; ESCORT, 1998; Franco, 1997; Katz, 2000; and Willig & Lee, 1996):

Objective assessment refers to testing that requires the selection of one item from a list of choices provided with the question. This type of assessment includes true-false responses, yes-no answers, and questions with multiple-choice answers.

Alternative assessment refers to other (non-traditional) options used to assess students' learning. When using this type of assessment, the teacher is not basing student progress only on the results of a single test or set of evidence. Some of the forms of this type of assessment include portfolios, journals, notebooks, projects, and presentations.

under alternative

Authentic assessment is a form of alternative assessment that incorporates real-life functions and applications.

CLOZE (gap-filling) tests or dictations (Katz, 2000, p. 143) "are examples of integrative tests. On these tests, students draw on several language skill areas — for example, reading, syntax, and morphology — as well as the context of the language text used in the testing situation." In some cases, more than one correct answer might be acceptable. They are reading tests that also provide an indication of overall language ability and consist of passages from which words are omitted at regular intervals.

Performance assessment (often used interchangeably with authentic assessment) requires the completion of a task, communicating information, or constructing a response that demonstrates knowledge or understanding of a skill or concept.

Naturalistic assessment involves evaluation that is based on the natural setting of the classroom. It involves the observation of students' performance and behavior in an informal context. The students' use of language in the classroom is assessed through observation.

A test of language dominance evaluates listening, speaking, reading, and/or writing skills in two languages by focusing on language contrasts rather than absolute levels of competence. The teacher can compare the performance, judge the relative strengths between the oral and written dimensions of both languages, and then decide which language best conveys content in the subject areas.

A test of language competence assesses vocabulary, control of structure, understanding of words in context, awareness of sounds, grammar, and syntax, or any combination of language skills. The content and form of this type of test depends on the purpose for its administration.

An achievement test battery is composed of sub-tests of language and usually includes the testing of reading comprehension, parts of speech, spelling, punctuation, and/or other technical aspects of language.

A **diagnostic language test** is developed to identify a student's strengths and weaknesses. The test content may be selected from a variety of language dimensions, depending upon the kind of information sought and the completeness of the diagnosis needed. Speech therapists or psychologists in clinical settings administer most of these tests individually.

A **language proficiency test** assesses how well students have met predetermined standards in language with the content specifically matched to the curriculum. The current trend is to require that students pass this type of proficiency test to demonstrate certain language skills required to receive a high school diploma. These tests usually use locally set criterion-referenced measures.

Standardized language tests include syntax measures, vocabulary tests, reading tests, tests of basic skills, and other published measures, and provide useful information about students' language skills. Their validity and reliability depends on three basic assumptions: a) students have been equally exposed to the test content in an instructional program, b) students know the language of the test directions and the test responses, and c) students just like those taking the test have been included in the standardization samples to establish norms and make inferences.

In general, the following considerations should be taken into account when selecting a language test:

- the nature of the information it may provide (more than two hundred dimensions of language can be appraised and most of the language instruments now available assess fewer than twelve of them),

Soundness of a lang. test or what is known as the instrument.

reliability validity

- the soundness (including validity and reliability) of the instrument, and

- the appropriateness of the test content.

Language tests should be used cautiously and supplemented by structured observations and interviews, consideration of family life variables, review of school records, and combination of different assessment methods. The student should be considered as a whole.

The assessment of ESOL students should include traditional and alternative assessment techniques. The assessment tasks should match the lesson taught.

Teachers should not teach one way and assess another way. Some **evaluative techniques** to use **with LEP students** are:

1. Observation (including observational checklists to observe behaviors and record correct oral responses)

2. Oral responses

3. Dramatizations

4. Drawings

5. Interviews

6. Demonstrations: Have the student(s) demonstrate understanding of procedures and/or skills

7. Projects

8. Checklists

9. Multiple Choice

10. Fill-in-the-blank with word banks

Always be aware that many LEP students are from cultures where students do not question a teacher, which includes asking questions when they do not understand. They may understand the concept but not the words. Try to make sure they understand both the concept and the words.

References

Further reading of these references may enhance understanding of the competency and may also increase performance on the examination.

Asher, J. *Learning Another Language Through Actions: The Complete Teacher's Guidebook* 2nd ed. Los Gatos, California: Sky Oaks Publications, Inc., 1982.

Badia, A. *Language Arts Through ESOL: A Guide for ESOL Teachers and Administrators.* Florida Department of Education, Office of Multicultural Student Language Education, 1996. [Also from World Wide Web: http://www.firn.edu/doe/omsle/egtoc.htm]

Cazden, C. B. "Adult Assistance to Language Developments: Scaffolding, Models and Direct Instruction." In *Developing Literacy: Young Children's Use of Language*, edited by R. P. Parker and F. A. Davis. Newark, DE: International Reading Association, 1983.

Chamot, A. U., and O'Malley, J. M. *The CALLA Handbook: Implementing the Cognitive Academic Language Learning Approach.* New York: Addison-Wesley Publishing Company, 1994.

Collier, V. P. *Promoting Academic Success for ESL Students: Understanding Second Language Acquisition for School.* NJTESOL-BE, 1995.

Collier, V. P. "A Synthesis of Studies Examining Long-term Language Minority Student Data on Academic Achievement." *Bilingual Research Journal,* 16 (1-2), (1992): 187-212.

Collier, V. P., and Thomas, W. P. "Two Languages Are Better Than One." *Educational Leadership* (55), (4), (December 1997/January 1998): 23-26.

Cummins, J. "The Role of Primary Language Development in Promoting Educational Success for Language Minority Students." In *Schooling and Language Minority Students: A Theoretical Rationale* (3-49), ed. by California State Department of Education. Los Angeles, CA: California State University, 1981.

Cummins, J. "Tests, Achievement, and Bilingual Students." *Focus,* No. 9. February 1, 1982. Wheaton, MD: National Clearinghouse for Bilingual Education.

Diaz-Rico, L. T., and Weed, K. Z. *The Crosscultural, Language and Academic Development Handbook: A Complete K-12 Reference Guide.* Boston: Allyn Bacon, 1995.

Dixon, C., and Nessel, D. *Language Experience Approach to Reading (and Writing).* Hayward, CA: The Alemany Press, 1983.

Eastern Stream Center on Resources and Training (ESCORT) (1998). Help! They Don't Speak English Starter Kit: A Resource Guide for Educators of Limited English Proficient Migrant Students, Grades Pre-K-6 (3rd Ed.). Charleston, West Virginia: AEL (Region IV Comprehensive Center: http://www.ael.org/ourwork or Region XIV Comprehensive Center: http://www.ets.org/ccxiv

Franco, L. "A Guide to Assist Parents in Understanding Alternative Assessments Which Focus on Limited English Speaking Students." In *Center for Applied Linguisics and Region XIV Comprehensive Center – ETS,* 1997.

Goodman, K. S.; Goodman, Y. M.; and Hood, W. J. (Eds.). *The Whole Language Evaluation Book.* Portsmouth, NH: Heinemann Educational Books, Inc., 1989.

Jameson, J. "From Theory to Practice: Three Principles for Success: English Language Learners in Mainstream Content Classes." *Center for Applied Linguisics and Region XIV Comprehensive Center – ETS, 1998.* [World Wide Web document retrieved October 23, 2003: http://www.cal.org/cc14/ttp6.htm]

Katz, A. "Changing Paradigms for Assessment." In *Implementing the ESL Standards for Pre-K-12 Students Through Teacher Education* edited by Snow, M. A. Bloomington, Illinois: Teachers of English to Speakers of Other Languages (TESOL), 2000.

Krashen S. D. *The Input Hypothesis: Issues and Implications*. New York: Longman, 1985.

Ninio, A., and Brunner, J. S. "The Achievements and Antecedents of Labeling." *Journal of Child Language,* 5, 1-15, 1976.

Nunan, D. "Closing the Gap Between Learning and Instruction." *TESOL Quarterly*, 29 (1), 133-158, 1995.

Schultz, R. A. "Foreign Language Education in the United States: Trends and Challenges." *ERIC Review*, 6 (1), 6-13, 1998.

Tomas, E., and Robinson, H. *Improving Reading in Every Class: A Source Book for Teachers*. Boston: Allyn & Bacon, 1972.

Vygotsky, L. S. *Mind in Society: The Development of Higher Psychological Processes* (M. Cole, V. John-Steiner, S. Scribner & E. Souberman, Eds. & Trans.). Cambridge, MA: Harvard University Press, 1978. (Original work published, 1955)

West Virginia Department of Education (2003). West Virginia Connections: Bridging Linguistic and Cultural Differences: Toolkit for Connecting Classroom Best Practices and Limited English Proficient Students. Retrieved September 22, 2003 from http://wvconnections.k12.wv.us

Willig, A., and Lee, C. (Eds.) (1996). Empowering ESOL Teachers: An Overview. Tallahassee: Florida Department of Education.

FTCE

Florida Teacher Certification Exam
Professional Education Test

Practice Tests

Practice Test 1

(handwritten: 120 / -95 / (75) passed   35 wrong)

(handwritten: 2nd take   24 wrong   120 / -24 / (96) passed)

(Answer sheets appear in the back of this book.)

TIME: Two and one-half hours
120 Questions

DIRECTIONS: Read each item and select the best response. Mark your responses on the answer sheet provided.

---

1. A student portfolio

   (A) contains artwork by a student.

   (B) is used to compare student work.

   (C) is graded on a scale.

   (D) contains documents and/or products to show the student's progress.

2. What is the narrative report approach?

   (A) Students describe how they feel they are doing.

   (B) A formal report card written by the teacher.

   (C) Teachers provide parents with a written assessment of a student's progress.

   (D) Parents and teacher discuss a student's attitudes about learning.

3. A student's permanent school record should be discussed with the

   (A) student's parents/legal guardians, current teachers, and school administrators.

   (B) parents only.

   (C) school administrators only.

   (D) school administrators and parents only.

4. When are students more likely to score higher on a test?

   (A) When the questions are multiple choice.

   (B) When they are not coached by a teacher.

   (C) When they are familiar with the test format and content.

   (D) When the format is always changing.

5. Teachers can provide a positive testing environment by

   (A) encouraging students to be anxious about a test.

   (B) providing a comfortable physical setting.

   (C) surprising students with disruptions and distractions.

   (D) emphasizing the consequences for poor performance.

6. If mastery level for a skill is set at 75%, what does the student need to accomplish to exhibit mastery?

   (A) a grade of C or higher.

   (B) a grade of B or higher.

   (C) answer 75% of all of the particular skill questions correctly.

   (D) answer 75% of all of the skills correctly.

7. When a teacher asks the class if they agree or disagree with a student's response, the teacher is using

    (A) redirect.

    (B) corrective.

    (C) positive feedback.

    (D) direct response.

8. Written academic feedback is most productive when it

    (A) is delayed by a day.

    (B) is uniform.

    (C) includes at least one positive remark.

    (D) is not specific.

9. Before working with mathematical word problems, a teacher needs to determine that

    (A) the student can complete the math unit.

    (B) the student is at a high enough reading level to understand the problems.

    (C) the math textbook mirrors the skills used in the word problems.

    (D) the class will be on-task for the problems.

10. Goals for individual students

    (A) should be based upon the student's academic record.

    (B) should be the same for all students.

    (C) are created from individual observations only.

    (D) are developed after considering the student's history and motivation.

11. Feedback sessions for a test are most effective

    (A) when they are immediate.

    (B) when they are delayed by a day or so.

    (C) when they are delayed for a few weeks.

    (D) when the feedback is written on paper only.

12. Good and Gouws found that effective teachers reviewed

    (A) verbally.

    (B) at the end of a lesson.

    (C) as students showed weaknesses in specific areas.

    —(D) daily, weekly, and monthly.

13. A student describes an analysis of a recent Presidential address for the class. The teacher replies, "You have provided us with a most interesting way of looking at this issue!" The teacher is using

    (A) simple positive response.

    (B) negative response.

    (C) redirect.

    (D) academic praise.

14. Effective praise should be

    (A) authentic and low-key.

    (B) used sparingly.

    (C) composed of simple, positive responses.

    (D) used to encourage high-achieving students.

15. While waiting for students to formulate their responses to a question, a student blurts out an answer. The teacher should

    (A) ignore the answer entirely.

    (B) respond immediately to the student's answer.

    —(C) silently acknowledge the student's response, and then address the response after the question has been answered by someone else.

    (D) move on to another question without comment.

16. What is one way of incorporating non-performers into a discussion?

    —(A) Ask a student to respond to a previous student's statement.

    (B) Name a student to answer a question.

    (C) Only call on students with their hands raised.

    (D) Allow off-topic conversations.

17. When a teacher leads choral chants, the teacher is

    (A) practicing aural skills.

    (B) practicing vocal exercises.

    (C) having students repeat basic skills orally.   *5X10=50*

    (D) repeating what the students answer.

18. If a teacher asks, "Does everyone understand where to place their answers?" the teacher is probably

    (A) using a transition between lessons.

    (B) determining if the class understands the directions.

    (C) assuming that the students were off-task.

    (D) introducing a new skill.

19. Teachers convey emotion through

    (A) body language, eye contact, and verbal cues.

    (B) verbal contact and cues.

    (C) voice levels.

    (D) the way they listen.

20. Controlled interruptions

    (A) can be positively directed with procedures already in place.

    (B) should be monitored on a case-by-case basis.

    (C) are inevitable in a classroom.

    (D) do not disrupt the classroom.

21. "You seem to feel that you aren't doing well in this subject" is an example of a(n)

    (A) evaluative statement.

    (B) directive statement.

    (C) nondirective statement.

    (D) judgment.

22. Which of the following is a trait of effective professional development?

    (A) a continuous plan of lifelong learning

    (B) activities developed solely by the principal

    (C) a one-hour stand-alone workshop

    (D) a totally theory-based program

23. The method by which teachers gather information on their teaching through the use of audio and video tapes is called

    (A) case methods

    (B) action research

    (C) reflective learning communities

    (D) mentors

24. Student data such as scores on tests and assignments would be the best criteria for determining which of the following?

    (A) only the students' academic grades

    (B) behavior assessment

    (C) student grades and the teacher's quality of instruction

    (D) student grades and behavior assessment

25. Results of the FCAT test indicate that a teacher's students did poorly on the mathematics problem solving section, while students in another class-room in the same school did much better. What would be the best action for the teacher of the students who did poorly to take?

    (A) Look at her students' scores from last year to justify their poor achievement.

    (B) Tell future students to study harder because that section is hard.

    (C) Suggest that parents hire a math tutor.

    (D) Ask the other teacher to share strategies that she used to help make her students successful.

26. The purpose of a mentor is to

    (A) supervise new teachers.

    (B) inform the principal of problems.

(C) keep track of resources given to a new teacher.

(D) promote and support peer teacher growth.

27. Teachers, researchers and policymakers have indicated the greatest challenge to implementing effective professional development is due to the lack of

(A) presenters

(B) time

(C) resources

(D) interested teachers

28. The question, "What was the name of Hamlet's father?" is

(A) a high-order question of evaluation.

(B) a low-order question that can be used to begin a discussion.

(C) a transition.

(D) questioning a skill.

29. Piaget's theory of cognitive development states that

(A) children should be able to understand complex directions.

(B) younger children are unable to understand complex language.

(C) younger children will be unable to understand directions, even in simple language.

(D) directions should not be given to young children.

30. Children under the age of eight

(A) are unable to answer questions.

(B) process information more slowly than older children.

(C) can answer the same questions as slightly older children.

(D) cannot learn in a cooperative environment.

31. Marshall Rosenberg categorized learners as

(A) rigid-inhibited, undisciplined, acceptance-anxious, and creative.

(B) undisciplined and high-achieving.

(C) undisciplined, disciplined, and high-achieving.

(D) fearful, undisciplined, and disciplined.

32. Inductive thinking can be fostered through which activity?

(A) choral chanting of skill tables

(B) computer experience

(C) multiple-choice questions

(D) personal-discovery activities

33. How can a teacher elicit a high-order response from a student who provides simple responses?

(A) Ask follow-up questions.

(B) Repeat the questions.

(C) Ask the same questions of a different student.

(D) Ask another student to elaborate on the original response.

34. Bloom divided educational objectives into which of the following domains?

(A) knowledge, affective, and evaluation

(B) cognitive, affective, and psychomotor

(C) affective, value judgments, and psychomotor

(D) knowledge, comprehension, and application

35. Long-term memory

(A) will disappear in approximately 20 seconds unless rehearsed.

(B) is very limited.

(C) is permanent and appears unlimited.

(D) will exist for a few months unless rehearsed.

36. Students are presented with the following problem: "Bill is taller than Ann, but Ann is taller than Grace. Is Ann the tallest child or is Bill the tallest?" This question requires students to use

(A) inductive reasoning.

(B) deductive reasoning.

(C) hypothesis formation.

(D) pattern identification.

37. A teacher asks her eighth-grade English students to select a career they would enjoy when they grow up and then find three sources on the World Wide Web with information about that career. She tells the students that they must find out how much education is required for this career. If the career requires post-secondary education, then the student must find a school or college that provides this education and find out how long it will take to be educated or trained for this career. Through this assignment, the teacher is helping her students to

(A) explore short-term personal and academic goals.

(B) explore long-term personal and academic goals.

(C) evaluate short-term personal and academic goals.

(D) synthesize long-term personal and academic goals.

38. When a teacher asks a student, "When you were studying for your spelling test, did you remember a mnemonic we talked about in class for spelling principal that 'a principal is your pal'?," the teacher is

(A) leading the student in a divergent thinking exercise.

(B) teaching the student mnemonics, or memory devices.

(C) asking questions to guide the student in correcting an error.

(D) modeling inductive reasoning skills for the student.

39. Using student ideas and interests in a lesson

(A) takes students off-task.

(B) detracts from the subject content.

(C) does not allow for evaluation of students' prior knowledge.

(D) increases learning and student motivation.

40. If a child in your class suffers from serious emotional disturbances, it is important to

(A) maintain open communication with the parents.

(B) keep the child separate from the other students.

(C) only discuss the student with other teachers.

(D) keep an eye on attendance.

41. When working with ESL students, the teacher should be aware that

(A) students should only speak English in class.

— (B) an accepting classroom and encouraging lessons will foster learning.

(C) the student should be referred to a specialist.

(D) limiting the number of resources available is beneficial to the students.

42. Student Teams-Achievement Divisions (STAD) uses

(A) homogeneous groups, elements of competition, and rewards.

(B) preparation, presentation, practice, and evaluation.

(C) heterogeneous groups, elements of competition, and rewards.

(D) description, content, practice, review, and follow-up.

43. Sequential language acquisition occurs when students

(A) learn a second language after mastery of the first.

(B) learn a second language at the same time as the first.

(C) learn two languages in parts.

(D) develop language skills.

44. Teachers should provide a variety of experiences and concrete examples for children with reading difficulties since some children

(A) come from environments with limited language exposure.

(B) have poor learning habits.

(C) have trouble distinguishing letters.

(D) can speak well, but have difficulty reading.

45. A teacher writes on the board "All men are created equal" and asks each student to explain the meaning of the statement. One student says that it means that all people are equal, but another student says that it just applies to men, and a third student says that it is a lie because not all people are equally good at all things; for example, some people can run faster than others and some can sing better than others. The teacher's instructional aim is to

    (A) see if students can reach consensus on the meaning of the statement.

    (B) see how well students can defend their beliefs.

    (C) provoke the students to disagree with the statement.

    (D) engage the students in critical thinking and to allow them to express their opinions.

46. If the other students laugh when a first-grade girl says, "I want to be a truck driver when I grow up" and tell her that "Girls can't drive big trucks," what should the teacher do?

    (A) Tell the class to quiet down, that the student can be whatever she wants to be when she grows up.

    (B) Tell the class that most truck drivers are men.

    (C) Tell the class that women and men can both be truck drivers, depending on their skills.

    (D) Ask the class to vote on whether women should be truck drivers.

47. An educator in the State of Florida has obligations to the student, the public community at large, and to

    (A) the administration.

    (B) fellow professionals.

    (C) the profession.

    (D) the body of students that advocates school policies.

48. The State of Florida Code of Ethics mandates that the student

    (A) have encouragement from the teacher to be well-rounded.

    (B) have protection from illegal substances.

(C) should not be restrained from individual pursuit of learning outside the classroom.

(D) seek protection in the teacher from a difficult home environment.

49. An educator in the State of Florida should do all of the following EXCEPT

(A) allow students full access to diverse points of view.

(B) not harass a student on the basis of race, color, religion, or sex.

(C) not discriminate against a student based on race, color, religion, or sex.

(D) make the effort to ensure every student's protection from harassment or discrimination.

50. A senior in high school who runs for the track team is drafted by one of the major colleges. The student has become something of a celebrity now. The student's coach, who was instrumental in ensuring the placement at the top college, plans to ask the student to speak with incoming freshmen and their parents to recruit for the high school's track team. The coach

(A) should have reservations about this course of action, because the Code of Ethics dictates that the student deserves protection from the public.

(B) should follow through with this plan, because the Code of Ethics says that identifiable information can be disclosed for professional purposes.

(C) should not follow through, because the educator should not exploit the relationship with the student for personal gain or advantage.

(D) should have reservations about this plan, because an educator should not intentionally expose a student to unnecessary embarrassment or disparagement.

51. A high school student approaches a teacher who is considered to be a student mentor. The teacher generally does what she can for the students, speaks with the administration about fundraisers and stands behind the students' freedom of speech. The student wants the teacher to help start a tradition at the high school: a Christmas tree that could stand at the front of the school from Thanksgiving vacation until the start of the New Year. The teacher, who likes the idea,

   (A) should help support the tree, as an ethical teacher should not reasonably deny a student access to diverse points of view.

   (B) should direct the student's conversation to the principal, because her own views should not be revealed to the student.

   (C) should support the tree, because the student has a legal right to freedom of speech.

   (D) should carefully tell the student that her own views are irrelevant to the matter and that she supports the idea, but professionally, she cannot help.

52. A teacher leaving for school in the morning promises his wife that he will make copies of their son's birthday party invitations and then fax his medical records to the insurance company. As he rushes out to his car at 6:00 P.M., he realizes that he has done neither of these things. This teacher

   (A) should hurry if he wants to make it home for dinner.

   (B) would be violating the Code of Ethics if he walked back into the school to copy the invitations, though the medical records are a necessity and considered to be ethically sound.

   (C) would be violating the Code of Ethics to fax the medical records, as the teacher must follow all legal guidelines concerning public documents, though the party invitations are minor, and therefore, ethically sound.

   (D) would be violating the Code of Ethics to use his fax and copy privileges at the school for personal gain.

53. Which of the following can we conclude from Jean Piaget's theory of human development?

   (A) Children cannot learn a given concept until they learn the concepts that sequentially precede it.

   (B) Judgments are made on the basis of physical consequences.

   (C) The classroom should be arranged to facilitate learning.

(D) Humans are born with an innate ability to recognize letters and numbers.

54. According to Erikson's theory of social development, when will students begin to develop a sense of initiative?

(A) birth to two years of age

(B) two to six years of age

(C) six to twelve years of age

(D) twelve years of age to adult

55. A student is intrinsically motivated to participate in a given activity if the student

(A) participates in the activity because he or she enjoys the activity.

(B) participates in the activity because he or she enjoys the consequence or result of the activity.

(C) refuses to participate in the activity because he or she does not enjoy the consequence of the activity.

(D) refuses to participate in the activity because he or she does not enjoy the activity.

56. Goals for individual students should be

(A) based upon the student's academic record only.

(B) the same for all students.

(C) created from individual observations only.

(D) developed using information from their academic ability, developmental level, and individual experience.

57. An essential component to providing appropriate accommodations is to

(A) treat everyone the same.

(B) provide individualized assessment to identify the individual needs for each student.

(C) use a token economy.

(D) reinforce attempts for appropriate behavior in the classroom setting.

58. Teachers who apply behavioral learning theory in practice

    (A) create educational environments in which educational stimuli can be presented and behavioral responses can be observed and measured.

    (B) focus on academic and cognitive developmental stages to guide instruction and lesson planning.

    (C) teach students by modeling and using individual students as examples for others to follow.

    (D) use manipulatives to teach math for students under the age of eleven.

59. An example of cognitive learning theory in practice would be using

    (A) drill and practice.

    (B) peer examples.

    (C) manipulatives to teach math for students under the age of eleven.

    (D) a reward system.

60. According to social learning theory, students learn by

    (A) observing the behavior of others.

    (B) completing drill and practice activities.

    (C) using manipulatives.

    (D) focusing on academic and cognitive developmental stages.

61. While the teacher is reading aloud to the class, Linda is telling jokes to get her peers to laugh. According to behavioral theory, what is a possible hypothesis for the function of Linda's behavior?

    (A) Linda tells jokes to make her peers laugh, which may serve to gain attention for Linda or may serve to distract the teacher from the lesson, which allows Linda to escape academic tasks.

    (B) Linda tells jokes to make the teacher angry.

    (C) Linda obviously has trouble at home and therefore this is an issue her parents need to deal with.

    (D) Linda enjoys the performing arts.

62. According to the operant model in behavioral theory, negative reinforcement is

    (A) operant behavior.

    (B) stimulus for operant behavior.

    (C) unknowingly strengthening negative behavior.

    (D) removing a stimulus which causes a behavior to increase.

63. Students diagnosed with autism spectrum disorder would NOT exhibit which of the following due to the disorder

    (A) a delay in communication/language.

    (B) a delay in social skill development.

    (C) stereotyped or repetitive behaviors.

    (D) a delay in physical growth and development.

64. If a teacher notices that her/his students are having difficulty with reading from the textbook, she/he needs to

    (A) determine if the text is at an appropriate reading level for the students.

    (B) encourage the students to raise questions about the material.

    (C) suggest the students reread the material.

    (D) all of the above

65. In order to help students learn strategies to improve reading comprehension of subject area material, the teacher should

    (A) help them remember skills taught in earlier grades.

    (B) explicitly teach the strategies.

    (C) explain that the reading is not as hard as it seems.

    (D) call attention to the problems the students are having.

66. When the teacher uses graphic organizers to present a topic, he/she is

    (A) trying to make the presentation more attractive.

    (B) attempting to use scientific methodology in teaching.

    (C) helping to make learning more visual and concrete.

(D) appealing to the artistic talent of some students.

67. In using audio-visual aids, the teacher should

(A) use those that were recommended by friends and colleagues.

(B) carefully screen them prior to use to make sure they enhance curricular objectives.

(C) use at least one per lesson and several per unit.

(D) be sure to use them at the beginning of the period.

68. Cooperative learning is an example of a

(A) strategy applicable to interdisciplinary instruction.

(B) classroom management strategy.

(C) strategy only to be used in secondary classrooms.

(D) time-saving technique.

69. When using videos or films in the classroom, it is best to

(A) show the film completely from beginning to end.

(B) make sure it will take up the entire period.

(C) show the film without introduction for maximum effect.

(D) stop the film from time to time for discussion and note-taking.

70. In the middle of a discussion, a student asks to sharpen a pencil in response to an academic question. The teacher should

(A) see if the pencil needs to be sharpened.

(B) allow the student to sharpen the pencil.

(C) signal no, and then ask someone else the question.

(D) repeat the question to the student.

71. "After you finish reading the passage, get out your history books and read the next section" is a

(A) teacher redirect.

(B) high-order activity.

(C) transition statement.

(D) test of complex skills.

72. One benefit of using transition statements is that

— (A) students are oriented to the classroom pace.

    (B) non-performers are being tested.

    (C) it enables high-order questioning.

    (D) it determines if students understand the directions.

73. Changing to an interactive approach, switching to a cooperative group activity, and incorporating manipulatives during the course of a lesson are examples of

    (A) alternate behavior.

    (B) getting students back on-task.

    (C) management transition.

    (D) skill practice.

74. Which of the following is a useful way of bringing a daydreaming student back on-task?

    (A) Call on the student.

— (B) Walk over and stand near the student.

    (C) Question the class.

    (D) Stop and stare at the student.

75. A teacher tells a class that when a task is completed, book exercises should be worked on. This teacher is using

    (A) a transition.

    (B) wait-time avoidance.

    (C) taking students off-task.

    (D) wait time.

76. If a teacher is considered to be "with it," that teacher

— (A) is always aware of what is going on in the classroom.

    (B) wears modern clothes.

    (C) understands student trends.

    (D) uses language that the students relate to.

77. "Invitational learning" is the result of

    (A) a well-built classroom space.

    (B) use of good teaching voice.

    (C) fun classroom exercises.

    (D) good lighting.

78. What is one skill demonstrated by invitational teachers?

    (A) They are separate from the students.

    (B) They ignore student feelings.

    (C) They use the behavioral method approach.

    (D) They are active listeners.

79. Cooperative groups help to develop the students' abilities to

    (A) avoid misbehavior.

    (B) develop logic skills.

    (C) interact with their peers.

    (D) stay on-task.

80. What is the self-fulfilling prophecy?

    (A) Students produce work that matches their personal expectations.

    (B) Teachers can predict student progress.

    (C) Incorrect assumptions or beliefs become true because they are expected.

    (D) Students are unable to understand teacher expectations.

81. Kallison Jr. found that subject retention increased when lessons included

    (A) reviews.

    (B) comprehension checks.

    (C) outlines at the beginning and a summary at the end.

(D) lesson-initiating reviews.

82. What is one benefit of practice activities?

_   (A) The teacher can observe where students need additional instruction.

(B) The students can develop their creative writing skills.

(C) Students can revisit previously learned skills.

(D) Students can learn new concepts.

83. One use of homework is to

(A) introduce new concepts.

(B) provide structure to the classroom.

(C) develop short-term retention.

(D) revisit learned skills and concepts.

84. When assigning a specific writing exercise, it is best to

(A) assign a clear due date.

(B) describe what should be included and how it will be graded.

(C) allow students to write what they wish.

(D) describe how the paper was graded when it is returned.

85. If a teacher introduces a concept using examples and non-examples and asks the class to provide a definition of the concept, the teacher is considered to be teaching

(A) deductively.

(B) inductively.

(C) using definitions.

(D) using examples.

86. When teaching a concept, the teacher should provide

(A) examples and non-examples.

(B) several examples.

(C) only interesting examples.

(D) definitions.

87. Student learning is most successful when

~ (A) objectives are clearly outlined.

(B) colorful graphs and maps are used.

(C) the same examples are used.

(D) the classroom size is small.

88. How should learning activities be designed?

(A) They should be selected by the students.

⌐ (B) The activities should be based on specific objectives.

(C) They should test for knowledge.

(D) They should be used on a daily basis.

89. Objectives given to a class for student mastery

_ (A) should be tailored to students at all levels.

(B) should only be expected of certain students.

(C) should be ignored.

(D) are unnecessary.

90. A teacher ran out of copies of a worksheet before handing them out to the entire class, thus interrupting

(A) materials.

(B) class interest.

⌐(C) instructional momentum.

(D) passing out the papers.

91. A lesson where students are given a tankful of water and various objects and are asked to order the objects by weight would be considered a(n)

(A) science lesson.

— (B) discovery-learning lesson.

(C) inductive-reasoning lesson.

(D) eg-rule lesson.

92. When introducing academic laws, the teacher should

(A) teach related rules at the same time.

(B) state the rule and have the class repeat it.

(C) provide several examples.

(D) state the rule, provide examples, and provide exercises.

93. If a student incorrectly answers a question during a discussion, the teacher can guide the student to the correct answer by

(A) asking another student.

(B) providing the correct answer.

(C) asking the student a series of questions to guide him or her to the correct answer.

(D) assigning the question as homework.

94. In the beginning of the year, David was a quiet child. However, in the middle of the year he is starting to frequently shout out and cause disruptions. What should an effective teacher do first?

(A) Send David to the office.

(B) Talk to the school administration.

(C) Use verbal and nonverbal cues to try to modify the behavior.

(D) Contact David's parents.

95. When reprimanding a class, which is most effective?

(A) loud shouting

(B) the threat of harsh consequences

(C) using a soft voice

(D) angry outbursts

96. Canter and Canter's assertive discipline asserts that positive behavior should be

(A) the standard.

(B) positively reinforced.

(C) part of the classroom rules.

(D) not met with consequences.

97. Using the operant behavior model, what is negative reinforcement?

    (A) operant behavior

    (B) stimulus for operant behavior

    (C) unknowingly strengthening negative behavior

    (D) removing something unpleasant after the asserted or expected behavior has occurred

98. Robert always calls out answers to questions without raising his hand. The teacher always ignores his answers. The teacher is trying to use

    (A) negative reinforcement.

    (B) extinction.

    (C) noninterventionism.

    (D) punishment.

99. According to Rath's values clarification, most student misbehavior is the result of

    (A) a student's cognitive deficits.

    (B) the student's inability to view alternatives.

    (C) students not knowing or thinking about their values.

    (D) a lack of indicators.

100. Rules for computer use in a classroom should be determined and explained

    (A) before any student reaches a computer.

    (B) as students show their skill levels.

    (C) to each student individually.

    (D) six weeks after things have settled down.

101. How can computer software be used in a classroom?

    (A) to explore the Internet

(B) to record class computer skill growth

(C) for the class newspaper

(D) all of the choices listed are ways computer software can be used in a classroom.

102. If only one computer is available to a class, students should be able to use the computer

(A) singly or in small groups.

(B) if they are familiar with computers.

(C) only during full class instruction.

(D) to record class progress.

103. You suspect that one of your students suffers from some form of psychotic disorder. You should first

(A) talk to the student.

(B) contact your school administration.

(C) get a second opinion from another teacher.

(D) set up a meeting with the parents and the student.

104. If there is a tornado warning, your class should be

(A) evacuated from the building.

(B) on the top level of the building.

(C) in your classroom.

(D) in a first-floor room away from windows.

105. When teaching cooperative learning skills, the teacher should

(A) foster student independence.

(B) set up practice situations for skill mastery.

(C) allow the students to foster the skill on their own.

(D) form groups of students with various backgrounds.

106. The first Kindergarten was started by

(A) Benjamin Franklin.

(B) Friedrich Froebel.

(C) Maria Montessori.

(D) Johann Pestalozzi.

107. According to the Socratic method, teachers should

    (A) impart all of their knowledge to their students in ways they deem most appropriate.

    (B) ask questions to get students to think about universal truths.

    (C) ask questions so that students can show how much they know.

    (D) encourage students to ask questions which will enable them to learn.

108. The first children's book, Orbis Pictus, which could be used as an instructional tool, was written by

    (A) John Calvin

    (B) John Amos Comenius

    (C) Desiderius Erasmus

    (D) Jean-Jacques Rousseau

109. Johann Friedrich Herbart made all of the following contributions to education EXCEPT

    (A) the use of concrete objects called "gifts" to teach concepts.

    (B) the founding of a pedagogical seminary.

    (C) the founding of a demonstration school.

    (D) a five step teaching process including preparation, presentation, association, generalization, and application.

110. The first compulsory education law was passed in

    (A) Connecticut

    (B) Delaware

    (C) Massachusetts

    (D) New York

111. All of the following were true of education in the Southern colonies EXCEPT

    (A) private tutors were used to educate the sons of wealthy plantation owners.

    (B) the education of girls was limited to the knowledge of how to manage a household.

    (C) slaves were taught to read so that they could study the Bible.

    (D) teaching a slave to read or write was a criminal act.

112. An ESOL student is proficient in oral language; however, he continues to experience difficulty with academic language used in Science and Social Studies classes. The teacher believes academic proficiency correlates with oral language proficiency. What has the teacher failed to acknowledge in her analysis of the student's language proficiency?

    (A) Both basic interpersonal communication skills and cognitive academic language proficiency are needed for successful academic performance.

    (B) Basic interpersonal communication skills develop equally with cognitive academic language proficiency.

    (C) Basic interpersonal communication skills are criteria for successful academic performance.

    (D) Cognitive academic language proficiency is primary to basic interpersonal communication skills.

113. The two receptive basic language skills are

    (A) speaking and listening.

    (B) reading and writing.

    (C) reading and listening.

    (D) speaking and writing.

114. A student from a Hispanic culture is being reprimanded for fighting at school. Which of the following actions is the most culturally representative?

    (A) the child cries

    (B) the child looks downward

(C) the child looks at the teacher

(D) the child laughs

115. A school board committee from a district of a mixed population of English and Spanish speakers wants to set up a program at a local elementary school that includes the following components:

- Reading instruction in Spanish for all students

- Use of a Spanish-speaking teacher

- Delay of English reading until grade 2

- Pull-out ESOL for limited-and non-English speakers

- Conscious attention to Hispanic cultures

Which of the following models fits this committee's specifications?

(A) transitional bilingual education

(B) maintenance bilingual education

(C) one-way Spanish immersion

(D) two-way Spanish immersion

116. Which of the following are components of the natural approach?

(A) grammatical sequencing of material; reading and writing activities based on the grammar rules presented; bilingual vocabulary lists

(B) limited error correction; use of realia; lowered affective filter

(C) dialogues and pattern practice; sequencing of material based on contrastive analysis; aural-oral language

(D) use of conversations, games, and plays; new material introduced via dialogues; use of music and rhythmic breathing

117. Which is the national professional organization that represents teachers of students who speak another language?

(A) IRA

(B) FFLA

(C) NABE

(D) TESOL

118. An elementary school wishes to choose a social studies textbook to be used by mainstream classroom teachers that are working with native speakers of English and ESOL students at different language proficiency levels. Which features would be the most appropriate for the selection?

    (A) Review questions and a vocabulary list at the end of each chapter unit reviews that include a variety of research questions for individual or group investigation and an activity book with vocabulary activities and essay prompts.

    (B) vocabulary list and pretest at the beginning of each chapter; review questions, posttest, and cooperative activities at the end of each chapter with full-page illustrations.

    (C) large boldface section headings in each chapter; review questions at the end of each section, summary questions at the end of each chapter with important vocabulary highlighted in blue.

    (D) an overview and activity to build schema at the beginning of each chapter; summaries, questions, and extension activities at the end of each chapter; pictures, graphs, and charts.

119. A high school teacher wants to help her LEP students with an American history unit. Which of the following is the best strategy?

    (A) Providing a translation of the American history book.

    (B) Highlighting main ideas and key concepts in the textbook.

    (C) Keeping students after school for individual tutoring.

    (D) Showing history films and videos.

120. Which of the following is the first step a teacher should take for a student with possible exceptionalities?

    (A) Making an appointment with the principal.

    (B) Testing the student for an exceptionality.

    (C) Placing the student in an appropriate ESL program.

    (D) Contacting the parents to schedule a LEP conference.

Answer Key

1. (D)	31. (A)	61. (A)	91. (B)
2. (C)	32. (D)	62. (D)	92. (D)
3. (A)	33. (A)	63. (D)	93. (C)
4. (C)	34. (B)	64. (D)	94. (C)
5. (B)	35. (C)	65. (B)	95. (C)
6. (C)	36. (B)	66. (C)	96. (B)
7. (A)	37. (B)	67. (B)	97. (D)
8. (C)	38. (C)	68. (A)	98. (B)
9. (B)	39. (D)	69. (D)	99. (C)
10. (D)	40. (A)	70. (C)	100. (A)
11. (B)	41. (B)	71. (C)	101. (D)
12. (D)	42. (C)	72. (A)	102. (A)
13. (D)	43. (A)	73. (B)	103. (B)
14. (A)	44. (A)	74. (B)	104. (D)
15. (C)	45. (D)	75. (A)	105. (D)
16. (A)	46. (C)	76. (A)	106. (B)
17. (C)	47. (C)	77. (A)	107. (B)
18. (B)	48. (C)	78. (D)	108. (B)
19. (A)	49. (D)	79. (C)	109. (A)
20. (A)	50. (C)	80. (C)	110. (C)
21. (C)	51. (D)	81. (C)	111. (C)
22. (A)	52. (D)	82. (A)	112. (D)
23. (B)	53. (A)	83. (D)	113. (C)
24. (C)	54. (B)	84. (B)	114. (B)
25. (D)	55. (A)	85. (B)	115. (B)
26. (D)	56. (D)	86. (A)	116. (B)
27. (B)	57. (B)	87. (A)	117. (D)
28. (B)	58. (A)	88. (B)	118. (C)
29. (B)	59. (C)	89. (A)	119. (B)
30. (B)	60. (A)	90. (C)	120. (D)

Detailed Explanations
of Answers

FTCE

PRACTICE TEST 1

1. **D**

   A portfolio keeps a collection of dated samples of a student's work over time. There can be a single portfolio for all subjects, or portfolios for specific subjects. The work contained in a portfolio then becomes an accurate representation of a student's progress. It may contain artwork by a student, but is not limited to artwork (A). It is not used to draw comparisons between students (B), nor is the project graded on a scale (C).

2. **C**

   Teachers compose narrative reports which describe a student's strengths, weaknesses, behaviors, progress, and any other information to supplement the information that is conveyed in a report card. They can be used if a parent cannot attend a parent-teacher conference, for example. (A) is incorrect because it is the teacher, not the student, who describes how the student is performing. It is not a formal report card (B), but is used to supplement the information on the report card. (D) is also incorrect because narrative reports can be used as an alternative to parent-teacher conferences.

3. **A**

A student's permanent record, which is a file containing all aspects of a student's background, should only be discussed with the student's parents, legal guardians, teachers, and school administrators. It is a highly personal and comprehensive student record. It may be discussed with the student's parents (B), or the school administrators (C), but is not limited only to school administrators and parents (D). Teachers also have the right to discuss the student's record. Therefore, (B), (C), and (D) are incorrect.

4. **C**

Research has shown that students perform better on tests when they are familiar with the test content and test format. It does not matter if the test contains a particular type of question (A), as long as the students know what to expect. Students have greater success in testing situations when their teacher is enthusiastic about their results (B). Students perform poorly when the test format changes frequently (D).

5. **B**

Students are able to perform better on tests when their physical setting, which includes lighting, temperature, and seating, is favorable. When students feel anxious over a test (A), or when teachers threaten against poor performances (D), students do not perform as well. Outside disruptions (C) can break a student's concentration, most specifically in younger children.

6. **C**

When a teacher sets a mastery level at a certain percentage and the student reaches that percentage, he or she is considered to have mastered that skill and receives a grade of "A" for his or her efforts. Therefore, (A) and (B) are incorrect. Answering 75% of all of the skills correctly (D) is also incorrect because in order to master a particular skill, the student does not need to master all of the skills.

7. **A**

A redirect (A) occurs when a teacher asks one student to react to the response of another student. A corrective (B) occurs when a teacher responds to a student error by explaining why it is an error and then provides a correct answer. When teachers are redirecting, they are not giving any feedback (C), nor are they directly responding to the student comments (D).

8. **C**

Written academic feedback should contain specific comments on errors and how to improve them. It should also contain a positive remark that notes an aspect of the assignment that was done well. Therefore, delaying feedback by a day (A), specifying uniform guidelines (B), and presenting feedback in a vague manner (D) are not the correct answer choices.

9. **B**

It is important to ensure that the word problems given to students are at their reading level; otherwise, a teacher will be unable to evaluate their successes with these problems accurately. (A), (C), and (D) are not the best answers to the question.

10. **D**

Individual goals for a student should be developed after reviewing both the student's history and assessing the student's motivation. This will ensure that the goals can be met by the student. Goals should not be based solely on the student's academic record (A) or created from individual observations only (C). They should also not be the same for all students (B) since students learn at different levels and aim for different goals.

11. **B**

Research has shown that it is favorable to provide feedback in test situations when the feedback is delayed by a day or so, rather than giving immediate feedback (A). Delaying the feedback session for a few weeks is not beneficial to the students because too much time has elapsed (C). A class review of the test has been shown to be more beneficial in clearing up misunderstandings than handwritten notations (D).

12. **D**

Good and Gouws found that effective teachers conducted reviews as part of their daily, weekly, and monthly routines. Therefore, (A), (B), and (C) are incorrect because they were not findings in their study.

13. **D**

Academic praise is composed of specific statements that give information about the value of the object or about its implications. A simple positive response (A) does not provide any information other than the praise, such as the example, "That's a good answer!" There is nothing negative (B) about the teacher's response. A redirect (C) occurs when a teacher asks a student to react to the response of another student.

14. **A**

Praise has been shown to be the most effective when it is authentic and low-key (A). It should be used frequently; therefore (B) is incorrect. It should consist of complex responses that provide information about the reasons for the quality of the student response; therefore (C) is incorrect. It should be used to provide all students with positive experiences; therefore (D) is incorrect.

15. **C**

If the teacher ignores the answer entirely (A) or moves on to another question (D), it devalues the student response. If the teacher responds immediately to the digression (B), the disruptive behavior has been rewarded. The correct answer is (C).

16. **A**

Non-performers are students who are not involved in the class discussion at that particular moment. Asking students to respond to student statements (A) is one way of incorporating non-performers into a class discussion. Therefore, (B), (C), and (D) are incorrect.

17. **C**

When students repeat basic facts, spellings, and laws, it is called a choral chant.

18. **B**

It is important to make sure that students understand directions so as to limit any factors that may prevent a successful lesson. This question is not a transition between tasks (A) and does not assume that the students were not paying attention (C). It is a way of monitoring something that has already been explained. (D) is incorrect because the teacher is not introducing a new skill.

19. **A**

Even without saying a word, teachers can communicate a variety of emotions with their body language and eye contact. Verbal cues (such as the intonation of voice), smiles, movement, posture, and eye contact with students can all convey the enthusiasm of an effective teacher. Body language can even convey that teachers are actively listening to their students by maintaining eye contact and leaning into the conversation.

20. **A**

Controlled interruptions include students that are missing supplies, are late to class, and are returning after an absence—minor disruptions that can be minimized with procedures that are already in place. For example, if a student is missing a supply needed for a class, he or she would know to sign out for a replacement from the supply shelf. These types of disruptions are inevitable, but can be managed.

21. **C**

Nondirective statements are a way of showing a student that the teacher is listening, but not making a judgment or pointing the conversation in a specific direction. Directive statements (B) do just the opposite. The statement is also not evaluating (A) or judging (D), so these answers are incorrect.

22. **A**

Effective professional development is not a one-time workshop, nor can it be satisfied within a specified amount of time (C). To affect growth in children, teachers must grow and develop as well. This learning must extend throughout the teacher's career and beyond. In addition, effective professional development relies on meeting the needs of those involved and, therefore, cannot be dictated solely by one individual (B). Finally, in addition to being theory and research-based, the learning gained from professional development activities must be practical and applicable (D). Otherwise, it cannot be used at the school site, and the training is rendered useless.

23. **B**

Action research allows teachers to carry out research investigations in their own classroom. In case methods (A), teachers are encouraged to analyze a "case" within a group discussion, role play or writing and use the situations to gain new knowledge, evoke problem solving techniques, or stimulate reflection. Reflective learning communities (C) consist of dialogue by teachers about particular topics, issues, lessons or a book that all in the group have read. The conversation revolves around the art of teaching. Mentors (D) promote and support teachers that are new to the school, grade level, profession, or subject area. It is generally a one-to-one relationship in which the more experienced mentor helps the less experienced teacher develop his/her talents in a secure environment.

24. **C**

Data gathered within the learning environment resulting from day-to-day activities could also provide a means for reflection and discussion. This includes using student scores in class not only for their most recognized use, student academic grades, but also using the success of students to guide a teacher's professional development plan. Looking for inconsistencies in grading can be a basis for teachers to explore their teaching practices while looking for new and more effective methods. In considering answers (B) and (D), student academic grades should never be used in behavior assessment.

25. **D**

All teachers have different strengths and weaknesses. By working collaboratively, they can share their strengths to create more strengths and fewer weaknesses. If a teacher has found a method of teaching a concept that is successful, it is worth trying. Viewing the students' scores from the previous year would assist in seeing if they had made any progress since their last test, but should not be used to justify their poor scores (A). This does nothing to assist students in improving their academic achievement. Telling future students to study harder (B) or suggesting math tutors (C) is always good advice but should not be the only course of helping students improve in a certain area.

26. **D**

A mentor relationship supports the teacher who is new to the profession, school, grade level, or subject area. The mentor is to promote and support peer teacher growth, not inhibit it by creating an adversarial relationship with the teacher (B). Any supervisory functions such as overseeing or resource allocation should be done by administrative personnel (A).

27. Ⓑ

School schedules do not usually include time for teachers to engage in professional development activities such as consulting, observing colleagues, engaging in research, learning and practicing new skills, curriculum development, or professional reading. Contributing to this lack of time given to teachers for professional development is the prevailing school culture which considers a teacher's proper place during school hours to be in front of the class. This isolates teachers from one another and discourages collaborative work. Presenters (A) for professional development are plentiful and creative school administrators can even use their own cache of teachers to deliver very effective in-service and workshops. Also, there are plenty of interested teachers (D), provided the professional development activities correspond to the needs of the teachers. Finally, while there will generally always be a certain lack of resources (C) in education, this problem is not as pronounced as the lack of time.

28. Ⓑ

A high-order question (A) tests the student's ability to apply information, evaluate information, create new information, etc., rather than to recall simple content. Transitions (C) are used to connect different ideas and tasks. The information that the question is looking for is one of content, not skill (D). The question presented here is a low-order question that ensures that a student is focused on the task at hand and can be used to develop into higher questioning.

29. Ⓑ

Piaget developed four stages of cognitive development. As children go through each stage new abilities will have been developed, but they will be unable to have this ability until they reach that particular stage. Children under the age of eight do not have the understanding of language that grasps complexities (A). Accordingly, teachers should use simple language when working with these children (C, D).

30. Ⓑ

When designing learning activities, teachers should be aware that younger students process information more slowly than their older counterparts. Activities for younger children should be simple and short in duration.

31. A

Teachers need to stimulate all types of students and be aware of their needs. Marshall Rosenberg has categorized them as rigid-inhibited, undisciplined, acceptance-anxious, and creative.

32. D

In inductive thinking, students derive concepts and definitions based upon the information provided to them, which can be fostered through personal-discovery activities (D) where students try to determine the relationships between the objects given to them. Choral chanting (A) practices skills; multiple-choice questions (C) test objective knowledge; general computer experience (B) fosters computer knowledge.

33. A

A teacher can guide a student to a higher-level answer through questioning. Repeating the question (B) would probably elicit the same response, and asking a different student (C, D) would not help the original student who provided the simple response.

34. B

Bloom classified educational objectives into a classification system that was divided into three domains—cognitive (memory and reasoning), affective (emotions), and psychomotor (physical abilities).

35. C

Long-term memory is thought to be unlimited and permanent. Short-term memory is limited in capacity (B). (A) and (D) are not characteristics of long-term memory.

36. B

The example illustrates a deductive reasoning task. Inductive reasoning (A) would be giving the class some information and asking them to form a rule or generalization. (C) and (D) are examples of inductive tasks.

37. B

This assignment asks students to gather information or explore long-term goals, goals many years in the future. Short-term goals (A, C) are those which can be achieved in days, weeks, or maybe months. Answer (D), synthesize, is a more complicated process than merely gathering information.

38. C

The teacher is asking the student questions to allow the student to correct a spelling error. Spelling does not allow for divergent or creative thinking (A). Although the teacher reminds the student of a mnemonic, the teacher is not teaching the mnemonic (B); finally, applying spelling rules or guides to improve spelling would be an example of deductive reasoning, not inductive reasoning (D).

39. D

Students are more likely to be more enthusiastic when things that they enjoy are the subject or focus of a lesson, which in turn helps to build the academic success of the lesson.

40. A

It is important to keep strong communication lines open with the parents so that the child can get the best possible care and understanding from both the parents and the teacher.

41. B

It is very important that all students feel welcome, but it is especially effective for ESL students to feel comfortable and welcomed in the classroom.

Voyager

42. C

The Student Teams-Achievement Divisions (STAD) is a cooperative learning approach that places students in teams of mixed abilities and has rewards for individual and group effort.

43. A

Students speaking two languages learn one of two ways: sequentially, in which one language is mastered before the study of the second language has begun (A), and simultaneously, in which both languages are learned concurrently (B). Sequential language acquisition does not mean a student learns two languages in parts (C) or develop language skills (D).

44. **A**

Some students may not speak English at home, or may have limited exposure to the vocabulary of the classroom. It is important to be aware of these factors and provide the materials appropriate to help guide mastery.

45. **D**

The teacher hopes to engage the students in critical thinking allowing them to express their opinions and realizing that students will have different interpretations of the statement. (A), (B), and (C) are possible outcomes, but (D) is the best answer since it relates specifically to the teacher's aim.

46. **C**

The best response is to emphasize that occupations are open to both men and women and that most people make career choices based on their abilities and their preferences. (A) and (B) fail to take advantage of the opportunity to teach the class about equal opportunity in career choices, and (D) implies that popular opinion determines career choices.

47. **C**

Although the educator has a responsibility to the administration (A), fellow professionals (B) and the student government that may advocate school policy (D), the third area under the Code of Ethics in Florida specifies that all professional, ethical educators are obligated to the profession.

48. **C**

The educator has legal obligations to protect a student from an abusive home environment (D), but is not required to report the abuse through the State of Florida Code of Ethics. Similarly, student encouragement (A) and protection from illegal substances (B) are important to education, but are not a component of the Code of Ethics.

49. **D**

Some of the educator's objectives under the Code of Ethics are to provide access to diverse points of view (A), and to not personally discriminate against a student based on race, color, religion, or sex (C). While the educator should not harass any student (B), it is not the educator's responsibility to actively ensure each student's protection from harassment or discrimination.

50. **C**

In the State of Florida, it is never ethical to exploit a student for the school's or the educator's personal gain and/or advantage.

51. **D**

The educator is not denying students access to diverse points of view by allowing the inquiring student to pursue the idea independently from her guidance (A). Equally, the educator in the scenario is not denying freedom of speech (C). The educator's personal views should not be hidden (B), but similarly should not interfere with his or her professional decisions. In this scenario, she is obligated to give her verbal support but to reserve her personal views from blending with those of the school's.

52. **D**

All educators' privileges should be reserved for service to the school, the students, and the classroom—not for personal gain.

Chomsky's – human learning = innate ability to recognize symbols

53. **A**

Jean Piaget developed stages of human development in which children must master one stage before moving on to the next. This idea of sequence was part of this theory. Innate abilities to recognize symbols comes from Chomsky's theory on human learning (D). The other choices refer to Behavioral or Social Learning theories (B), (C).

54. **B**

According to Erikson's theory of social development, students begin to develop a sense of initiative between the ages of two and six years of age. Prior to initiative, they are developing trust. After initiative they develop a sense of industry and, finally, identity.

Erikson's theory of social dev't.
1. trust
2. initiative 2-6
3. sense of industry
4. identity

55. **A**

Students are intrinsically motivated to participate in a given activity if they participate in the activity because they enjoy it. Participating because of consequences of an activity indicates extrinsic motivation (B), (C), while students who refuse to participate are simply not motivated (D).

56. **D**

Goals for individual students should be individually based and be based on more than an academic record or observation. Thus, (D) is the best description.

57. **B**

An essential component to providing appropriate accommodations is to provide individualized assessment to identify the individual needs for each student. Token economies (C) treat everyone the same and do not address accommodations (A). Reinforcing attempts (D) may be good practice in behavioral learning theory but it does not address accommodations.

58. **A**

Teachers who apply behavioral learning theory in practice create educational environments in which educational stimuli can be presented and behavioral responses can be observed and measured. Cognitive theory focuses on cognitive developmental stages and may suggest using manipulatives (D). Social learning theory promotes use of modeling (C).

59. **C**

An example of cognitive learning theory in practice would be using manipulatives to teach math for students under the age of eleven. The other options are examples of behavioral or social learning theories.

60. **A**

According to social learning theory, students learn by observing the behavior of others. The other options are examples of cognitive and behavioral theories.

61. Ⓐ

Linda's behavior serves a purpose or function. To assess the purpose or function of a behavior, teachers can use a functional behavioral assessment. Students normally do not exhibit behaviors for the purpose of making others angry (B). While it is possible that Linda just simply enjoys telling jokes, it is unlikely that she chooses to do so in the midst of a class lesson for the sheer enjoyment of performing (D). Hypotheses about the functions of behaviors address why the person might be exhibiting the behavior and what they are accomplishing or avoiding by exhibiting it.

Reinforcement:
positive ↓ applied
negative ↓ removed

62. Ⓓ

According to the operant model in behavioral theory, negative reinforcement is removing a stimulus, which causes a behavior to increase. Reinforcement can be positive or negative in that is it applied or removed. All reinforcement, positive or negative, increases the likelihood that the behavior will occur again. Likewise, punishment can be positive or negative, but all punishment decreases the likelihood that the behavior will occur again.

63. Ⓓ

Students diagnosed with autism spectrum disorder would not exhibit a delay in physical growth due to the diagnosis of autism. The other choices are symptoms of the disorder.

64. Ⓓ

There are many strategies teachers can use to assist student comprehension of text. However, not all strategies will work with all students, nor will all strategies work for every reading situation. The effective teacher has a repertoire of strategies to help students understand subject area text in order to select the strategy most effective for the students and the reading situation.

65. Ⓑ

Research is very clear that strategies must be explicitly taught in response to reading problems. Teachers cannot assume that students will have learned such skills at an earlier time or that they have generalized the use of strategies in response to a variety of reading needs. (A) would be helpful but not practical since students frequently learn skills in isolation and do not generalize them to a variety of subject areas. (C) will likely make the student who is having trouble understanding the text feel even less capable. (D) will make students aware of the reading problem but will offer no help in response to it.

66. C

Subject area material is often of an abstract nature and therefore difficult for many students to grasp without visual cues. Because of their visual nature, graphic organizers offer tremendous assistance in making the material more concrete. (A) is incorrect because, while graphic organizers are visual and often attractive, their purpose is to organize material for better comprehension. (B) is incorrect because, while they could be very useful in the science classroom, graphic organizers have little to do with scientific methodology. (D) is incorrect because, like (A), graphic organizers are often visually attractive, but their purpose lies in concretizing the material, not making it prettier.

graphic organizers to organize mat'l for better comprehension

67. B

One of the cardinal rules of teaching is to make sure that all materials are (a) suitable for the students, (b) related to the curriculum, and (c) an effective use of school time. Unless the teacher carefully screens the material, he/she will be unaware of either blatant or subtle pieces of information or pictorial matter that may be objectionable and violate one or more of the factors of the rule stated above. (A) is incorrect because, while friends and colleagues may be entirely trustworthy, their use of the material may have been different from the teacher's intended use. (C) is incorrect because there is no rule governing the use of audio-visual aids. They should be used only when they enhance learning. (D) is incorrect for the same reason. The effective teacher will select the best time to use the audio-visual aid so that its use enhances learning.

68. A

Properly used, cooperative learning requires students to utilize numerous skills and material in solving problems in a cooperative fashion. Because the real world is interdisciplinary and learning in a cooperative group is closer to real-world learning than individual sit-in-your-seat-and-do your-own-work learning, the teacher is able to mix and mingle a variety of subject areas in a single problem solving session. (B) is incorrect because, while cooperative learning activities tend to engage students and often lessen adverse behavior, their purpose is cooperative problem solving, not classroom management. (C) is incorrect because cooperative learning can be used at any grade level. (D) is incorrect because cooperative learning activities often take more time to complete than paper-and-pencil activities.

69.

In the effective classroom videos and films are used to enhance understanding of the curriculum. Learning will be facilitated when the students can assimilate small bits of information at a time. By stopping the film from time to time for discussion and note-taking, the effective teacher provides scaffolding of information in incremental but connected steps leading to better understanding of the whole. (A) is incorrect because showing the film from beginning to end makes it difficult for many students to mentally go back and recall specific scenes that are important. (B) has no place in the effective classroom. (C) is incorrect because it will not give the students any point of reference or target for learning through viewing.

70.

Body language is an effective way of avoiding digressions in class. This answer choice provides the best method of dealing with the disruptive behavior while maintaining the class momentum. Checking to see if the pencil needs to be sharpened (A) and repeating the question to the students (D) disturb the class momentum. Allowing the student to sharpen the pencil (B) rewards the student's disruptive behavior.

71.

This transition statement is used to inform the student of what the expected tasks are as the class moves from one subject to another. A redirect (A) occurs when a teacher asks one student to react to the response of another student. A high-order activity (B) tests the student's ability to apply information, evaluate information, create new information, etc., rather than simple content or simple skills. Transitions (C) are used to connect different ideas and tasks. (D) is incorrect because this is a statement and is not intended to test the students.

72.

Transitions allow students to be aware of future events, topics, and expectations (A). Transitions are not class discussions, so students cannot be classified as either performers or non-performers (B). Transitions set up events rather than questions (C) and are generally supplemented by formalized instructions for each topic or event (D).

73. **B**

Changing to an interactive approach, switching to a cooperative group, and using manipulatives are all methods of getting students more actively involved in a lesson because it forces them to be occupied with the task at hand.

74. **B**

If a teacher notices that a student is daydreaming, walking over to the student or placing a hand on his or her shoulder are ways of bringing the student back on-task without disrupting the flow and the momentum of the lesson. Calling on the student (A), who will probably be unable to answer, or stopping and staring at the student (D) will result in lost momentum. Asking questions of the class (C) may not bring the student back on-task.

75. **A**

The teacher is using a transition to keep the momentum of the class going. Students now know what is expected of them, and those that finish the first task early will be able to move onto the next task easily.

76. **A**

A teacher's "with it"-ness relates to the ability to observe and manage disruptions quickly, quietly, and at all times. For example, a "with it" teacher that is helping a student with deskwork would be able to detect and distinguish any disruptive behavior in a different part of the room.

77. **A**

Invitational learning takes place in a classroom that is welcoming; that is, one that is adequately sized, well-built, and properly equipped. The physical setting of a classroom can greatly influence learning. Special attention should also be paid to lighting, ventilation, and proper exit and entry locations.

78. **D**

Invitational teachers display behaviors and attitudes that are inviting, rather than disinviting, to students. Some of these behaviors include reaching out to each student, listening with care, and being "real" with students and with themselves. Invitational teachers do not separate themselves from the students (A), ignore student feelings (B), or use the behavioral method approach (C).

79. C

One of the main goals of cooperative learning is to have students work together and teach one another for improved peer interaction.

80. C

It has been shown that students can internalize what a teacher expects of them and will perform at that level, whether it is positive or negative.

81. C

Kallison Jr. found that subject-matter retention was increased when the teacher provided an outline detailing what would be discussed during a lesson and a summary of the lesson at the end. Therefore, answers (A), (B), and (D) are incorrect because they were not part of the findings.

82. A

Practice activities provide an opportunity for teachers to monitor students to see if additional instruction is needed after a lesson (A). Practice activities are used for any subject matter just featured in the class lesson; therefore, (B) is incorrect. Practice activities reinforce skills that the students have just learned, rather than reviewing old material (C) or introducing new concepts (D).

83. D

Homework should be used to reinforce the learning done in the classroom (D), rather than to start new lessons (A). This will help to place the skills learned in long-term memory (C). Effective classroom management is needed to form structure in a classroom (B).

84. B

It is very important to outline what is expected from students, especially in writing assignments where the grading can be more subjective. This overshadows announcing a due date (A), and while it is important to give feedback on how something was graded (D), this information should be outlined when work is assigned. Students will be able to find a balance between writing what they want (C) and meeting their writing objectives.

85. B

In inductive teaching, the students are provided with examples and non-examples and are expected to derive the definition from this information. In deductive teaching (A), the teacher defines a concept and provides a few examples and non-examples. Definitions (C) and examples (D) are important parts of inductive and deductive teaching.

86. A

It has been found that it is most effective to provide a few examples and non-examples in teaching a concept. The actual number of examples (B) does not make a difference, nor do the examples all have to be interesting (C). From the examples and non-examples, students can inductively determine the definition (D) of the concept.

87. A

Students are able to learn the most when they are aware of and understand exactly what is expected of them. This overshadows the use of special materials (B), repetition of examples (C), or classroom size (D).

88. B

The learning activities in class should be based on specific objectives, preferably ones that are closely related to the recent objectives of the class.

89. A

The objectives given to a class should be applicable for all of the levels within the class to be fair and effective. It is necessary to detail these objectives to the class so that they are aware of what is expected of them. Objectives should not only be expected of certain students (B), but should be expected of the entire class. They also should not be ignored (C) and are important for the class and should not be deemed unnecessary (D).

90. C

To keep students on-task, it is very important to keep any distractions to a minimum, or else the instructional momentum will be lost. Always be sure to have enough copies of materials, and check to see if audio-visual equipment is working properly.

91. B

A discovery-learning lesson is one where the class is organized to learn through their own active involvement in the lesson. In inductive-reasoning lessons (C), the students are provided with the examples and non-examples and are expected to derive definitions from this information. The eg-rule method (D) moves from specific examples to general rules or definitions. The lesson may take place in a science class (A), but is still a discovery-learning lesson.

92. D

When introducing an academic law, the teacher should use the multistep process of stating the rule, providing examples, and then providing exercises. Thus, students are introduced to the concept, can see how it relates to the examples given, and can then try to apply the law on their own. It is a process that requires higher-level thought, rather than just repetition (B). The teacher should not teach related rules (A) until the students are familiar with the initial concept. Only providing examples (C), without stating the rule and providing exercises, is not an effective way to introduce the law.

93. C

If a student answers a question incorrectly, it is possible to guide him or her to the correct answer by asking a series of questions. If a student is unsure of a particular historical figure, for example, and gives an incorrect name in response, the teacher can ask questions that are associated with the correct name.

94. C

A teacher should first try to modify the behavior in the classroom with management techniques. However, if the behavior continues to persist, the teacher should discuss the matter with the student's parents (D).

95. C

Studies have shown that reprimands are more effective when they are made in a soft, controlled manner. Loud shouting (A), threats (B), and angry outbursts (D) cause more anxiety in a classroom rather than effectively modify behavior.

96. B

Canter and Canter's assertive discipline is a system for teachers to maintain a positive classroom while managing misbehavior situations constructively. One of the fundamental ideas is that proper behavior in a classroom should result in positive consequences, which in turn promote a positive classroom environment.

97. D

A negative reinforcement occurs when an adverse stimulus is removed after the desired behavior has occurred.

98. B

The teacher is not providing any sort of reinforcement for Robert's behavior in the hope that, without reinforcement, Robert will lose interest, and the behavior will die out.

99. C

According to Rath, student misbehavior is the result of a student not knowing or thinking about his or her values. Rath considers this to be due to mental or physical abilities, emotional experiences, or a lack of values.

100. A

Whether in a classroom dedicated to computers or in a room with a computer center away from the main group, computer rules should be emphasized and then posted in the classroom to avoid any confusion or any experimentation with the machines. Therefore, answers (B), (C), and (D) are incorrect.

101. **D**

The Internet can be accessed using a browser program, such as Netscape® or Internet Explorer® (A). Class records can be maintained in a recordkeeping program, such as Excel® (B). Class newspapers can be created using desktop publishing programs (C).

102. **A**

As long as students are well-informed about procedures ahead of time, it is possible to rotate computer use among single students or small groups so that the class can optimize their experience with computers. Therefore, (B), (C), and (D) are not the best choices.

103. **B**

Psychotic disorders are rare in children, but if you do suspect that something is wrong you should contact your school administration.

104. **D**

In case of a tornado, you should evacuate everyone to the first floor of the building and then place students near walls that are away from windows. Everyone should crouch on the floor and then cover their heads with their hands. The teacher should evacuate students to the first floor of the building, but not outside the building (A). Students should also not be on the top level of the building (B) or in a classroom (C) unless the classroom is on the first floor and students are away from windows.

105. **D**

Cooperative learning requires that students work with their peers in heterogeneous groups, with each student adopting a strong role. This requires that the students first learn how to work with one another using cooperative skills. The students should see the need for these skills, should be able to understand and practice these skills, and should be able to practice these skills until they appear natural to the students. Since cooperative learning requires students to be in groups, it does not foster student independence (A) or allow the students to foster the skill on their own (C). Cooperative learning also does not set up practice situations for skill mastery (B).

106. **B**

Friedrich Wilhelm Froebel was a German philosopher and educator, and the founder of the modern kindergarten. Benjamin Franklin (A) was a political leader, philosopher, and scientist who developed the structure of the modern high school. Maria Montessori (C) was an Italian physician who developed an early childhood curriculum based on a structured environment. Johann Pestalozzi (D) established the first training schools for teachers in Prussia.

107. **B**

According to the Socratic Method, teachers should ask questions that allow students to find the truth within themselves.

108. **B**

Comenius wrote this illustrated book (*The Visible World in Pictures*) to use the sense of sight to teach. Comenius believed in using the senses to assist the intellect.

109. **A**

Friedrich Wilhelm Froebel used concrete objects called "gifts" to teach concepts. The remaining three accomplishments are accredited to Herbart.

110. **C**

Massachusetts enacted the first compulsory education law in 1642.

111. **C**

It was believed that the slaves would be more submissive if they remained illiterate, so most were never taught to read or write. Teaching a slave to read or write was, in fact, a criminal act.

112. **D**

In general, teachers believe that oral language proficiency correlates with academic proficiency. However, research indicates that oral language proficiency is easily acquired through daily living experiences, whereas, academic language proficiency requires an academic setting with context-reduced activities.

[Handwritten annotation: James Cummins → reading + listening – Receptive Skills EXCEED productive skills of speaking & writing]

113. C

According to James Cummins, reading and listening are receptive skills, which always exceed the productive skills of speaking and writing.

114. B

This is an example of a deep culture characteristic of the Hispanic culture. Educators do not easily recognize deep culture characteristics. In this situation, the student was demonstrating respect for an authority figure by looking downward when reprimanded.

115. B

The goal of the maintenance bilingual education model is to maintain the native language of the second-language learners. This model includes all of the components that are specified by the committee.

116. B

According to Krashen and Terrel (1983), the topic-centered language approach develops basic communication skills in accord with the way individuals naturally acquire language.

117. D

Among all of the nationally recognized professional organizations, Teachers of English to Speakers of Other Languages (TESOL) is identified as the organization that provides professional support for educators.

118. C

This example illustrates the necessary components for increasing comprehension and contextual support for all students, but especially for ESOL students, at different language proficiency levels.

119. B

The example given requires an instructional lesson modification, which includes providing the overview and identifying key concepts.

120. **D**

The best response is to emphasize that the teacher gathers as much information as possible to prevent an inappropriate referral of a language minority student to a special education program. Talking to the parents about the student will help the teacher to gather information.

Practice Test 2

TIME: Two and one-half hours
120 Questions

> **DIRECTIONS:** Read each item and select the best response. Mark your responses on the answer sheet provided.

1. A very bright student, scoring in the top 10 percentile on standardized achievement tests for children his age, is already well-known throughout the school for causing trouble because of behavior problems. To help this student, the teacher should suggest that

    (A) the student receive a prescription for Ritalin or another drug to control hyperactivity.

(B) the student be diagnosed as having attention deficit disorder (ADD).

(C) the student would be served best in a private school or by being home schooled.

(D) the student's parents come to school to meet and discuss his behavior at home.

2. At the end of class, the teacher asks the students to write a one-sentence summary. She writes on the board, "Who, What, When, Where, How, and Why," and tells the students to write one sentence answering those questions from the day's class. This is an effective way for the teacher to

(A) teach sentence structure.

(B) help students summarize the lesson.

(C) engage her students in journal writing.

(D) get feedback about how students feel about her class.

3. A teacher could expect to find all of the following in the student's permanent record EXCEPT

(A) standardized achievement test scores (such as the CAT).

(B) a record of disciplinary actions taken against the student during his or her enrollment.

(C) any intelligence or psychological tests documenting learning disabilities.

(D) samples of the student's written work.

4. Effective teachers understand that student performance on subject-matter tests indicates

(A) how innately intelligent or smart a student is.

(B) the student's general aptitude.

(C) how likely it is that a student will be successful on future tests.

(D) a student's particular skills or knowledge at a particular point in time.

5. A teacher usually stops her high school history class about five minutes before class time is over and asks the students to write a one-sentence summary of what they have learned in the class. When class is over, the students must turn in their summaries, which their teacher reads. By doing this, the teacher is

   (A) gathering data on students' writing skills.

   (B) using a classroom assessment technique to determine what her students are learning.

   (C) giving students a chance to unwind from classroom activities.

   (D) losing valuable and productive class time.

6. A teacher consistently returns graded papers to her students within three days of their turning their work in. She writes very complete comments on each paper to help students understand what they have done correctly or incorrectly on their assignments. Doing this is important to the teacher's instructional goals because

   (A) it is easy to fall behind in grading if a teacher does not keep up with the workload.

   (B) grading papers is an important part of a teacher's job performance.

   (C) students have a responsibility to keep track of their graded work.

   (D) providing students with information about their performance is one way to help them improve their performance.

7. If academic assessment reveals that a female student has a low range IQ (70–80), and the student (although in the sixth grade) has reading skills at the second-grade level and math skills at the first-grade level, the teacher should

   (A) continue with class as before, including the student in class activities but doing nothing special to draw attention to the student and her skill deficiencies.

   (B) investigate the possibility of sending the student to a lower-grade class where she can repeat some of the subjects she has had before.

   (C) meet with the student and her parents to discuss the best way to proceed with class instruction and make sure that their questions about their student's achievement are addressed.

   (D) encourage the student to try harder because if she really tries hard she can do better.

8. Mastery testing means that

    (A) students can retake tests until they achieve a specified standard.

    (B) all students achieve a 90 percent or higher on a test on their initial attempt.

    (C) students are allowed to use their books and other materials to help them when they take tests.

    (D) students with special needs are given accommodations or alternatives for testing.

9. The teacher's grade book is all of the following EXCEPT

    (A) a record of student attendance and performance on assignments and tests.

    (B) a confidential record of student and class performance.

    (C) a record of assignments, tasks, and tests given throughout the school year.

    (D) an open record of public information.

10. A student making top grades in class has received a percentile score of 63 on a nationally standardized math test. The best explanation of the student's score is

    (A) a percentile score of 63 means that on a scale of 1–100, the student is 37 points from the top.

    (B) a percentile score of 63 means that out of a group of 100 students, 37 would score higher and 62 would score lower, meaning that the student has done well by scoring in the top half of all students taking the test.

    (C) a percentile score of 63 is just like a grade of 63 on a test; it means that the student made a low D on the test.

    (D) a percentile score of 63 means that out of a group of 100 students, 37 would score higher and 62 would score lower, showing a big difference between the student's performance on the standardized test and in class.

11. "I" messages are a means of communicating effectively, especially in situations where confrontation is necessary or conflict is possible. "I" messages

   (A) require eye contact.

   (B) are statements beginning with the word "I" where the speaker states his or her thoughts and feelings.

   (C) are statements beginning with the word "I," where the speaker states his or her goals and expectations.

   (D) are incomplete messages where the speaker states, "I want..." and lets the other party complete the sentence.

12. A student asks, "Why do we have to write so many papers in this class?" A good response from the teacher would be to say

   (A) "You ask too many questions instead of doing your work."

   (B) "Next year you will have to write twice as many papers as you have written this year, and we have a big test coming up in two weeks. I want you all to be ready."

   (C) "The reason you have to write papers is because I've told you to and I'm the teacher."

   (D) "There is no reason. It's just something that all students have to do in school."

13. A communication tool or language device which teachers use to motivate, evaluate, practice, guide, and even invite students to the learning experience is the

   (A) declarative sentence.

   (B) exclamation of "Eureka!"

   (C) question.

   (D) common verb.

14. Which of the following teacher responses corrects a student response by giving correct information?

   (A) "Okay, Stacey, can you think of anything else you'd like to say?"

   (B) "Buster, your answer is wrong; *believe* is spelled 'b-e-l-i-e-v-e' not 'e before i.' "

(C) "Jill, that answer is incorrect; what made you think that was the way to spell *neighbor*?"

(D) "Elliot, that answer is wrong; does anyone know what the correct answer is?"

15. As the teacher distributes a test to the class, the best statement to make is

(A) "Students, I believe that you all are well-prepared for the test. I am confident that you will do your best."

(B) "Students, this is the hardest test I've ever given my students, so you must really work hard."

(C) "The last time I gave this test, no one passed. I'll be surprised if this class can do better."

(D) "Students, I doubt if anyone will be able to complete this test in the time allowed."

16. A student expresses concern to the teacher about his grade on his last test. The student is accustomed to making A's and is displeased that he earned a C on his last test. One way for the teacher to help the student understand his grade is to

(A) show the student the grade book so the student can see that few students made A's or B's on the test.

(B) go over the answer key with the student, explaining why he missed questions.

(C) tell the student that the grades in class ranged from C to F, that the median grade was an F and the top grade was a C.

(D) assure the student that the test was very hard and encourage him to study harder for the next exam.

17. If a teacher asks a question, calls on a student, and the student does not immediately answer, what should the teacher do?

(A) Say nothing, but give the student more time to think of an answer.

(B) Say, "We're waiting for an answer."

(C) Call on another student.

(D) Restate the question.

18. If a student is usually quick to attempt answers to questions, but often blurts out wrong responses, the teacher's best response to the student is to

(A) say, "Wrong answer, but better luck next time."

(B) say, "Well, not exactly. But, you're close."

(C) say nothing, but smile and call on someone else.

(D) say, "Why don't I give you another minute to think about that answer?"

19. Which of the following teacher responses more clearly provides student feedback that a response is correct?

(A) "Well, Adam that's something no one has thought of before."

(B) "Yes, Jennifer that is the correct answer."

(C) "Okay, Melissa. Next student?"

(D) "That's a very interesting idea, Billy."

20. A student says, "We're having a big test in two weeks! What kind of test will it be?" The best answer is

(A) "Let's not start worrying about the test. We have plenty of time to get ready."

(B) "You're asking questions when you should be writing. Get back to work."

(C) "The test will be to write a five-paragraph theme just like you've been writing in class the last four weeks. It will be graded the same way, and you will have the same amount of time as you have for all the papers you've practiced writing."

(D) "It's going to be a writing test."

21. A teacher wants to explain a reading score of 2.3 on a standardized reading test to a student's parents. The teacher teaches second grade, and it is March of the school year. The teacher's best explanation of a score of 2.3 is that the student is

(A) on the second-grade level and the student has strong reading skills for the grade.

(B) on the second-grade level, but slightly behind what is expected for the class.

(C) on the second-grade level, third month, and that since school started in August and the student was tested in March, the eighth month, it would be a good idea for the student to get extra help to improve reading skills.

(D) on the second-grade level, third month.

22. Effective professional development occurs when there is a commitment by educators to

(A) attend 70% of staff development activities.

(B) meet recertification requirements.

(C) continuous lifelong learning.

(D) join a professional organization.

23. A group of teachers are meeting together to have direct, honest, and productive conversations about the art of teaching. Today they are discussing a lesson that one of the teachers in the group taught and the others observed. This scenario best describes what method of professional development?

(A) case methods

(B) action research

(C) reflective learning communities

(D) mentors

24. Which of the following enables teachers to access professional journals and other pertinent educational information from their home or school for professional development?

(A) Internet

(B) public library

(C) professional organizations

(D) television

25. If several students miss the same question on a test, this should cause the teacher to

    (A) give all of the students who missed it zeros for cheating.

    (B) examine how the concept was taught and wording of the question.

    (C) throw out that question and ignore the concept.

    (D) not see it as a problem.

26. A career teacher may increase and vary his/her responsibilities without leaving the classroom. Within which of the following roles would the teacher be allowed to do this?

    (A) principal

    (B) assistant principal

    (C) mentor

    (D) guidance counselor

27. After a professional development activity, a teacher returns to her school and attempts to implement what was learned in her classroom. She is disappointed and frustrated, as she did not get the results that she had envisioned. What course of action should she take?

    (A) Abandon the idea because it does not work.

    (B) Report the ineffective professional development activity to the district.

    (C) Share her experience with another teacher and seek feedback.

    (D) Assume her students are the problem.

28. A teacher asks her class, "What do you think should happen if a student is caught cheating on a test?" By asking her students to participate in the process of establishing this rule, the teacher

    (A) ensures that few students in her class will attempt to cheat.

    (B) uses consensus to help build classroom support for the rule about cheating.

    (C) is certain that everyone in class understands that cheating is a serious offense.

    (D) has identified the students who will be most likely to cheat.

29. A teacher decides to show his class a video of *The Crucible* after they have read the play. All of the following are reasonable assumptions EXCEPT

    (A) he does this to help the students who are struggling with reading the play to understand it better.

    (B) he does this to reward his students by giving them a "day off."

    (C) he does this to help his students appreciate the visual presentation of the written word.

    (D) he does this to allow his students to critique the differences between the book and the video.

30. As a teacher explains to his class the biological concept of feedback systems (loops) involving the control center (which receives information and processes information), the receptor (which sends information), and the effector (which receives information and produces a response), he finds that using a metaphor (a comparison) is helpful. He decides that the best metaphor is

    (A) a computer with a monitor and a printer.

    (B) a computer with a floppy disk drive and a hard drive.

    (C) a telephone system, a person making a call, and the phone.

    (D) two audio speakers attached to a compact disc player.

31. An example of a question or task requiring synthesis (from Bloom's taxonomy) would be which of the following?

    (A) Here are five words. Write a sentence using these five words and adding any other words you might need.

    (B) Describe how Columbus, in his search for the New World, ended his journey in the Caribbean Islands.

    (C) Compare Freud's theory of psychosexual development to Erikson's theory of psychosocial development.

    (D) Diagram the sentence written on the board.

32. A teacher plays a piece of music for her music appreciation class, telling the students that it is an example from the Romantic period. She plays the piece again and asks the students to describe the piece. After students describe the music, she asks them to define "romance." The teacher is engaging her students in

    (A) inductive reasoning.

    (B) deductive reasoning.

    (C) oral interpretation.

    (D) evaluation.

33. In order to help a student who has very creative and sophisticated ideas improve his or her spelling (and, thus, his or her grades in English class), a teacher might suggest that

    (A) the student try typing his next paper on a word processor, using a spell checker.

    (B) the student use simpler words that are easier to spell.

    (C) the student write each misspelled word on the last paper 20 times.

    (D) spelling errors not count against the student on papers.

34. An English teacher wants to challenge his students to think critically. He has been teaching about the parts of speech. He writes the following sentence on the board, "The man ran down the street." He asks a student to identify the part of speech of the word "down." The student says that "down" is an adverb telling where the man ran. The teacher should respond

    (A) "No, *down* is not an adverb."

    (B) "Yes, *down* does tell where the man ran."

    (C) "*Down* is a preposition, and *down the street* is a prepositional phrase."

    (D) "Well, *down* does tell where the man ran which is what adverbs do. But in this case, *down* is part of the phrase *down the street*. Do you want to change your answer?"

35. A teacher writes this question on the board, "How do you know if someone is intelligent or not?" The class then is assigned to research the question and develop a list of all the traits and characteristics that define or describe someone who is intelligent. Through this exercise, the teacher has

   (A) led her students through an activity of developing criteria against which a judgment can be made.

   (B) led her students through an activity of gathering examples.

   (C) led her students through an activity of testing if someone is intelligent or not.

   (D) engaged her students in a creative-thinking activity.

36. Which of the following is an example of a question or task requiring application thinking skills according to Bloom's taxonomy of learning?

   (A) Demonstrate how to fill the printer tray with paper.

   (B) What kind of paper is needed to fill the printer tray?

   (C) Describe how to load the printer tray with paper.

   (D) If the printer does not print after loading the paper tray, what could be the problem?

37. Why is it a good idea for a teacher to give students options and allow them to make choices?

   (A) Some teachers dislike telling students what to do.

   (B) Some teachers like to give students different options so they can exercise their decision-making skills.

   (C) Teachers know different students are motivated and stimulated by different tasks.

   (D) Students deserve a break from all the rules and regulations in most classes.

38. Which of the following requires the higher-order thinking skill according to Bloom's taxonomy of learning?

   (A) Demonstrate how to change the printer cartridge.

   (B) State what kind of cartridge the printer needs.

   (C) Describe how to change the printer cartridge.

(D) If the printer does not print after the cartridge has been changed, figure out what the problem is.   *analysis*

39. A bright and cheerful student with a flair for the dramatic is confined to a wheelchair as a result of a birth defect. Her junior high speech teacher would like to recommend that this student try out for the school play. The teacher should

a

(A) tell the student about the play and let the student decide whether or not to try out for a part.

(B) encourage the student to try out for the play, assuring her that she can win a part.

(C) be sure that the student knows all about the behind-the-scenes roles to be played, so if she does not get a stage role she can still be part of the crew.

(D) wait to see if the student shows any interest in being in the play.

C 40. Pat was given a test which consisted of being asked to repeat several digits forward and backward. Additionally, Pat was given some vocabulary questions. What kind of test was Pat given?

(A) A vocabulary test

(B) An achievement test

(C) An intelligence test

(D) An arithmetic placement test

C 41. A teacher asks his students to name great Americans who have made significant contributions to American culture. As students start calling out names of people, the teacher notices that all the names are those of white men. The teacher then

(A) chastises the students for their bigotry.

(B) adds the names of some men and women of other cultures and races to the list.

(C) asks the students to think of some women and people of other cultures and races to add to the list.

(D) asks the students if they have ever heard of Dr. Martin Luther King, Jr.

42. School policy states that, "All students will be treated with dignity and respect." Which of the following would be an exception to this policy?

    (A) The teacher requests that students reply "Yes, sir" or "No, sir" when answering questions.

    (B) The teacher requests that students reply simply "Yes" or "No" when answering questions.

    (C) The teacher addresses students as "Mr. last name" or "Ms. last name."

    (D) The teacher addresses the male students as "Mr. last name" and the female students by their first names.

43. A teacher overhears a group of students discussing their favorite foods. One student says, "I can't believe that people in China eat dogs." Another student of Indian heritage and Hindu religious training says, "That's the way I feel when I see people eating steak." The teacher, in an effort to show an appreciation of cultural and religious differences, says

    (A) "Some people have difficulty understanding why Americans eat so much meat in their diets."

    (B) "Different people in different cultures and religious backgrounds have different customs when it comes to eating and drinking certain foods and beverages."

    (C) "Everyone knows that a dog is man's best friend."

    (D) "Research shows that it is healthier to not eat meat, but to have a vegetarian diet."

44. When a teacher includes short stories by authors from various ethnic groups for the class to read, the teacher is demonstrating to her students that

    (A) some cultures produce better writers than others.

    (B) the short story, as a genre, has certain basic characteristics.

    (C) people of different nationalities have vastly different concerns when it comes to human values.

    (D) Russian writers are more difficult to understand than Mexican or Japanese authors.

45. A high school Spanish teacher is leading the class through a conversational exercise. A student in the class asks, "Do they eat pizza in Mexico?" The teacher's best response is to

    (A) ask (in Spanish), "Are you nuts? We're not talking about pizza!"

    (B) ask the student (in Spanish) to repeat the question in Spanish.

    (C) ask another student in class (in English), "What do you think?"

    (D) say (in English or Spanish), "That question is irrelevant to the discussion."

46. "Imagine that you are on the first space shuttle to Mars. What do you think you will see and do when you arrive on Mars?" This is an example of a question requiring

    (A) critical thinking.

    (B) creative thinking.

    (C) convergent thinking.

    (D) cause and effect thinking.

47. A teacher's primary objective when serving the public is to

    (A) always be available and open to questions and authentication of statements.

    (B) attend all functions relating to the school and the community to indicate support of the institution.

    (C) give the public discerning and responsible citizens through education.

    (D) always use precautions and research when representing the institution and when dealing with the public.

48. A new school is opening on the poor side of town. There are no teachers who are willing to transfer and leave their current position. The principal, who is given the authority to hire the needed teachers, offers a bonus of five thousand dollars to any teacher who is willing to leave his/her post and fill the new school. An ethical teacher

    (A) would take the money for the first year only, in order to fill this school.

    (B) would refuse to go. Five thousand dollars is not worth the time or energy it would take to develop a new functional school.

(C) would have taken the job before being offered the money. The incentive is to teach the child, anywhere, any time.

(D) would refuse the money, though reconsider the job. The true incentive is teaching, and an ethical teacher would never accept gifts or favors or special advantages.

49. A teacher's obligation to the profession is to

(A) teach the most recent material.

(B) provide instruction that is professional.

(C) focus on the children before oneself or the public.

(D) be aware of and adhere to professional behaviors such as reporting harassment and criminal acts.

50. Within how many hours is a teacher required to report any arrests/charges involving abuse of a child or the sale and/or possession of a controlled substance?

(A) 24 hours

(B) 48 hours

(C) 72 hours

(D) 96 hours

51. Which of the following areas is one that a professional administrator may NOT single out in teachers and fellow administrators?

(A) GPA

(B) socio-economic status

(C) family connections

(D) attitude

52. The educator values all of the following, EXCEPT

(A) the worth and dignity of every person.

(B) the pursuit of truth.

(C) nurturing of democratic citizenship.

(D) the facilitation of professional development.

53. An overall lack of interest in activities, constant crying, or talk of suicide are indicators of

    (A) Autism

    (B) Communication disorders

    (C) Emotional behavioral disorders

    (D) Physical disability

54. A teacher's usual testing procedure is to give students a written exam. However, this semester, the teacher has a vision-impared student in her class who cannot read small print. Which of the following would be the most effective, efficient, and fair way to test this student?

    (A) Use the office copier to enlarge the print on the same tests that the other students will take.

    (B) Make an audio tape of the test questions and let the student take the tape to the library to listen and then record his or her answers.

    (C) Ask the student to come early or stay later and give him or her a shorter, oral test.

    (D) Send the student to the resource room to let the resource teacher or the counselor read the test to him or her.

55. What is the purpose of a functional behavioral assessment?

    (A) To determine why inappropriate behaviors are occurring and design a behavioral intervention plan that logically follows from the assessment intervention

    (B) To apply time out to those students who make learning difficult for others in the class

    (C) To assess the functional behavior of students in a play group

    (D) To design academic content

56. An example of social learning theory in practice would be using

    (A) drill and practice.

    (B) modeling as an instructional strategy.

    (C) a zone of proximal development.

    (D) manipulatives.

57. Teachers who apply cognitive learning theory in practice

   (A) create educational environments in which educational stimuli can be presented and behavioral responses can be observed and measured.

   (B) focus on academic and cognitive developmental stages to guide instruction and lesson planning.

   (C) employ modeling as an instructional strategy.

   (D) use direct observations and operational definitions to measure learning objectives.

58. An example of behavioral learning theory in practice would be using

   (A) manipulatives.

   (B) peer examples.

   (C) drill and practice.

   (D) a zone of proximal development.

59. The first standard for math class is, "The student understands how to use math to solve problems in the real world." Which of the following would be the best way to test the students' performance on this standard?

   (A) Give the students ten addition and ten subtraction problems to solve.

   (B) Give the students ten addition and ten subtraction problems to solve using a calculator.

   (C) Give students a matching test where they must match the standard numeral with its Roman numeral equivalent.

   (D) Give students a newspaper ad, and ask them to calculate the cost of several items if those items were on sale for 20 percent off.

60. Learning objectives created for a classroom of students

   (A) should be tailored to students at all levels.

   (B) should only be expected of certain students.

   (C) should be the same for all students regardless of developmental level, academic ability, or personal experience.

   (D) are unnecessary.

61. According to Jean Piaget's theory of human development, between which ages should students develop the ability to solve abstract problems logically?

    (A) birth to two

    (B) two to seven

    (C) seven to eleven

    (D) eleven to adult

62. According to Erikson's theory of social development, when will students begin to develop a sense of industry?

    (A) birth to two years of age

    (B) two to six years of age

    (C) six to twelve years of age

    (D) twelve years of age to adult

63. A student's self-concept, whether positive or negative

    (A) is the result of feelings of superiority over the rest of the class.

    (B) is an important factor in the student's ability to learn.

    (C) is a reflection of the parent's opinion.

    (D) will be the same for everyone in an entire class.

64. A Venn diagram is an example of

    (A) a complicated chart of social interaction.

    (B) a graphic organizer.

    (C) a model used in social studies to determine the rate of immigration.

    (D) a technique useful only in mathematics.

65. Computer-assisted instruction aids the teacher because it

    (A) reduces testing required to assess students' skills.

    (B) ensures students are working at a similar rate.

    (C) decreases administrative work necessary for managing the class.

    (D) increases time for providing students with individualized instruction.

66. Ms. Jaynes spends much of her instructional time teaching her students different reading strategies and giving them opportunities to practice using these strategies in class. By teaching her students reading strategies they can use on their own, she is

    (A) creating a quiet classroom environment conducive to learning.

    (B) able to spend more class time on grading student work.

    (C) stressing to her students the importance of reading as a social activity.

    (D) promoting students' sense of responsibility for their own learning and equipping them with the tools to become independent readers.

67. Ms. Clampmeyer is a fourth-grade schoolteacher at an inner city school. She asks her students to go to their homes and their library and find four different kinds of people in the workplace who use potatoes or the word "potato." When the students come back with their assignments, answers range from "Mom" to "farmers" to "potato chip bags." Ms. Clampmeyer then points out how many different people need to know how to read the word "potato," and be able to put it to good use, even if they are not just being asked to spell it right for English class. By using this exercise, Ms. Clampmeyer is primarily

    (A) showing students the amount of times potato is used in the culture.

    (B) demonstrating the value of the potato to the economy.

    (C) allowing students to learn in their own way.

    (D) revealing how knowing English is important in all walks of life, not just for school.

68. Ms. Harlow is a chemistry teacher of seniors at a public high school. She wants her chemistry students to understand how to produce nitrous oxide safely in the lab. She has them take notes as she demonstrates by her example how to produce the result in the lab. Next, she discusses how Mr. Jones, the English teacher, has volunteered to allow the requirement for a paper written about a process to be satisfied by a paper from Ms. Harlow's chemistry class. Ms. Harlow teaches them how to write the paper for chemistry, and the grade is shared with their English course. In carrying out this activity, Ms. Harlow is achieving what instructional objective above all?

    (A) She is demonstrating the value and necessity of writing well in professional disciplines or hard science.

(B) She is showing how clever she can be at integrating course material.

(C) She is primarily creating a collaborative learning activity that will provide peer learning.

(D) She is showing students how to get an "A" in English.

69. Mr. Pike teaches an eleventh grade class in biology. In planning his unit on the principle of natural selection, he asks students to make note of the old saying that "big fish eat little fish," and working in groups, to show in a brief essay how that old saying may or may not apply to Darwin's theory of evolution, both literally or by analogy. In so doing, Mr. Pike is

(A) encouraging an understanding of diversity in the culture.

(B) using independent study, collaborative learning and writing as a form of learning to enhance retention.

(C) showing how Darwin's theory is unscientific and illogical.

(D) promoting primary learning through group interaction.

70. An instructionally effective way for a teacher to maximize student recall is to begin class by

(A) engaging the students in singing a song to make them feel more comfortable.

(B) conducting a review of previously studied material.

(C) giving a "pop" test or quiz to see how much the students remember from the last class.

(D) asking students if they have any questions about their homework assignment.

71. An effective way for teachers to establish standards for student behavior in the classroom is to

(A) adopt the same rules and regulations that were enforced in school when they were students.

(B) survey the literature to develop a comprehensive list of standards.

(C) consider the characteristics and socially-accepted norms of the school community.

(D) borrow ideas from the major religions of the world.

72. Classroom control is integral to successful instruction because

    (A) the teacher cannot dispense knowledge in a chaotic environment.

    (B) students cannot learn in a noisy classroom.

    (C) the teacher has to establish that he or she is the "boss" or leader, and the class has to follow the leader.

    (D) the teacher and the students must work in tandem, each having certain rules and protocols to follow.

73. Drill and practice exercises, such as the use of flashcards, are appropriate activities for

    (A) task analysis.

    (B) divergent thinking.

    (C) memory work.

    (D) critical thinking.

74. Two students always finish their assigned work before their classmates. Consequently, they are usually disruptive to the rest of the class, who are still working. An effective way to help the two students learn time-management skills and to keep them out of trouble would be for the teacher to

    (A) send them to the principal's office for their horseplay.

    (B) point out the careless errors they make on their assignments for not taking their time and for not giving more thought to their work.

    (C) plan activities for students who finish their classwork early.

    (D) count 10 points off their assignment for each time he has to tell them to quiet down.

75. A teacher makes sure that the aisles between the desks in her high school classroom are at least three feet wide in order to

    (A) make sure that desks are accessible to all students in her class, including those using crutches or wheelchairs.

    (B) promote a feeling of interdependence among students.

    (C) provide individual attention to each student.

    (D) discourage collaborative learning.

76. A teacher wants to start the semester by providing students with complete and explicit guidelines to follow regarding their behavior in class. He decides that the most effective way to communicate this information to his students is to

    (A) make a big poster with all the rules listed, display the poster in class, and discuss each rule with the students.

    (B) ask the students what they think would help everyone in class get along with each other.

    (C) survey what the other teachers are doing with regard to classroom management.

    (D) present a few of the rules on the first day of each week and then reinforce those rules throughout the week.

77. A teacher has a routine for distributing papers to the class, for having students get their books, and for writing on the board. The routine is one way the teacher demonstrates that he or she

    (A) uses class time efficiently.

    (B) has good problem-solving skills.

    (C) is a rigid and unreasonable teacher.

    (D) expects his/her students to do their best.

78. A teacher tells the class, "Tomorrow you will have a test on chapters 5 and 6. There will be 50 matching questions and 10 short answer questions. You will have 45 minutes to take the test." What other important information about the test should the teacher tell the students?

    (A) "You should bring two No. 2 lead pencils with you. I will provide the answer sheets."

    (B) "Don't forget to study! This will be a very hard test!"

    (C) "This will be your third test this term."

    (D) All of the above.

79. At random and without announcement, students are required to pass through metal detectors as they enter the school. This procedure is used to

    (A) alert students to the possibility that classmates are carrying weapons to class.

(B) make sure students are not carrying weapons to class.

(C) remind students that someone is watching them.

(D) promote school safety.

80. A teacher begins class by checking attendance. She tells the students that while she is checking attendance, they should get out their books and review what they had studied during the last class meeting. All of the following are instructional benefits to this practice EXCEPT

(A) it keeps students from talking while the teacher takes attendance.

(B) it provides students with time to review before the class "officially" begins.

(C) it helps the students to focus their attention.

(D) it helps prepare the student to connect new material with previously learned information.

81. Which of the following are the components of the process approach model?

(A) Transform and teach

(B) Sensing and acting

(C) Reach, touch, and teach

(D) Reaching and teaching

82. Which of the following contributes to the development of student responsibility?

(A) clear requirements, specific assignments, progress monitoring, and feedback

(B) frequent feedback, continual assessment, and student-developed assignments

(C) student portfolios and frequent feedback

(D) student self-management, monitored progress, and frequent feedback

83. Which is an example of specific praise?

(A) "I really like the way that Alice is doing her work!"

(B) "Good for you! That is the top grade in the class!"

(C) "I am very pleased to say that everyone did a great job on the test!"

(D) "Your careful work made this special, especially in your artwork!"

84. A teacher begins a lesson with the following: "Today I want to briefly go over yesterday's problems before we introduce a few new algebraic laws. You will then have the opportunity to work with your partner on proving these laws." What is this teacher doing?

(A) Cooperative learning

(B) Giving a pep talk

(C) Informing the students of what the objectives for the day will be

(D) Reviewing yesterday's work

85. When assigning seatwork exercises, an effective teacher always

(A) provides corrective feedback.

(B) includes review questions.

(C) allows students to grade their neighbors' papers.

(D) introduces new concepts.

86. In selecting materials for a heterogeneous class, the effective teacher will look at

(A) the ratio of pictures to text.

(B) the size of the font used.

(C) if the material can hold the attention of learners of all types.

(D) the size of the material.

87. What are the essential components of cooperative learning tasks?

(A) reward systems and prizes

(B) individual students selecting teammates

(C) pairs of students teaching each other

(D) heterogeneous teams working toward goals

88. To encourage students to read more books on their own time, a teacher develops a reward system to give students tokens for the books they read depending on the difficulty and the length of the book. At the end of the semester, students will be able to use their tokens to purchase "rewards" from the school store (pens, pencils, erasers, notebooks, and so forth). This reward system appeals to students who are

    (A) intrinsically motivated.

    (B) extrinsically motivated.

    (C) reading below grade level.

    (D) able to purchase their own school supplies.

89. When a teacher uses a student's response as a springboard to ask additional, more detailed questions, the teacher is

    (A) correcting student answers.

    (B) elaborating on student answers.

    (C) accepting student answers.

    (D) affirming student answers.

90. In order to provide appropriate motivation for everyone in class, an English teacher assigns the class to write a 300-word essay and specifies that

    (A) there are two different topics from which students may choose to write.

    (B) there are two different topics from which students may choose to write, and if a student wants to write about another topic, then he or she should get approval from the teacher for that topic.

    (C) every student will write about the same topic.

    (D) each student must find a topic to write about and get it approved in advance.

91. A junior high science teacher was encouraged to relate instructional objectives and activities to the interests, feelings, and experiences of her students. One way that she was able to do this was by

    (A) giving her students an interest survey to determine their interests, preferences, likes and dislikes, and experiences.

(B) allowing students to select the assignments they would complete.

(C) encouraging students to do their best.

(D) creating a progress chart to allow each student to graph his or her class performance.

92. Until recently, a very quiet, reserved student had completed all her work on time and was making satisfactory progress. Lately, however, she has been erratic in her class attendance, and when she comes to class, she appears distracted. She is having trouble staying on-task and finishing her work. She has failed to turn in several recent assignments. On the last writing assignment, she wrote a very graphic poem about a girl who is sexually assaulted. The level of details used in the poem was shocking to the teacher. Her teacher should

(A) ignore the topic of the poem, grade it on its poetic merit only, and return it to the student, waiting to see what will happen with the next assignment.

(B) grade the poem on its poetic merit and return it to the student with a written comment that she would like to talk to her about the poem.

(C) ask the student to stay after class, return the poem, and ask the student about it.

(D) make a copy of the poem and distribute it to other teachers to solicit their opinions about the poem.

93. An effective way to check students' understanding of directions or an assignment is to

(A) ask, "Does everyone understand?"

(B) ask, "Are there any questions?"

(C) say, "Student Name, do you know what you're supposed to do?"

(D) move around the room and check to make sure that everyone has started the assignment and is doing it correctly.

94. When a teacher suspects that a student is using drugs, the teacher, as a conscientious professional, should

(A) contact the appropriate school authorities in order to protect other students and secure help for the student in question.

(B) contact the student's parents to let them know that their son or daughter is in trouble.

(C) alert other teachers to the situation so they can be watching for unusual behaviors.

(D) keep quiet about her suspicions until she has collected enough evidence to prove that the student has a drug problem.

95. Two weeks after a student writes a poem about a rape, she comes to the teacher and confides that she was the girl in the poem. She tells the teacher that her mother's new boyfriend raped her (the student) and that she is afraid her mother will be mad if she tells her what happened. The teacher should

(A) tell the student to go ahead and tell her mother what happened.

(B) call the student's mother on the phone and tell her what the student said.

(C) report the student's sexual assault to the appropriate authorities.

(D) tell the student that she needs to talk to a school counselor.

96. When a student writes about attempting suicide in a journal, the best way for the teacher to deal with the situation is to

(A) write encouraging notes to the student in the margins of the journal.

(B) ask the student to come over to his or her house after school to spend some time together.

(C) suggest that the student read some inspirational and motivational books.

(D) take the student's threats of suicide seriously and report the situation to the appropriate school authorities.

97. A very outgoing and friendly student seems insecure at times, and "fitting in" with her clique is very important to her. She does not like for people to disagree, and she has shown that she is willing to give in to others to avoid a conflict. The teacher becomes very concerned when she sees the student spending time with students who appear to be involved in gang-related activities. The teacher is

(A) jumping to conclusions by assuming that the student will also become involved in gangs.

(B) justified in worrying that the student will be influenced by her friends.

(C) involving herself in something that is really none of her concern.

(D) underestimating the student's ability to make decisions for herself.

98. A student is misbehaving in class, so the teacher institutes an exclusionary time-out. What will happen?

(A) The student will sit out in the hallway for a period of ten minutes.

(B) The student will observe the class, but without any reinforcement.

(C) The student will ask to be alone.

(D) The student will be unsure of what the reinforcement will be.

99. A female student comes up to a teacher and says that a relative has been touching her in a way that makes her uncomfortable. What do you do?

(A) Contact the school administration.

(B) Talk to her and call her parents.

(C) Nothing.

(D) Talk to another teacher.

100. A teacher says, "We have just finished reading *Sense and Sensibility*. Let's go through our notes and review the traits of each character in the novel." This is an example of

(A) lesson-end review.

(B) lesson-initiating review.

(C) month-end review.

(D) topic summary.

101. Research supports all of the following statements about the use of computers in education EXCEPT

(A) computers in the classroom have a motivational effect on many students.

(B) students who use computers to write papers in class write longer papers.

(C) computerized tests cannot measure higher-order thinking skills.

(D) when utilizing technology (such as computers), the teacher needs a back-up plan in case the technology fails.

102. A teacher encourages students to use a spell checker when they write papers. If the teacher allows students to write and prepare typed papers at home, the first thing to consider is

(A) whether or not students have access to a computer and/or word processor at home.

(B) whether or not students' parents would end up writing the paper.

(C) whether or not the students can be trusted to do their own work.

(D) whether or not the students will have time to do extra work at home.

103. The purpose of Glasser's reality therapy is to

(A) guide students toward realistic behavior by using reinforcements.

(B) incorporate psychoanalytical and educational techniques.

(C) clarify value systems.

(D) aid the student in behaving responsibly.

104. Students start using drugs and alcohol

(A) due to curiosity, desire for pleasure, peer pressure, and/or problem avoidance.

(B) to deal with stress from school.

(C) due to parental influences.

(D) depending on social groups.

105. Social isolation, unwarranted nausea, headaches, and irrational fears or obsessions are symptoms of

(A) nerves.

(B) nothing.

(C) tall tales.

(D) neurotic disorders.

106. All of the following were true of education in the Middle Atlantic colonies, EXCEPT

    (A) Pennsylvania established the first parochial schools.

    (B) Virginia established the first private schools.

    (C) a single public school system was established to educate the large homogeneous population of children.

    (D) the first vocational schools were established to meet the needs of businesses and trades in these colonies.

107. As secretary of the Massachusetts State Board of Education, Horace Mann advocated all of the following EXCEPT

    (A) free circulating libraries in every school district.

    (B) private academies to replace public high schools.

    (C) women's wages equal to those of men.

    (D) the need for teacher-training institutions.

108. The launching of Sputnik by the Soviet Union in 1957 triggered increased emphasis on all of the following areas of study EXCEPT

    (A) world history.

    (B) math.

    (C) science.

    (D) foreign language.

109. The ruling of the Supreme Court in *Brown v. Board of Education of Topeka, Kansas* (1954), found that

    (A) separate educational facilities could offer equal educational opportunities to students.

    (B) students could be placed in segregated tracks within desegregated schools.

    (C) segregated schools resulted in unequal educational opportunity but caused no psychological effects.

    (D) separate educational facilities were inherently unequal and violated the Fourteenth Amendment.

110. President Lyndon B. Johnson's "War on Poverty" resulted in all of the following EXCEPT

   (A) the Peace Corps.

   (B) Head Start.

   (C) VISTA (Volunteers in Service to America).

   (D) The Elementary and Secondary Education Act.

111. The Education for All Handicapped Children Act of 1975 mandates that schools provide free and appropriate education for all of the following except,

   (A) mentally handicapped.

   (B) physically handicapped.

   (C) socially-emotionally handicapped.

   (D) learning disabled.

112. In a fifth-grade ESOL class, Karen is holding three similar but different pictures. Enrique is looking at a copy of one picture that Karen is holding. Neither student can see the other's pictures. Enrique spends 60 seconds describing the picture he is holding while Karen listens and asks questions for clarification. When time is up, Karen identifies the pictures Enrique described.

   What features of the communicative approach does this activity employ?

   (A) information gap

   (B) question and answer

   (C) vocabulary practice

   (D) pronunciation opportunities

113. What must schools do to meet the needs of LEP students?

   (A) Have high expectations for the academic achievement of all students.

   (B) Keep the parents out of the classroom so there is more use of English.

   (C) Refuse the development of programs that address multicultural concerns as they are only a waste of the teacher's time.

(D) Downplay the home languages and cultures of the students. They are in an American school so they should adhere to an American way of thinking and living.

114. The Florida Consent Decree

  (A) is an agreement between the Florida State Board of Education and a coalition of eight organizations represented by Multicultural Education, Training, and Advocacy, Inc. (META).

  (B) provides a structure for compliance of the jurisprudence insuring the rights of LEP students in Florida, and quality in educational opportunities as afforded to all native English-speaking students.

  (C) has as one result that all teachers must receive some type of training in teaching ESOL students.

  (D) All of the above.

115. The four quadrants depicting Cognitively Undemanding (Easy) to Cognitively Demanding (Hard) and Context-Embedded (Clues) to Context-Reduced (No Clues) was developed by

  (A) Stephan Krashen.

  (B) Noam Chomsky.

  (C) James Cummins.

  (D) James Asher.

116. Which of the following is an example of an instructional modification for an ESOL student in a mainstream sixth-grade class?

  (A) The teacher develops schema and vocabulary, and then discusses important questions from the lesson; finally, students read the chapter in cooperative groups.

  (B) The students read the chapter individually, and then write out the answers to the questions at the end of the chapter; finally, the teacher leads a discussion of the highlights of the chapter.

  (C) The students write out definitions to the vocabulary from the chapter, and then read the chapter aloud in class; finally, the teacher leads a discussion of the highlights of the chapter.

  (D) The teacher writes notes from the chapter on the board, which all students copy into their notebooks, and then all students read the chapter silently and ask questions about what they do not understand.

117. Placement tests designed to place students into ESOL programs in Florida schools should

 (A) be entirely in each student's native language.

 (B) be the same as for English-only students.

 (C) focus on items about U. S. culture.

 (D) focus on language and content skills.

118. Which strategy is the most appropriate when introducing writing to an ESOL student at the pre-literate stage of development?

 (A) The student copies a passage from a story the teacher has read recently.

 (B) The student dictates a story about a recent event to the teacher.

 (C) The teacher dictates a story about a favorite subject to the entire class.

 (D) The teacher asks the entire class to watch while she writes a story on the board.

119. Which organization is responsible for the involvement and participation of families of ESOL students' education?

 (A) Parent leadership council

 (B) LEP committee — no parents

 (C) School advisory council

 (D) School improvement team

120. According to the Florida Consent Decree, the first step in the process of the placement of an ESOL student is the

 (A) placement test.

 (B) personal interview.

 (C) home language survey.

 (D) review of school records.

Answer Key

1.	(D)	31.	(A)	61.	(D)	91.	(A)
2.	(B)	32.	(A)	62.	(C)	92.	(C)
3.	(D)	33.	(A)	63.	(B)	93.	(D)
4.	(D)	34.	(D)	64.	(B)	94.	(A)
5.	(B)	35.	(A)	65.	(D)	95.	(C)
6.	(D)	36.	(A)	66.	(D)	96.	(D)
7.	(C)	37.	(C)	67.	(D)	97.	(B)
8.	(A)	38.	(D)	68.	(A)	98.	(B)
9.	(D)	39.	(A)	69.	(B)	99.	(A)
10.	(D)	40.	(C)	70.	(B)	100.	(A)
11.	(B)	41.	(C)	71.	(C)	101.	(C)
12.	(B)	42.	(D)	72.	(D)	102.	(A)
13.	(C)	43.	(B)	73.	(C)	103.	(D)
14.	(B)	44.	(B)	74.	(C)	104.	(A)
15.	(A)	45.	(B)	75.	(A)	105.	(D)
16.	(C)	46.	(B)	76.	(A)	106.	(C)
17.	(A)	47.	(D)	77.	(A)	107.	(B)
18.	(D)	48.	(D)	78.	(A)	108.	(A)
19.	(B)	49.	(D)	79.	(D)	109.	(D)
20.	(C)	50.	(B)	80.	(A)	110.	(A)
21.	(C)	51.	(B)	81.	(C)	111.	(C)
22.	(C)	52.	(D)	82.	(A)	112.	(A)
23.	(C)	53.	(C)	83.	(D)	113.	(A)
24.	(A)	54.	(A)	84.	(C)	114.	(D)
25.	(B)	55.	(A)	85.	(A)	115.	(C)
26.	(C)	56.	(B)	86.	(C)	116.	(A)
27.	(C)	57.	(B)	87.	(D)	117.	(D)
28.	(B)	58.	(C)	88.	(B)	118.	(B)
29.	(B)	59.	(D)	89.	(B)	119.	(A)
30.	(C)	60.	(A)	90.	(B)	120.	(C)

Detailed Explanations
of Answers

FTCE

PRACTICE TEST 2

1. (D)

The teacher should determine if the student's behavior is consistent in different settings, asking about his behavior at home and in other environments. Although the other options (A), (B), (C) might be viable possibilities for future action, the first step is to explore his present behavior.

2. (B)

One-sentence summaries are effective tools for students to use in summarizing a lesson. Answering the questions the teacher wrote on the board is not necessarily a good way to teach students about sentence structure (A) as their writing may or may not be complete, grammatical sentences; the point is for the students to summarize the main ideas or main points. Journal writing is a more personal activity (versus factual recall) and the sentence, if the students have followed the directions, will not provide the teacher any information about how students feel about the class (C, D).

3. **D**

The student's permanent record does not include samples of the student's written work. It should, however, contain achievement test results (A), disciplinary measures (B), and other test results (C).

4. **D**

Performance on subject-matter tests indicates a student's skills or knowledge at a particular point in time. They do not measure intelligence (A) or aptitude (B), nor do they predict how well a student will perform in the future (C).

5. **B**

The teacher is getting feedback to help her know what her students have learned and whether they have missed key points. This helps the teacher increase her teaching effectiveness. (A) and (C) may be by-products of the teacher's classroom assessment technique; however, they are not the best answers. (D) is incorrect; getting student feedback is not a waste of time.

6. **D**

The outcome or product of an instructional activity is to help students improve their work. (A), (B), and (C) may be true statements, but they describe a teacher's priorities or expectations, rather than an instructional goal.

7. **C**

Now that the student has been diagnosed, it is important that she and her parents understand the educational implications and options available to them. (A) is wrong as it fails to address the problem. Although (B) and (D) might be possibilities, they are not the best answers to the question. After meeting with the student and her parents, the teacher will want to explore other ways to meet the student's educational needs (B) and continue to encourage her (D); however, the student may already be trying hard and doing the best she can.

8. **A**

Mastery teaching and testing allows students to rework and retake tests until they have achieved a specified standard of performance. Although attaining high scores on tests is an indicator of a high-achieving class, it does not necessarily mean mastery testing (B). When students use books and materials, the test is described as being an open-book test (C). Students with special needs may require testing accommodations, but that is not a characteristic of mastery testing (D).

9. **D**

The teacher's grade book is confidential (B) and not open to the public. It is also a record of student performance and attendance (A) and a record of all graded items given throughout the school year (C).

10. **D**

This is the best answer because it contains information which is technically correct and which expresses a concern about the difference in the student's standardized test score and usual performance in math class. (A) is technically correct; however, it does not really provide as much complete information as (D). (B) tends to provide the student with a false impression; while it is true that the student scored in the top half, as one of the best students in class, the student could have expected to have scored perhaps in the top ten percent or at least the top quartile. (C) is a false statement.

11. **B**

"I" statements begin with the word "I" and express the individual's thoughts or feelings. They are not statements of goals and/or expectations (C). "I" statements are not incomplete statements (D), nor are they called "I" statements because eye contact is involved (A).

12. **B**

An honest and complete rationale for writing papers is the answer the student deserves. (A), (C), and (D) ignore the student's need to know why he has to write papers and, thus, fail to provide the motivational rationale the student may require in order to do his best work. (C) and (D), furthermore, are insulting, failing to show the student respect for his inquiry.

13. **C**

Teachers spend a great deal of their time asking questions, answering questions, and listening to questions. Questions are an important tool for teachers. Teachers use sentences (A), exclamations (B), and verbs (D) in a variety of ways, but questions are essential to the learning process.

14. **B**

This provides specific information to correct a student's mistake. (A) is a response to a correct answer (not incorrect, as specified in the question). (C) and (D) do not provide specific information.

15. **A**

A positive statement of encouragement will boost the confidence of some students and will not undercut anyone's self-esteem. (B), (C), and (D) are almost certain to generate anxiety that will interfere with test performance for some students.

16. **C**

If the top grade in the class was a C, then the student is still at the top of the class. The teacher cannot show the grade book without violating students' rights of confidentiality of grades (A). Going over the answer key with the student will merely show which answers were missed and will not allay his concerns over his ranking in the class (B); encouraging the student to work harder also fails to address his concerns (D).

17. **A**

Many students need time to reflect before they give an answer, and teachers often fail to allow enough time to elapse before they give an example or ask another question. (D) would be appropriate if the teacher gave the student ample time and the student still did not answer. If, after the example, the student still did not answer, then the teacher could call on another student (C). (B) is an inappropriate response.

18. **D**

Many times, teachers fail to give students enough time to think about their answers, especially if their first response is incorrect. (A) and (C), while not technically incorrect, are not as good as (D) because they fail to provide the student with any feedback or chance to self-correct his/her answer. (B) gives the student a false impression that he or she almost had the correct answer.

19. B

This is clear and unequivocal feedback. (A) and (D) are unclear as to whether they are correct or not. While (C) indicates acceptance of the answer, it is not as clear as (B).

20. C

A full and complete answer is required to allay the student's worries and help him/her prepare for the test. (D) is inadequate. (A) and (B) are not really answers to the question; they are, instead, attempts to evade answering the question.

21. C

The technical information about second grade, third month of instruction as the meaning of the 2.3 grade equivalency score is correct in answers (C) and (D); however, (D) is not as good a choice as (C) because (D) does not explain the meaning of the score. (A) is false. (B) could be considered a correct or truthful answer; however, it does not suggest a remedy or imply that the student needs to improve to be on grade level. (C) is the best answer because it contains factual information, and it explains that the student's parents and the teacher need to work together to help the student improve his/her reading.

22. C

To affect growth in children, teachers must grow and develop as well. Effective professional development must extend throughout the teacher's career and beyond. The other choices (A, B, D) are good approaches to professional development, but are only part of what an effective professional development plan should be. While teachers should attempt to attend 100% of staff development activities, keep their teaching credentials current and are encouraged to join professional organizations, a continuous lifelong commitment to learning must be the main goal of the individual.

23. C

Reflective learning communities consist of dialogue by teachers about particular topics, issues, lessons or a book that all in the group have read. The conversation revolves around the art of teaching. In case methods (A), teachers are encouraged to analyze a "case" within a group discussion, use role play, writing, and the situations to gain new knowledge, evoke problem solving techniques, or stimulate reflection. Action research (B) allows teachers to carry out research investigations in their own classroom. Mentors (D) promote and support teachers that are new to the school, grade level, profession, or subject area. It is generally a one-to-one relationship in which the more experienced mentor helps the less experienced teacher develop his/her talents in a secure environment.

24. **A**

Teachers can access professional journals, educational websites, and other educational information from their school or home through the use of the Internet. The public library (B) and professional organizations (C) also have educational materials available, but if these are not accessed through the Internet or by mail, they must be obtained in person. Television (D) does offer information on educational topics, but it is a one-way process with the options for topics left up to the network or station programmer.

25. **B**

Student test data can be an effective tool for teachers to reflect on their own practice of instruction, review information, help students process information, and to construct test questions. If many students miss the same question on a test, it should not be viewed as a coincidence and the cause of this event should be investigated. There could be many reasons for this to happen such as the students not understanding the concept, the concept not being taught, poor wording of the question, or even cheating on the part of the students. However, none of these should be assumed without analysis (A), (C), (D).

26. **C**

Opportunities to expand the teaching role while remaining a classroom teacher are achievable through a mentoring program where established teachers are allowed to assist in the development of new teachers. The other positions (A), (B), (D) require the teacher to give up classroom responsibilities to attend to one's new administrative roles.

27. **C**

A great part of professional development is the collegial aspect. Teachers are very fortunate to be in a profession where they are constantly surrounded by professional teachers. After any professional development activity, it is important that cooperation amongst the teachers be strongly encouraged. Sometimes it is difficult to implement something in a classroom that has just been learned outside of the classroom environment. The other teachers at a school site can serve as support. If a new idea does not work the first time, it should not be abandoned *without further thought (A). That would mean that the training received was a waste of time. After further thought, the teacher may come to the conclusion that it was a poor idea or that it is not appropriate for her particular students (D), and at that time discontinue it and inform her colleagues (B).*

28. **B**

This is an example of consensus building. There is no evidence in the scenario described that supports answers (A), (C), or (D).

29. **B**

Showing a video can help students who are not strong readers to understand a written text (A) as well as allow students to see a story (C) and to become aware of the differences in text and film (D). However, a teacher does not use visual media to simply kill time or give students a "day off."

30. **C**

Teachers often teach through example or metaphor. The best metaphor is the telephone system (which sends and processes information), a person making a call (who sends information), and the telephone instrument itself (which receives the information and sends it through the system). (A), (B), and (D) describe a system and two information receivers/senders.

31. **A**

Putting together or arranging elements to make a whole pattern or product is synthesis. (B), (C), and (D) are examples of tasks requiring analysis, not synthesis.

32. **A**

Inductive reasoning involves making generalizations based on a particular fact or example. Deductive reasoning (B) would be used if students were to discuss the characteristics of romance and then compose a musical piece encompassing those characteristics. Oral interpretation (C) is a type of dramatic speech, and evaluation (D) involves judging the quality or merits of a work or product.

33. **A**

New technologies can be helpful to students in many ways. (B) would stifle the student's creativity and result in less sophisticated writing. (C) has not been proven effective as a technique to help students improve their spelling. (D) means that the teacher would not be applying standards of good writing in evaluating the student's work.

34. **D**

The teacher gives the student appropriate feedback and still gives the student a chance to think about the correct answer without simply providing the correct answer. The other choices (A), (B), (C) are correct (at least, in part), but none is the best answer.

35. **A**

The students have developed criteria against which they can decide or judge if someone is intelligent. The students were gathering characteristics, not examples (B), and the students have yet to test their criteria (C). Instead of creative thinking, in this activity students are engaged in critical thinking (D).

36. **A**

"Demonstrate" is a word used to show application or that the student has learned to apply knowledge to perform a task. The other questions deal with other aspects of Bloom's taxonomy—(B) and (C) with the knowledge and comprehension levels, respectively, and (D) with analysis.

37. **C**

Different students respond differently to different kinds of stimuli. (A) and (B) are basically the same answer, just worded differently. (D) is a poor choice because even when teachers plan an activity that is different than the norm, there should be an instructional principle or rationale behind the activity.

38. **D**

This question requires an analysis of the situation or problem in order to answer. (A) requires application, the level below analysis; (C) requires comprehension, the level below application, and (B) requires knowledge, the lowest level, according to Bloom's taxonomy.

39. **A**

The teacher should give the student the information and let her make her own decision, just as the teacher should do for all her students. In open competition, there is no way for a teacher to know who will earn parts (B) or to assume that the student should ask for a job on the crew (C). The student may not know enough to ask about the play (D).

40. **C**

Pat was given an intelligence test. A vocabulary test (A) would not ask for the repetition of digits; an achievement test (B) would evaluate what the student had learned about a particular subject; math questions were not included on the test (D).

41. **C**

The teacher should allow the students to evaluate the list and add some names to show that they do recognize the diversity of individuals who have contributed to America's greatness. (D) is sarcastic, and (A) is too harsh. (B) does not allow the students to amend their list.

42. **D**

(A) and (B) describe different cultural responses or customs; generally speaking, in the South, there is greater use of the terms "sir" and "ma'am," but a simple "Yes" or "No" does not indicate disrespect. Neither does calling students by a title ("Mr." or "Ms.") show disrespect (C). However, addressing one group of students by a title ("Mr.") and not using an equivalent title ("Ms.") with another group of students shows differential treatment, implying that one group (male) is due more respect than the other group (female).

43. **B**

This answer addresses an appreciation of cultural and religious differences as indicated in the question. (C) is a cliché or adage, not a statement of fact. (A) and (D) are factual statements, but they do not address the question posed.

44. **B**

In teaching literature, different genres share basic characteristics regardless of the writer's culture or nationality (A, C). Writers from any culture may be easier or more difficult to understand, depending on the writing style and features of the individual writer (D).

45. **B**

Since the teacher is engaging the class in conversation, they might as well discuss the question in Spanish. (A) is demeaning to the student, and although (D) is accurate, it fails to take advantage of the opportunity to teach the student something about which he or she is interested. Resorting to English (C) in a Spanish class is not as effective as continuing the discussion in Spanish.

46. **B**

Asking students to imagine is a creative act or task. Critical thinking would require analysis and evaluation (A). Convergent thinking would require synthesis or a bringing together of elements (C). Cause-and-effect thinking requires sequential analysis of a process or processes (D).

47. **D**

The teacher has no ethical obligation to be available for questions or authentication (A), or to attend all school related functions (B). The teacher has a social obligation to give the public discerning and responsible citizens in the students he/she teaches (C), but, again, the only ethical obligation is to provide truthful and complete information when representing the school to the public.

48. **D**

The ethical teacher should never accept gifts, favors, or special advantages.

49. **D**

The Code of Ethics dictates that the teacher has dual obligations to the public and to the students (C), but states nothing about personal knowledge (B) or state of materials (A). The professional educator has an awareness and knowledge of the practices that perpetuate education's professionalism such as reporting harassment and personal acts of a criminal nature.

50. **B**

The Code of Ethics explicitly states that the teacher has 48 hours to self-report criminal acts.

51. **B**

Teachers may not be discriminated against for socio-economic status, though college GPA (A), family connections (C), and personal attitude (D) can be assessed during an interview and at any point after to determine eligibility for the a position in an educational institution.

52. **D**

The Preamble to the Principles in the Code of Ethics details that dedication to the worth and dignity of the person (A), the pursuit of truth (B), and democratic citizenship (C) are all qualities that an ethical educator in the State of Florida possesses. The Code of Ethics does NOT require that the educator continue to facilitate him- or herself through professional development.

53. **C**

An overall lack of interest in activities, constant crying, or talk of suicide are specific indicators of depression which is an emotional disorder that should be taken seriously by teachers. Diagnoses of autism (A), communication disorders (B), or physical disabilities (D), are not indicated by these behaviors.

54. **A**

This is the most effective and efficent way to provide this student with the same testing opportunity that his or her classmates will have. The other methods suggested (B), (C), (D) would allow the student to have possible advantages and/or disadvantages as compared to the other students.

55. **A**

Functional behavioral assessments are useful tools for assessing inappropriate behaviors, why they occur, and how a plan can be created to address the needs of the person exhibiting the behaviors. (B), (C), and (D) may be part of the assessment or intervention but are far too focused to be considered the purpose of the assessment.

56. B

Drill and practice (A) is an example of behavioral theory. Zone of proximal development (C) is an example of Vygotsky's cognitive theory. Manipulatives (D) are an example of Piaget's cognitive theory. Modeling is an instructional strategy in which an observer learns by watching another person perform. This is an example of social learning theory.

57. B

Cognitive theories of learning do not focus on behaviors (A), social modeling (C), or operational definitions of behaviors (D). These are examples of behavioral and social learning theory. Cognitive theories focus on academic and cognitive developmental stages to guide instruction and lesson planning.

58. C

Behavioral learning theory focuses on the observable and measurable behaviors of students for learning. Drill and practice (C) is a behavioral teaching strategy. Zone of proximal development (D) is an example of Vygotsky's cognitive theory. Manipulatives (A) are an example of Piaget's cognitive theory. Modeling or peer examples (B) are an instructional strategy in which an observer learns by watching another person perform.

59. D

This answer is an example of using a "real world" problem, determining the price of items on sale. (A) and (B) are not "real world" examples. (C), likewise might have little to do with the real world today, and a matching test measures recognition or memory, not understanding.

60. A

Learning objectives created for a classroom of students should be tailored to students at all levels. Learning objectives are necessary to effective learning and cannot be the same for all students if individual differences exist.

61. D

According to Jean Piaget's theory of human development, students develop the ability to solve abstract problems logically as they mature into adulthood. The other ages reflect stages in which students are developing other component skills.

62. **C**

According to Erikson's theory of social development, students begin to develop a sense of industry between the ages of six and twelve years of age. After industry, they are focused on developing their identity. Prior to industry they are focused on issues of trust and initiative.

63. **B**

A student's self-concept, whether positive or negative is an important factor in the student's ability to learn. Class competition (A) and parental opinion (C) may help contribute to self-concept, but the self-concept is influenced by so many factors that to choose one as the cause of someone's self concept would be naive. It is highly unlikely that all of the students in the class would have the same self-concept (D).

64. **B**

A Venn diagram is a very useful graphic organizer in which students can compare two subjects by identifying both their individual characteristics and those characteristics they have in common. (A) is incorrect because a chart of social interaction is usually called a sociogram. (C) is incorrect because a Venn diagram is a graphic organizer designed to facilitate comparison of subjects, not occurrence rate of an event. (D) is incorrect because, while it may be used in mathematics, the Venn diagram has broad application to many subject areas. The effective teacher will use it widely.

65. **D**

Computer-assisted instruction (CAI) is often formatted in a behavioristic or programmed manner presenting small segments of learning followed by a test and self-assessment before going on to the next segment. Effectively used, CAI can provide the teacher with opportunities for specific students to individually work with problematic areas and receive rapid assessment. (A) is incorrect because regardless of the use of CAI, the teacher is still responsible for making the final assessment of student learning. CAI programming is usually designed for a specific skill or purpose. The teacher should assess the student perhaps using some of the CAI information but with other information as well. (B) is incorrect because not all students need CAI nor will all benefit from it. Its best use is for students who need additional and more individualized instruction. (C) is incorrect because it means the teacher is using CAI for administrative purposes rather than learning purposes.

66. D

By explicitly teaching students strategies they can use in a variety of reading situations, the teacher helps students begin to develop a repertoire of strategies to use whenever they encounter reading/comprehension difficulties. (A) is incorrect because the learning and application of strategies is likely to produce a more dynamic classroom. (B) is incorrect because the effective teacher who teaches her students a variety of strategies will be highly engaged in their learning at all times. (C) is incorrect because stressing the importance of reading will not help students become good readers. For this they need a variety of strategies and lots of practice.

67. D

She is helping the students bridge learning from school to reality by taking an abstract word and putting it in a concrete context. (A) and (B) are incorrect because the focus is not on the use of potatoes as a commodity but the variety of life situations in which a common word like "potato" is used. (C) is incorrect because, while this exercise does allow for a variety of learning styles to be used, the main purpose is on the broad use of words in realistic settings.

68. A

Far too often writing has become an "assignment" in language arts. Students need to recognize that writing is an act of communication in all walks of life. This activity provides an opportunity for the students to "think and write" in science. (B) is incorrect because the integration itself is less important than the real-life writing/learning that the activity will provide. (C) is incorrect because there is no evidence that this activity will include peer learning. (D) is incorrect because the grade is not emphasized, while the style of scientific writing is emphasized.

69. B

The teacher has designed a problem-solving activity that must be completed by the group requiring them to use writing, talking, and reasoning in different modes. In order to provide a response to the question, the group will need to share their knowledge and skills in formulating the essay. Mr. Pike is utilizing multiple approaches to instruct effectively. (A) is incorrect because the focus is on the utilization of group knowledge rather than on cultural diversity. (C) is incorrect because Darwin's theory forms a backdrop for this assignment. The students may or may not support the theory. The focus of the activity is upon their collective analysis and application of knowledge. (D) is incorrect because it is not the only approach integrated into the exercise by Mr. Pike.

70. **B**

Providing a review of previously studied material is a method of maximizing student recall. Some students might not feel very comfortable about singing a song (A), depending on their age, the subject matter, and so forth. Without a review, students would not be expected to perform well on a quiz or test (C), and without a review or time to look over their homework, it is unlikely that they would have many questions to ask on their own (D).

71. **C**

Teachers must take into consideration the values and norms of the school community and its special characteristics. The standards by which student behaviors are judged must be acceptable to the community. Although there may be value to the ideas offered in the other answers (A), (B), (D), they are not as good as answer as (C).

72. **D**

Learning is a partnership, with both teacher and students playing important parts; classroom control is dependent on both the teacher and the students. The other statements (A), (B), (C) are false.

73. **C**

Drill and practice is a good way for students to acquire memory skills or attain knowledge. Analysis (A), divergent thinking (B), and critical thinking (D) require more complex skills than those addressed in drill and practice.

74. **C**

The best teachers should plan activities for students who finish their classroom work before their peers. (A) and (D) are merely punitive measures and are not instructive regarding time management. Although (B) may imply a need for better time management, it does not provide the students with a remedy for staying out of trouble.

75. **A**

This is the best answer since it demonstrates that the teacher is making her classroom fully accessible for students with special needs. Having desks spaced three feet apart would not contribute to feelings of interdependence (B). Spacing of the desks has nothing to do with providing students with individual attention (C). Collaborative learning is an effective instructional technique, so the teacher would not want to discourage collaborative learning (D).

76. A

In order to communicate completely and explicitly what the rules and expectations are, the teacher would select answer (A). (B), (C), and (D) would not accomplish what the teacher has identified as his aim.

77. A

Using class time efficiently is an important part of successful teaching. (B) and (D) are irrelevant to the situation described. The information provided is insufficient for concluding that the teacher is rigid or unreasonable (C).

78. A

The question asks about additional information that the teacher should provide. (B) could create debilitating anxiety for students and (C) does not really provide any additional information about the upcoming test. A teacher should describe a test in positive terms that will motivate and encourage students to do their best.

79. D

At best, this procedure can be said to promote school safety. It cannot be assumed that the procedure is sufficient to accomplish the goal of school safety (B). (A) and (C) are not desirable consequences.

80. A

Although the teacher may prefer a quiet class, keeping the class quiet is not necessarily an instructional benefit. (Some experts say that "Students who talk are students who learn.") (B), (C), and (D) are instructional benefits. A review of previously learned material (B) is beneficial for learning new material (D), and having direction gives students a purpose to focus their attention (C).

81. **C**

The process approach can be used in a variety of fields. It uses a sensing function (reach), a transforming function (touch), and an acting function (teach). Students take in information, abstract and add value to this information, and then act on an alternative that is based upon the information.

82. **A**

Students will be able to develop their responsibility in classrooms that provide clear objectives and assignments, are monitored for progress, and where students are given frequent feedback on their actions.

83. **D**

Specific praise should compliment the specific behavior that is being rewarded, and comment on how the specific behavior resulted in good work. (A), (B), and (C) are examples of praise, but they are not specific.

84. **C**

The teacher is outlining the plans for the day so that the students will be aware of what is expected of them.

85. **A**

Teachers should always provide corrective feedback to student work. Seatwork may or may not consist of review material (B), can be graded by other students if the teacher reviews the results (C), and should not introduce new concepts (D).

86. **C**

Since a teacher will be working with students of all levels and abilities, it is important to select texts that can be useful to all students.

87. **D**

Cooperative learning techniques all have in common the use of heterogeneous groups working toward goals.

88. **B**

Providing external rewards (such as tokens and prizes) for reading appeals to students who are extrinsically motivated. Intrinsically motivated students (A) read for the pleasure and self-satisfaction of reading. Students who read below, at, and above grade level (C) may be motivated extrinsically or intrinsically. Some students may be uninterested in earning tokens to acquire school supplies whether or not they are able to purchase their own supplies (D).

89. **B**

The examples given all require students to elaborate on previous responses. Correcting a student answer (A) would be saying, "No, that is not the answer." (C) and (D) mean the same thing; an example of accepting or affirming an answer would be saying, "Yes, good answer."

90. **B**

This is the best answer because it identifies two topics for students to have a choice if they prefer that the teacher provide the writing prompt and still it provides an opportunity for those students who like to choose their own topic. (A) and (C) are limited in that they fail to provide an option for the student who wants to choose his/her own topic, and (D) fails to take into account those students who prefer to have a teacher suggest a topic for their writing. (B) provides the best option for all learning styles and preferences.

91. **A**

This method allows the teacher to gather information about each student that can be used to tailor assignments to each individual's interest and experiences. (B) is a poor answer because it abdicates the teacher's responsibility for directing and guiding students. (C) and (D) describe motivational activities which may or may not have anything to do with the interests, feelings, or experiences of students.

92. **C**

There is sufficient evidence to suggest that the student is a victim of sexual abuse. The situation is too serious to delay action (A) or to remain passive (B). In no case would it be appropriate to copy and distribute the poem to other teachers (D).

93. **D**

An inspection of students' work is the most effective way to check their understanding. Asking questions (A), (B), (C) rarely provide the feedback the teacher needs to assess students' understanding.

94. **A**

A teacher has a responsibility to make immediate referrals when he or she suspects that a student is using drugs. (B) and (C) are inadequate and inappropriate responses. If the teacher waits until he or she has conclusive evidence (D), it may be too late.

95. **C**

Although the student should seek counseling (D) and will eventually need to tell her mother what happened (A), the teacher's legal responsibility is to report the assault to the appropriate authorities. It would not be appropriate for the teacher to call the student's mother (B).

96. **D**

Students' threats of suicide must be taken seriously and teachers must refer to trained professionals to take action in the face of such threats. (A), (B), and (C) are inadequate responses to threats of suicide.

97. **B**

Students who are social individuals, who avoid conflicts and try to placate others are especially susceptible to peer pressure. The teacher is justified in being concerned. (A), (C), and (D) are unsupported by the scenario described.

98. **B**

In an exclusionary time-out, which is generally used for less severe misbehaviors, the student will be placed where the class can be observed, but will not receive any reinforcement. Exclusionary time-outs usually last five to ten minutes.

99. **A**

The teacher should contact the school administration, who will then arrange for a trained professional to talk to the student. (B), (C), and (D) are not the correct actions to take.

100. A

The language that the teacher uses indicates that this is a lesson-end review that draws upon what the students have noted during the lesson. (B) is incorrect because the lesson has already been taught and, therefore, the teacher is not initiating the lesson. (C) is also incorrect because the teacher is not reviewing at the end of the month, but at the end of the lesson. (D) is incorrect because the students are not summarizing the novel, but are reviewing character traits.

101. C

Computerized tests can measure higher-order thinking skills. Research has supported that computers are motivational for many students (A), that students write longer papers when they use computers than when they write with pen and paper (B), and that, as wonderful as technology is, sometimes it fails, and teachers must have alternative plans (D).

102. A

This has to be the teacher's first consideration. The other options (B), (C), (D) are not viable if the students do not have access to technology at home. Although technology can be very helpful, many students have limited access to it.

103. D

Reality therapy is used to help the student to face reality and be responsible for his or her own actions. If a student misbehaves, the teacher should 1) help the student identify the problem; 2) aid the development of a value judgment about the behavior; and 3) assist the student in developing a plan to change the behavior.

104. A

All types of students start using drugs and alcohol out of curiosity, desire for pleasure, pressure from peers, and/or to avoid problems.

105. D

These are symptoms of a neurotic disorder. A neurotic disorder is an emotional disorder that endangers a child's well-being and should be taken very seriously.

106. **C**

The population of the Middle Atlantic colonies was heterogeneous in terms of religion, ethnicity, and language. Therefore, a single public school system would not have served the varied needs and desires of this population.

107. **B**

Mann did not advocate this concept. Instead, during the years following his tenure as secretary of the Massachusetts State Board of Education, high schools began to replace academies because of increases in urbanization and industrialization.

108. **A**

The United States was shocked by the launching of Sputnik by the Soviet Union in 1957. Comparisons between Soviet education and that available in the public schools of the United States indicated a need to emphasize math (B), science (C), and foreign language (D) for us to compete with other countries and to remain a world power.

109. **D**

In handing down its decision in Brown v. Board of Education of Topeka, Kansas in 1954, the Supreme Court stated that "Separate but equal has no place ... Separate educational facilities are inherently unequal and violate the equal protection clause of the Fourteenth Amendment."

110. **A**

The Peace Corps was established by President John F. Kennedy. Johnson's VISTA (C) was modeled after it. Head Start (B) and the Elementary and Secondary Education Act (D) were also put into effect as part of Johnson's "War on Poverty."

111. **C**

The Education for All Handicapped Children Act of 1975 provides for mentally (A) and physically (B) handicapped as well as learning disabled children (D). It does not include socially-emotionally handicapped youngsters.

112. A

The outcome of the communicative approach is social interaction requiring a minimum of two way oral communication with two active participants. The best interaction occurs when there is some need to communicate, some information gap between the communicators.

113. A

A careful reading of federal case law suggest districts should provide an affirmative program that assures that LEP students do not learn less because of their lack of knowledge of English.

114. D

These are all examples of the components of the Florida Consent Decree, which is a court enforced agreement regarding the identification and provision of services to students whose native language is other than English.

115. C

According to James Cummins (1981), there are appropriate tasks and strategies to help LEP students at varying proficiency levels. His second language framework differentiates students' social language and academic language.

116. A

This illustrates an example of increasing comprehensibility using Teach the Text Backwards, an instructional modification often used with secondary ESOL students in mainstream classrooms.

117. D

This provides specific information necessary to determine the students' ability to profit from instruction delivered in English. Documentation must justify the decision, as required by state rule.

118. B

This illustrates an example of the Language Experience Approach, which makes meaningful speech-print connections and introduces the ESOL student at the pre-literate stage to written discourse and its conventions.

119. **A**

It is this organization that is charged with encouraging parental involvement and participation in the implementation of LEP programming and academic achievement initiatives.

120. **C**

The best response illustrates the first step in identifying potential ESOL students as required by the Florida Consent Decree. The home language survey must be administered to all students; it may be included on the registration form or as a separate survey.

FTCE

Florida Teacher Certification Exam
Professional Education Test

Answer Sheets

FTCE
Practice Test 1

1. Ⓐ Ⓑ Ⓒ Ⓓ
2. Ⓐ Ⓑ Ⓒ Ⓓ
3. Ⓐ Ⓑ Ⓒ Ⓓ
4. Ⓐ Ⓑ Ⓒ Ⓓ
5. Ⓐ Ⓑ Ⓒ Ⓓ
6. Ⓐ Ⓑ Ⓒ Ⓓ
7. Ⓐ Ⓑ Ⓒ Ⓓ
8. Ⓐ Ⓑ Ⓒ Ⓓ
9. Ⓐ Ⓑ Ⓒ Ⓓ
10. Ⓐ Ⓑ Ⓒ Ⓓ
11. Ⓐ Ⓑ Ⓒ Ⓓ
12. Ⓐ Ⓑ Ⓒ Ⓓ
13. Ⓐ Ⓑ Ⓒ Ⓓ
14. Ⓐ Ⓑ Ⓒ Ⓓ
15. Ⓐ Ⓑ Ⓒ Ⓓ
16. Ⓐ Ⓑ Ⓒ Ⓓ
17. Ⓐ Ⓑ Ⓒ Ⓓ
18. Ⓐ Ⓑ Ⓒ Ⓓ
19. Ⓐ Ⓑ Ⓒ Ⓓ
20. Ⓐ Ⓑ Ⓒ Ⓓ

21. Ⓐ Ⓑ Ⓒ Ⓓ
22. Ⓐ Ⓑ Ⓒ Ⓓ
23. Ⓐ Ⓑ Ⓒ Ⓓ
24. Ⓐ Ⓑ Ⓒ Ⓓ
25. Ⓐ Ⓑ Ⓒ Ⓓ
26. Ⓐ Ⓑ Ⓒ Ⓓ
27. Ⓐ Ⓑ Ⓒ Ⓓ
28. Ⓐ Ⓑ Ⓒ Ⓓ
29. Ⓐ Ⓑ Ⓒ Ⓓ
30. Ⓐ Ⓑ Ⓒ Ⓓ
31. Ⓐ Ⓑ Ⓒ Ⓓ
32. Ⓐ Ⓑ Ⓒ Ⓓ
33. Ⓐ Ⓑ Ⓒ Ⓓ
34. Ⓐ Ⓑ Ⓒ Ⓓ
35. Ⓐ Ⓑ Ⓒ Ⓓ
36. Ⓐ Ⓑ Ⓒ Ⓓ
37. Ⓐ Ⓑ Ⓒ Ⓓ
38. Ⓐ Ⓑ Ⓒ Ⓓ
39. Ⓐ Ⓑ Ⓒ Ⓓ
40. Ⓐ Ⓑ Ⓒ Ⓓ

41. Ⓐ Ⓑ Ⓒ Ⓓ
42. Ⓐ Ⓑ Ⓒ Ⓓ
43. Ⓐ Ⓑ Ⓒ Ⓓ
44. Ⓐ Ⓑ Ⓒ Ⓓ
45. Ⓐ Ⓑ Ⓒ Ⓓ
46. Ⓐ Ⓑ Ⓒ Ⓓ
47. Ⓐ Ⓑ Ⓒ Ⓓ
48. Ⓐ Ⓑ Ⓒ Ⓓ
49. Ⓐ Ⓑ Ⓒ Ⓓ
50. Ⓐ Ⓑ Ⓒ Ⓓ
51. Ⓐ Ⓑ Ⓒ Ⓓ
52. Ⓐ Ⓑ Ⓒ Ⓓ
53. Ⓐ Ⓑ Ⓒ Ⓓ
54. Ⓐ Ⓑ Ⓒ Ⓓ
55. Ⓐ Ⓑ Ⓒ Ⓓ
56. Ⓐ Ⓑ Ⓒ Ⓓ
57. Ⓐ Ⓑ Ⓒ Ⓓ
58. Ⓐ Ⓑ Ⓒ Ⓓ
59. Ⓐ Ⓑ Ⓒ Ⓓ
60. Ⓐ Ⓑ Ⓒ Ⓓ

61. Ⓐ Ⓑ Ⓒ Ⓓ
62. Ⓐ Ⓑ Ⓒ Ⓓ
63. Ⓐ Ⓑ Ⓒ Ⓓ
64. Ⓐ Ⓑ Ⓒ Ⓓ
65. Ⓐ Ⓑ Ⓒ Ⓓ
66. Ⓐ Ⓑ Ⓒ Ⓓ
67. Ⓐ Ⓑ Ⓒ Ⓓ
68. Ⓐ Ⓑ Ⓒ Ⓓ
69. Ⓐ Ⓑ Ⓒ Ⓓ
70. Ⓐ Ⓑ Ⓒ Ⓓ
71. Ⓐ Ⓑ Ⓒ Ⓓ
72. Ⓐ Ⓑ Ⓒ Ⓓ
73. Ⓐ Ⓑ Ⓒ Ⓓ
74. Ⓐ Ⓑ Ⓒ Ⓓ
75. Ⓐ Ⓑ Ⓒ Ⓓ
76. Ⓐ Ⓑ Ⓒ Ⓓ
77. Ⓐ Ⓑ Ⓒ Ⓓ
78. Ⓐ Ⓑ Ⓒ Ⓓ
79. Ⓐ Ⓑ Ⓒ Ⓓ
80. Ⓐ Ⓑ Ⓒ Ⓓ

81. Ⓐ Ⓑ Ⓒ Ⓓ
82. Ⓐ Ⓑ Ⓒ Ⓓ
83. Ⓐ Ⓑ Ⓒ Ⓓ
84. Ⓐ Ⓑ Ⓒ Ⓓ
85. Ⓐ Ⓑ Ⓒ Ⓓ
86. Ⓐ Ⓑ Ⓒ Ⓓ
87. Ⓐ Ⓑ Ⓒ Ⓓ
88. Ⓐ Ⓑ Ⓒ Ⓓ
89. Ⓐ Ⓑ Ⓒ Ⓓ
90. Ⓐ Ⓑ Ⓒ Ⓓ
91. Ⓐ Ⓑ Ⓒ Ⓓ
92. Ⓐ Ⓑ Ⓒ Ⓓ
93. Ⓐ Ⓑ Ⓒ Ⓓ
94. Ⓐ Ⓑ Ⓒ Ⓓ
95. Ⓐ Ⓑ Ⓒ Ⓓ
96. Ⓐ Ⓑ Ⓒ Ⓓ
97. Ⓐ Ⓑ Ⓒ Ⓓ
98. Ⓐ Ⓑ Ⓒ Ⓓ
99. Ⓐ Ⓑ Ⓒ Ⓓ
100. Ⓐ Ⓑ Ⓒ Ⓓ

101. Ⓐ Ⓑ Ⓒ Ⓓ
102. Ⓐ Ⓑ Ⓒ Ⓓ
103. Ⓐ Ⓑ Ⓒ Ⓓ
104. Ⓐ Ⓑ Ⓒ Ⓓ
105. Ⓐ Ⓑ Ⓒ Ⓓ
106. Ⓐ Ⓑ Ⓒ Ⓓ
107. Ⓐ Ⓑ Ⓒ Ⓓ
108. Ⓐ Ⓑ Ⓒ Ⓓ
109. Ⓐ Ⓑ Ⓒ Ⓓ
110. Ⓐ Ⓑ Ⓒ Ⓓ
111. Ⓐ Ⓑ Ⓒ Ⓓ
112. Ⓐ Ⓑ Ⓒ Ⓓ
113. Ⓐ Ⓑ Ⓒ Ⓓ
114. Ⓐ Ⓑ Ⓒ Ⓓ
115. Ⓐ Ⓑ Ⓒ Ⓓ
116. Ⓐ Ⓑ Ⓒ Ⓓ
117. Ⓐ Ⓑ Ⓒ Ⓓ
118. Ⓐ Ⓑ Ⓒ Ⓓ
119. Ⓐ Ⓑ Ⓒ Ⓓ
120. Ⓐ Ⓑ Ⓒ Ⓓ

FTCE
Practice Test 2

1. Ⓐ Ⓑ Ⓒ Ⓓ
2. Ⓐ Ⓑ Ⓒ Ⓓ
3. Ⓐ Ⓑ Ⓒ Ⓓ
4. Ⓐ Ⓑ Ⓒ Ⓓ
5. Ⓐ Ⓑ Ⓒ Ⓓ
6. Ⓐ Ⓑ Ⓒ Ⓓ
7. Ⓐ Ⓑ Ⓒ Ⓓ
8. Ⓐ Ⓑ Ⓒ Ⓓ
9. Ⓐ Ⓑ Ⓒ Ⓓ
10. Ⓐ Ⓑ Ⓒ Ⓓ
11. Ⓐ Ⓑ Ⓒ Ⓓ
12. Ⓐ Ⓑ Ⓒ Ⓓ
13. Ⓐ Ⓑ Ⓒ Ⓓ
14. Ⓐ Ⓑ Ⓒ Ⓓ
15. Ⓐ Ⓑ Ⓒ Ⓓ
16. Ⓐ Ⓑ Ⓒ Ⓓ
17. Ⓐ Ⓑ Ⓒ Ⓓ
18. Ⓐ Ⓑ Ⓒ Ⓓ
19. Ⓐ Ⓑ Ⓒ Ⓓ
20. Ⓐ Ⓑ Ⓒ Ⓓ

21. Ⓐ Ⓑ Ⓒ Ⓓ
22. Ⓐ Ⓑ Ⓒ Ⓓ
23. Ⓐ Ⓑ Ⓒ Ⓓ
24. Ⓐ Ⓑ Ⓒ Ⓓ
25. Ⓐ Ⓑ Ⓒ Ⓓ
26. Ⓐ Ⓑ Ⓒ Ⓓ
27. Ⓐ Ⓑ Ⓒ Ⓓ
28. Ⓐ Ⓑ Ⓒ Ⓓ
29. Ⓐ Ⓑ Ⓒ Ⓓ
30. Ⓐ Ⓑ Ⓒ Ⓓ
31. Ⓐ Ⓑ Ⓒ Ⓓ
32. Ⓐ Ⓑ Ⓒ Ⓓ
33. Ⓐ Ⓑ Ⓒ Ⓓ
34. Ⓐ Ⓑ Ⓒ Ⓓ
35. Ⓐ Ⓑ Ⓒ Ⓓ
36. Ⓐ Ⓑ Ⓒ Ⓓ
37. Ⓐ Ⓑ Ⓒ Ⓓ
38. Ⓐ Ⓑ Ⓒ Ⓓ
39. Ⓐ Ⓑ Ⓒ Ⓓ
40. Ⓐ Ⓑ Ⓒ Ⓓ

41. Ⓐ Ⓑ Ⓒ Ⓓ
42. Ⓐ Ⓑ Ⓒ Ⓓ
43. Ⓐ Ⓑ Ⓒ Ⓓ
44. Ⓐ Ⓑ Ⓒ Ⓓ
45. Ⓐ Ⓑ Ⓒ Ⓓ
46. Ⓐ Ⓑ Ⓒ Ⓓ
47. Ⓐ Ⓑ Ⓒ Ⓓ
48. Ⓐ Ⓑ Ⓒ Ⓓ
49. Ⓐ Ⓑ Ⓒ Ⓓ
50. Ⓐ Ⓑ Ⓒ Ⓓ
51. Ⓐ Ⓑ Ⓒ Ⓓ
52. Ⓐ Ⓑ Ⓒ Ⓓ
53. Ⓐ Ⓑ Ⓒ Ⓓ
54. Ⓐ Ⓑ Ⓒ Ⓓ
55. Ⓐ Ⓑ Ⓒ Ⓓ
56. Ⓐ Ⓑ Ⓒ Ⓓ
57. Ⓐ Ⓑ Ⓒ Ⓓ
58. Ⓐ Ⓑ Ⓒ Ⓓ
59. Ⓐ Ⓑ Ⓒ Ⓓ
60. Ⓐ Ⓑ Ⓒ Ⓓ

Florida Teacher Certification Exam

61. Ⓐ Ⓑ Ⓒ Ⓓ
62. Ⓐ Ⓑ Ⓒ Ⓓ
63. Ⓐ Ⓑ Ⓒ Ⓓ
64. Ⓐ Ⓑ Ⓒ Ⓓ
65. Ⓐ Ⓑ Ⓒ Ⓓ
66. Ⓐ Ⓑ Ⓒ Ⓓ
67. Ⓐ Ⓑ Ⓒ Ⓓ
68. Ⓐ Ⓑ Ⓒ Ⓓ
69. Ⓐ Ⓑ Ⓒ Ⓓ
70. Ⓐ Ⓑ Ⓒ Ⓓ
71. Ⓐ Ⓑ Ⓒ Ⓓ
72. Ⓐ Ⓑ Ⓒ Ⓓ
73. Ⓐ Ⓑ Ⓒ Ⓓ
74. Ⓐ Ⓑ Ⓒ Ⓓ
75. Ⓐ Ⓑ Ⓒ Ⓓ
76. Ⓐ Ⓑ Ⓒ Ⓓ
77. Ⓐ Ⓑ Ⓒ Ⓓ
78. Ⓐ Ⓑ Ⓒ Ⓓ
79. Ⓐ Ⓑ Ⓒ Ⓓ
80. Ⓐ Ⓑ Ⓒ Ⓓ

81. Ⓐ Ⓑ Ⓒ Ⓓ
82. Ⓐ Ⓑ Ⓒ Ⓓ
83. Ⓐ Ⓑ Ⓒ Ⓓ
84. Ⓐ Ⓑ Ⓒ Ⓓ
85. Ⓐ Ⓑ Ⓒ Ⓓ
86. Ⓐ Ⓑ Ⓒ Ⓓ
87. Ⓐ Ⓑ Ⓒ Ⓓ
88. Ⓐ Ⓑ Ⓒ Ⓓ
89. Ⓐ Ⓑ Ⓒ Ⓓ
90. Ⓐ Ⓑ Ⓒ Ⓓ
91. Ⓐ Ⓑ Ⓒ Ⓓ
92. Ⓐ Ⓑ Ⓒ Ⓓ
93. Ⓐ Ⓑ Ⓒ Ⓓ
94. Ⓐ Ⓑ Ⓒ Ⓓ
95. Ⓐ Ⓑ Ⓒ Ⓓ
96. Ⓐ Ⓑ Ⓒ Ⓓ
97. Ⓐ Ⓑ Ⓒ Ⓓ
98. Ⓐ Ⓑ Ⓒ Ⓓ
99. Ⓐ Ⓑ Ⓒ Ⓓ
100. Ⓐ Ⓑ Ⓒ Ⓓ

101. Ⓐ Ⓑ Ⓒ Ⓓ
102. Ⓐ Ⓑ Ⓒ Ⓓ
103. Ⓐ Ⓑ Ⓒ Ⓓ
104. Ⓐ Ⓑ Ⓒ Ⓓ
105. Ⓐ Ⓑ Ⓒ Ⓓ
106. Ⓐ Ⓑ Ⓒ Ⓓ
107. Ⓐ Ⓑ Ⓒ Ⓓ
108. Ⓐ Ⓑ Ⓒ Ⓓ
109. Ⓐ Ⓑ Ⓒ Ⓓ
110. Ⓐ Ⓑ Ⓒ Ⓓ
111. Ⓐ Ⓑ Ⓒ Ⓓ
112. Ⓐ Ⓑ Ⓒ Ⓓ
113. Ⓐ Ⓑ Ⓒ Ⓓ
114. Ⓐ Ⓑ Ⓒ Ⓓ
115. Ⓐ Ⓑ Ⓒ Ⓓ
116. Ⓐ Ⓑ Ⓒ Ⓓ
117. Ⓐ Ⓑ Ⓒ Ⓓ
118. Ⓐ Ⓑ Ⓒ Ⓓ
119. Ⓐ Ⓑ Ⓒ Ⓓ
120. Ⓐ Ⓑ Ⓒ Ⓓ

Index

FTCE

Florida Teacher Certification Exam
Professional Education Test

Appendix:
Florida School Districts

Appendix

FLORIDA SCHOOL DISTRICT DATA

Bureau Chief
Education Information and Accountability Services
325 West Gaines Street, Suite 852
Tallahassee, Florida 32399-0400
Phone: 850/245-0400
Fax: 850/245-9097
3,934 Schools

SCHOOL DISTRICT & ADDRESS	PHONE	FAX	NO. OF SCHOOLS
Alachua County 620 East University Ave. Gainesville, FL 32601	352/955-7880	352/955-7873	73
Baker County 392 S. Boulevard East Macclenny, FL 32063	904/259-0401	904/259-1387	10
Bay County 1311 Balboa Ave. Panama City, FL 32401	850/872-7700	850/872-4367	46
Bradford County 501 West Washington St. Starke, FL 32091	904/966-6018	904/966-6030	15
Brevard County 2700 Judge Fran Jamieson Way Viera, FL 32940	321/631-1911	321/633-3432	125
Broward County 600 SE Third Ave. Ft. Lauderdale, FL 33301	754/321-2600	754/321-2701	270
Calhoun County 20859 East Central Ave. Room G-20 Blountstown, FL 32424	850/674-5927	850/674-5814	9

SCHOOL DISTRICT & ADDRESS	PHONE	FAX	NO. OF SCHOOLS
Charlotte County 1445 Education Way Port Charlotte, FL 33948	941/255-0808	941/255-7571	27
Citrus County 1007 West Main St. Inverness, FL 34450	352/726-1931	352/726-1246	27
Clay County 900 Walnut St. Green Cove Springs, FL 32043	904/284-6510	904/284-6525	37
Collier County 5775 Osceola Trail Naples, FL 34109	239/377-0212	239/254-4103	58
Columbia County 372 West Duval St. Lake City, FL 32055	386/755-8003	386/755-8008	19
Dade County 1450 NE Second Ave. #912 Miami, FL 33132	305/995-1430	305/995-1488	432
DeSoto County 530 LaSolona Ave. PO Drawer 2000 Arcadia, FL 34265	863/494-4222	863/494-0389	16
Dixie County PO Box 890 Cross City, FL 32628	352/498-6131	352/498-1308	8
Duval County 1701 Prudential Dr. Jacksonville, FL 32207	904/390-2115	904/390-2586	182
Escambia County 215 West Garden St. Pensacola, FL 32502	850/469-6130	850/469-6379	80

SCHOOL DISTRICT & ADDRESS	PHONE	FAX	NO. OF SCHOOLS
Flagler County PO Box 755 Bunnell, FL 32110	386/437-7526	386/437-7577	12
Franklin County 155 Avenue E Apalachicola, FL 32320	850/653-8831	850/653-3705	10
Gadsden County 35 Martin Luther King Blvd. Quincy, FL 32351	850/627-9651	850/627-0401	29
Gilchrist County 310 NW 11th Ave. Trenton, FL 32693	352/463-3200	352/463-3276	9
Glades County PO Box 459 Moore Haven, FL 33471	863/946-2083	863/946-2709	10
Gulf County 150 Middle School Rd. Port St. Joe, FL 32456	850/229-8256	850/229-6089	10
Hamilton County 4280 SW County Rd. 152 PO Box 1059 Jasper, FL 32052	386/792-1228	386/792-1231	11
Hardee County PO Drawer 1678 Wauchula, FL 33873	863/773-9058	863/773-0069	12
Hendry County PO Box 1980 LaBelle, FL 33975	863/674-4642	863/674-4090	20
Hernando County 919 North Broad St. Brooksville, FL 34601	352/797-7001	352/797-7101	29

SCHOOL DISTRICT & ADDRESS	PHONE	FAX	NO. OF SCHOOLS
Highlands County 426 School St. Sebring, FL 33870	863/471-5564	863/471-5622	21
Hillsborough County PO Box 3408 Tampa, FL 33601	813/272-4050	813/272-4038	275
Holmes County 701 East Pennsylvania Ave. Bonifay, FL 32425	850/547-9341	850/547-0381	11
Indian River County 1990 25th St. Vero Beach, FL 32960	772/564-3150	772/564-3128	30
Jackson County PO Box 5958 Marianna, FL 32447	850/482-1200	850/482-1299	24
Jefferson County 1490 West Washington St. Monticello, FL 32344	850/342-0100	850/342-0108	11
Lafayette County 363 NE Crawford St. Mayo, FL 32066	386/294-4107	386/294-3072	7
Lake County 201 West Burleigh Blvd. Tavares, FL 32778	352/253-6510	352/343-0594	62
Lee County 2055 Central Ave. Ft. Myers, FL 33901	239/337-8301	239/337-8378	89
Leon County 2757 West Pensacola St. Tallahassee, FL 32304	850/487-7147	850/487-7141	58

SCHOOL DISTRICT & ADDRESS	PHONE	FAX	NO. OF SCHOOLS
Levy County PO Drawer 129 Bronson, FL 32621	352/486-5231	352/486-5237	18
Liberty County PO Box 429 Bristol, FL 32321	850/643-2275	850/643-2533	11
Madison County 312 NE Duval St. Madison, FL 32340	850/973-5022	850/973-5027	12
Manatee County PO Box 9069 Bradenton, FL 34206	941-708-8770	941/708-8677	78
Marion County PO Box 670 Ocala, FL 34478	352/671-7702	352/671-7581	64
Martin County 500 East Ocean Blvd. Stuart, FL 34994	772/219-1200	772/219-1231	41
Monroe County PO Box 1788 Key West, FL 33041	305/293-1400	305/293-1408	26
Nassau County 1201 Atlantic Ave. Fernandina Beach, FL 32034	904/491-9901	904/321-5998	22
Okaloosa County 120 Lowery Place, SE Ft. Walton Beach, FL 32548	850/833-3109	850/833-3401	60
Okeechobee County 700 SW 2nd Ave. Okeechobee, FL 34974	863/462-5000	863/462-5204	22

SCHOOL DISTRICT & ADDRESS	PHONE	FAX	NO. OF SCHOOLS
Orange County PO Box 271 Orlando, FL 32802	407/317-3202	407/317-3401	207
Osceola County 817 Bill Beck Blvd. Kissimmee, FL 34744	407/870-4008	407/870-4010	65
Palm Beach County 3340 Forest Hill Blvd., C316 West Palm Beach, FL 33406	561/434-8200	561/434-8571	242
Pasco County 7227 Land O'Lakes Blvd. Land O'Lakes, FL 34639	813/794-2651	813/794-2326	85
Pinellas County PO Box 2942 Largo, FL 33779	727/588-6011	727/588-6200	176
Polk County PO Box 391 Bartow, FL 33831	863/534-0521	863/519-8231	155
Putnam County 200 South Seventh St. Palatka, FL 32177	386/329-0510	386/329-0520	27
St. Johns County 40 Orange St. St. Augustine, FL 32084	904-819-7502	904/819-7515	42
St. Lucie County 4204 Okeechobee Rd. Fort Pierce, FL 34947	772/429-3925	772/429-3916	48
Santa Rosa County 5086 Canal St. Milton, FL 32570	850/983-5010	850/983-5013	40

SCHOOL DISTRICT & ADDRESS	PHONE	FAX	NO. OF SCHOOLS
Sarasota County 1960 Landings Blvd. Sarasota, FL 34231	941/927-9000	941/927-2539	52
Seminole County 400 East Lake Mary Blvd. Sanford, FL 32773	407/320-0006	407/320-0281	78
Sumter County 2680 West County Rd. 476 Bushnell, FL 33513	352/793-2315	352/793-4180	18
Suwannee County 702 Second St. NW Live Oak, FL 32064	386/364-2604	386/364-2635	13
Taylor County 318 North Clark St. Perry, FL 32347	850/838-2500	850/838-2501	11
Union County 55 SW Sixth St. Lake Butler, FL 32054	386/496-2045	386/496-4819	9
Volusia County PO Box 2118 Deland, FL 32721	386/734-7190	386/734-2842	90
Wakulla County PO Box 100 Crawfordville, FL 32326	850/926-0065	850/926-0123	14
Walton County 145 S. Park St., Suite 3 DeFuniak Springs, FL 32435	850/892-1100	850/892-1191	19
Washington County 652 Third St. Chipley, FL 32428	850/638-6222	850/638-6226	15

REA's Test Preps
The Best in Test Preparation

- REA "Test Preps" are **far more** comprehensive than any other test preparation series
- Each book contains up to **eight** full-length practice tests based on the most recent exams
- **Every** type of question likely to be given on the exams is included
- Answers are accompanied by **full** and **detailed** explanations

REA publishes over 60 Test Preparation volumes in several series. They include:

Advanced Placement Exams(APs)
Biology
Calculus AB & Calculus BC
Chemistry
Computer Science
Economics
English Language & Composition
English Literature & Composition
European History
Government & Politics
Physics B & C
Psychology
Spanish Language
Statistics
United States History

College-Level Examination Program (CLEP)
Analyzing and Interpreting Literature
College Algebra
Freshman College Composition
General Examinations
General Examinations Review
History of the United States I
History of the United States II
Human Growth and Development
Introductory Sociology
Principles of Marketing
Spanish

SAT II: Subject Tests
Biology E/M
Chemistry
English Language Proficiency Test
French
German

SAT II: Subject Tests (cont'd)
Literature
Mathematics Level IC, IIC
Physics
Spanish
United States History
Writing

Graduate Record Exams (GREs)
Biology
Chemistry
Computer Science
General
Literature in English
Mathematics
Physics
Psychology

ACT - ACT Assessment

ASVAB - Armed Services Vocational Aptitude Battery

CBEST - California Basic Educational Skills Test

CDL - Commercial Driver License Exam

CLAST - College Level Academic Skills Test

COOP & HSPT - Catholic High School Admission Tests

ELM - California State University Entry Level Mathematics Exam

FE (EIT) - Fundamentals of Engineering Exams - For both AM & PM Exams

FTCE - Florida Teacher Certification Exam

GED - High School Equivalency Diploma Exam (U.S. & Canadian editions)

GMAT CAT - Graduate Management Admission Test

LSAT - Law School Admission Test

MAT- Miller Analogies Test

MCAT - Medical College Admission Test

MTEL - Massachusetts Tests for Educator Licensure

MSAT- Multiple Subjects Assessment for Teachers

NJ HSPA - New Jersey High School Proficiency Assessment

NYSTCE: LAST & ATS-W - New York State Teacher Certification

PLT - Principles of Learning & Teaching Tests

PPST- Pre-Professional Skills Tests

PSAT - Preliminary Scholastic Assessment Test

SAT I - Reasoning Test

TExES - Texas Examinations of Educator Standards

THEA - Texas Higher Education Assessment

TOEFL - Test of English as a Foreign Language

TOEIC - Test of English for International Communication

USMLE Steps 1,2,3 - U.S. Medical Licensing Exams

U.S. Postal Exams 460 & 470

REA's Test Prep Books Are The Best!

(a sample of the hundreds of letters REA receives each year)

" I am writing to congratulate you on preparing an exceptional study guide. In five years of teaching this course I have never encountered a more thorough, comprehensive, concise and realistic preparation for this examination. "
Teacher, Davie, FL

" I have found your publications, *The Best Test Preparation...* to be exactly that. "
Teacher, Aptos, CA

" I am writing to thank you for your test preparation... your book helped me immeasurably and I have nothing but praise for your GRE preparation. "
Student, Benton Harbor, MI

" Your GMAT book greatly helped me on the test. Thank you. "
Student, Oxford, OH

" I recently got the French SAT II Exam book from REA. I congratulate you on first-rate French practice tests. "
Instructor, Los Angeles, CA

" The REA LSAT Test Preparation guide is a winner! "
Instructor, Spartanburg, SC

" This book is great. Most of my friends that used the REA AP book and took the exam received 4's or 5's (mostly 5's which is the highest score!!) "
Student, San Jose, CA

(more on front page)